WITH BRIGHT WINGS

Agnolo Gaddi, THE TRINITY. Tempera on wood, c. 1369-1396. The Metropolitan Museum of Art. Gift of George Blumenthal.

WITH BRIGHT WINGS

A Book of the Spirit

A Collection of Texts
on the
Holy Spirit

compiled by

Mary Grace Swift O.S.U.

PAULIST PRESS
New York, N.Y./Paramus, N.J.

Library of Congress
Catalog Card Number: 75-44806

ISBN: 0-8091-1936-6

Published by Paulist Press
Editorial Office: 1865 Broadway, N.Y., N.Y. 10023
Business Office: 400 Sette Drive, Paramus, N.J. 07652

Printed and bound in the
United States of America

ACKNOWLEDGMENTS

Grateful acknowledgment is made for the use of the following works:

Poem, "Veni, Sancte Spiritus," by Sister M. Paulinus and *Documents of Vatican II*, trans. by Joseph Gallagher, reprinted with permission of *America,* 1960 and 1966. All Rights Reserved © by America Press, 106 W. 56th Street, New York, N.Y. 10019.

"Allocution, Second Vatican Council," from *Catholic Mind*, 1964. All Rights Reserved © by America Press, 106 W. 56th Street, New York, N.Y. 10019.

Robert E. Brennan's *The Seven Horns of the Lamb*; *The Great Encyclical Letters of Pope Leo XIII*; *The Raccolta*; Maurice Landrieux's *The Forgotten Paraclete*, trans. by E. Leahy; Raoul Plus' *Living with God: Cardinal Mercier's Conferences*, trans. by J. M. O'Kavanaugh, used with permission of Benziger, Bruce and Glencoe, Beverly Hills, California.

Cardinal Manning's *The Internal Mission of the Holy Ghost*, published by Burns & Oates, London.

Joseph Gill's *The Council of Florence*, published by Cambridge University Press.

"Act of Consecration to the Holy Ghost," in *Living with God*, published by Catholic Book Publishing Co., New York, N.Y. 10011.

Pius XII's "Mystici Corporis" published by Catholic Truth Society, London.

The Works of Saint Cyril of Jerusalem, trans. by Leo P. McCauley and Anthony A. Stephenson; St. Ambrose's *Theological and Dogmatic Works*, trans. by Roy J. Deferrari; *Saint Gregory the Great: Dialogues*, trans. by Odo J. Zimmerman; *Saint John of Damascus*, trans. by Frederick H. Chase—all used with permission of The Catholic University of America Press.

The Book of Divine Consolation of the Blessed Angela of Foligno, trans. by M. G. Steegman, published by Chatto and Windus, London.

Thomas Merton's *The Climate of Monastic Prayer*, used with permission of Cistercian Publications, Kalamazoo, Michigan.

The Works of William of St. Thierry, trans. by Theodore Berkeley, used with permission of Cistercian Publications, Spencer, Mass.

Yves Congar's *The Revelation of God*, trans. by A. Manson and L. C. Sheppard, used with permission of Darton, Longman, and Todd, London.

Lettres du Venerable Pere Libermann, published by Desclée de Brouwer.

Boris Bobrinskoi's "The Holy Spirit, Life of the Church," used with permission of *Diakonia*, George Maloney, editor.

"Invitation to the Paraclete," by Sister M. Madeleva, C.S.C. in *A Child Asks for a Star.* Copyright 1964 by Dimension Books, Inc., Denville, N.J. Used with permission.

John Donne's "The Litany," in *Poems*, ed. by Hugh l'Anson Fausset, published by E. P. Dutton, New York.

Cardinal Suenens, "Esprit-Saint et Renouveau Conciliare," published by *Documentation Catholique*, Paris.

Scriptural quotes in Chapter I are taken from *The Jerusalem Bible*, New York, Doubleday and Company, Inc. 1966 Copyright © 1966 by Darton, Longman and Todd Ltd. & Doubleday and Company Inc.

Albert Dondeyne's *Faith and the World* published by Duquesne University Press, Pittsburgh, Pa. Reprinted with permission. Copyright 1963, Duquesne University Press.

Frederick Dale Bruner's *A Theology of the Holy Spirit*, used with permission of Wm. B. Eerdman's Publishing Co., Kalamazoo, Mich.

Thomas Merton's *Thoughts in Solitude* (New York: Farrar, Strauss and Cudahy, 1958), p. 29; p. 36. *The New Man* (*Ibid.* 1962), pp. 199-200; 43-44; 169-170.

Leonce de Grandmaison's *Come, Holy Spirit*, trans. by Joseph O'Connell, published by Fides Publishers, South Bend, Indiana.

The Cure of Ars to His People published by Grail Publications, St. Meinrad, Indiana.

Origen and the Doctrine of Grace, trans. by Benjamin Drewery, published by The Epworth Press (Methodist Publishing House), London.

Thomas Merton's *The Sign of Jonas* published by Harcourt Brace Jovanovich, New York.

Teilhard de Chardin's *Hymn of the Universe* (abridged selections). Copyright © 1965 by William Collins Sons and Co., Ltd. By permission of Harper and Row, Publishers.

Meister Eckhart: A Modern Translation by Raymond B. Blakney. Copyright © 1941 by Harper and Row, Publishers. By permission of the publishers.

The Shepherd of Hermas, trans. by Kirsopp Lake, published by Harvard University Press.

Enchridion Symbolorum, used with permission of Verlag Herder, Freiburg.

Matthias Scheeban's *Mysteries of Christianity* and *Spiritual Journal of Lucie Christine.* Trans. by A. Poulain, published by B. Herder, St. Louis.

"Prayers for the Seven Gifts of the Holy Ghost," used with permission of Holy Ghost Fathers, Wheaton, Maryland.

The Collected Works of St. John of the Cross, trans. by Kieran Kavanaugh, published by the Institute of Carmelite Studies, Washington, D.C.

The Constitution of the Society of Jesus, trans. by George Ganss, published by Institute of Jesuit Cources, St. Louis.

English translation of excerpts from the Roman Missal and the Rite of Baptism for Children; rite for Confirmation, Holy Orders and Consecration of a Bishop. Copyright © 1969, 1973, 1975 by International Committee on English in the Liturgy, Inc., All rights reserved.

Prayer, "Pentecost," by Michael Walker in *Hear Me, Lord*, used with permission of Arthur James Ltd., Evesham, Worcester, England.

The Hours of the Divine Office in English and Latin. Published by The Liturgical Press. Copyrighted by the Order of St. Benedict, Inc., Collegeville, Minnesota.

Letters of St. Ignatius of Loyola, trans. by William J. Young, and *The Autobiography of Venerable Marie of the Incarnation*, trans. by John J. Sullivan, published by Loyola University Press, Chicago.

Karl Adam's *Christ Our Brother*, trans. Justin McCann, © 1931 by Macmillan Co., renewed by Justin McCann, 1959; Dietrich Bonhoeffer's *The Cost of Discipleship*, 2nd edition, © SCM Press Ltd. 1959—both used with permission, of Macmillan Publishing Co., New York.

John XXIII's *Journal of a Soul*, trans. by Dorothy White, used with permission of McGraw Hill Book Company.

Thomas Merton's *Life and Holiness* (New York: Herder and Herder, 1963), pp. 30-32; 37-38; 86-88. Copyright© by the Abbey of Gethsemani, Trappist, Ky. Used with permission of the Thomas Merton Legacy Trust.

Litany of the Holy Spirit, used with permission of Montefort Missionaries, Bay Shore, Long Island.

Meditations and Devotions from the Writings of Francois de Salignac de la Mothe Fenelon, trans. by Elizabeth C. Fenn. Copyright © Morehouse-Barlow, Co., Inc. 1952. Used by permission.

Karl Barth's *The Faith of the Church*, trans. by Gabriel Vahanian. Used with permission of New American Library, New York.

Thomas Merton's *Seeds of Contemplation.* Copyright 1949 by Our Lady of Gethsemani Monastery. Reprinted by permission of New Directions Publishing Corporation.

Paul Evdokimov's *The Struggle with God* and Karl Rahner's *On Prayer*, published by Paulist Press, New York.

Prayer of Pope Pius XII, trans. by Martin W. Schoenburg; *The Exercises of St. Gertrude*, trans. by a Benedictine Nun of Regina Laudis; the following volumes of *Ancient Christian Writers*: No. 1 *The Epistles of St. Clement of Rome and St. Ignatius of Antioch*; No. 6 *The Didache. The Epistle of Barnabas*, etc., trans. by James E. Kleist; No. 23 *Athenagoras*, trans. by J. H. Crehan; No. 36 *Letters of St. Paulinus of Nola*, trans. by P. G. Walsh; also, *Revelations of Divine Love Shewed to a Devout Ankress by Name Julian of Norwich*, Ed. Dom Roger Hudleston; *The Dialogue of the Seraphic Virgin Catherine of Siena*, trans. Algar Thorold; *St. Francis de Sales. Letters to Persons in Religion*, trans. Henry B. Mackey; *The Spiritual Doctrine of Father Louis Lallement*; Bartholomey Froget's *The Indwelling of the Holy Trinity in the Souls of the Just*, trans. by Sidney A. Raemers; *The Liturgical Year* by Abbot Gueranger, trans. by Laurence Shepherd; *The Cloud of Unknowing*, ed. Justin McCann; *The Trinity in Our Spiritual Life. An Anthology of the Writings of Dom Columba Marmion*, compiled by Dom Raymond Thibaut; St. Therese of Lisieux' *The Story of a Soul*, trans. by Michael Day; *The Collected Works of Abbot Vonier*; Eugene Vandeur's *Pledge of Glory*, trans. by Dominican Nuns; John T. MacMahon's *The Gift of God*; *The Spiritual Legacy of Sister Mary of the Holy Trinity*; Joseph Schryver's *The Gift of Oneself*, trans. by a Religious of Carmel; *Reminiscences of Sister Elizabeth of the Trinity, Servant of God*, trans. by a Benedictine of Stanbrook Abbey—all used with permission of Newman Press, New York.

Carlo Carretto's *The God Who Comes.* Copyright © 1974 Orbis Books, Maryknoll, N.Y. 10545.

"God's Grandeur," in *Poems of Gerard Manley Hopkins* and excerpts from *The Early Christian Fathers* and *The Later Christian Fathers*, trans. by Henry Bettenson, published by Oxford University Press.

Paul Claudel, "Pentecostal Hymn," trans. by Sister M. David; Romano Guardini's *Prayer in Practice*, trans. by Prince Leopold, and "Prayer to God, the Holy Spirit," by Symeon the New Theologian, taken from *Come, South Wind*—all published by Pantheon Books.

Letters of St. Athanasius, trans. by C. R. B. Shapland. Published by Philosophical Library, New York.

Addresses of John XXIII and Paul VI, used with permission of *The Pope Speaks*, Washington, D.C.

Simone Weil's *Waiting for God*, trans. by Emma Craufurd. Reprinted by permission of G. P. Putnam's Sons. Copyright © 1951 by G. P. Putnam's Sons.

Romano Guardini's *The Lord*, trans. by Elinor Castendynk; *Early Christian Prayers*, trans. by Walter Mitchell; *The Sunday Sermons of the Great Fathers*, trans. by M. F. Toal—all published by Henry Regnery, Chicago.

Fathers of the Church, trans. by F. A. Wright, used with permission of Routledge and Kegan Paul Ltd., London.

Luis Maria Martinez's *The Sanctifier*, trans. by Sister M. Aquinas, published by St. Anthony's Guild, Paterson, New Jersey.

The Catechetical Oration of St. Gregory of Nyssa, trans. by J. H. Srawley, published by The Society for Promoting Christian Knowledge, London.

The Anti-Nicene Fathers, trans. by Alexander Roberts and James Donaldson, and *From Glory to Glory. Texts from Gregory of Nyssa's Writings*, trans. by Herbert Masurillo; *The Mediaeval Mystics of England*, compiled by Eric Colledge, published by Charles Scribner's Sons.

"The Odes of Solomon" from Louis Bouyer's *The Meaning of Monastic Life*, used with permission of Search Press, Ltd., London.

"Pentecost" from *Hymns to the Church* by Gertrude Von Le Fort, trans. by Margaret Chanler; *The Passion of the Infant Christ* by Caryll Houselander. Copyright 1949, Sheed and Ward; *The Holy Ghost* by Edward Leen, C.S.S.P., copyright 1937 Sheed and Ward; *A Theology of History* by Hans Urs Von Balthasar, trans. by John Moriarty and Alexander Dru, copyright 1963 by Sheed and Ward; *The Church* by Hans Kung, © Verlag Herder, R.G., Freiburg im Brusgau, 1967, English trans.© Burns and Oates Ltd., 1967; *Women in Wonderland* by Dorothy Dohen, copyright Sheed and Ward, Inc. 1960—all published by Sheed and Ward, New York.

"Pentecost" by Daniel Berrigan, used with permission of *Spirit. A Magazine of Poetry*, The Catholic Poetry Society of America, Seton Hall University, South Orange, New Jersey.

"The Church Militant Mobilizing," by Father Cyril Papali, O.C.D., in *Spiritual Life*, Washington, D.C.

"Pentecost," by Dorothy Holland, in *Torch Magazine*, used with permission of Third Order of St. Dominic, New York.

Pius XII, "Haurietis Aquas," in *Selected Documents of His Holiness Pope Pius XII*, used with permission of United States Catholic Conference, Washington, D.C.

The Prayers of Kierkegaard, by Søren Kierkegaard, published by The University of Chicago Press.

St. Madeline Sophie Barat. Her Life and Letters. Used with permission of Margaret Williams, R.S.C.J.

Karl Rahner's *Spiritual Exercises*, trans. by Kenneth Baker. Used with permission of Oberdeutsche Provinz, S.J., Munich.

David Wilkerson's *The Cross and the Switchblade*, used with permission of Chosen Books, Chappaqua, New York.

The Teaching of the Catholic Church as Contained in Her Documents, originally prepared by Josef Neuner and Heinrich Roos, ed. by Karl Rahner, published by Alba House, Staten Island, N.Y.

Extracts from the *Prison Meditations/Letters from Prison* of Alfred Delp S.J.© Search Press, London 1962/1976.

this book is dedicated

to the

mother

of

grace

Because the Holy Ghost over the bent

World broods with warm breast and with ah! BRIGHT WINGS

GERARD MANLEY HOPKINS

CONTENTS

Foreword

This collection of texts on the Holy Spirit was assembled principally as an aid to further devotion to the Holy Spirit, and not as a new revelation of scholarship. Texts were selected because they were either (1) significant or (2) appealing. It is hoped that the book might provide a source of inspiration for meditation, that it might be useful for pastors composing sermons, and in general provide a concise sampling of devotion to the Holy Spirit through the centuries for any interested reader. Unfortunately, only short passages could be taken from many authors who wrote voluminously on the subject.

Therefore, I would like this volume to serve the same purpose that the currently popular wine-tasting parties serve: to give the reader merely enough of the essence of a spiritual writer to entice him to imbibe more, so whetting his thirst for the very Spirit of God himself that he may someday experience the plenitude of His ineffable presence and power. After all, we live in an age when many people of high and low rank are feeling the blissful intoxication that comes from being touched by the Spirit of God. Lest the analogy seem facetious in regard to a subject about which I am most in earnest, I could point out that for long ages those living a monastic life chanted at Lauds the phrase:

> Laeti bibamus sobriam
> Ebrietatem Spiritus.*

May this book somehow be a channel for the Holy Spirit to touch more hearts, so that we may all drink joyfully of the sober inebriety of the Spirit.

I would like to thank many people who have assisted me with this book. Loyola University has continually supported and encouraged my research, chiefly for this project by granting a sabbatical leave, during which it was finished. I am thankful for the use of the libraries of

*Let us all joyfully drink of the sober inebriety of the Spirit.

Fordham University, Union Theological, and Notre Dame Seminary, New Orleans.

Fathers George Maloney and Gerald Fagin, S.J. assisted me with their advice; other friends assisted me more than they realize simply by their encouragement. I will not name all my sisters in religion who granted me hospitality in New York to do my research, but without their help, my task would have been much more difficult. May the Spirit of God reward them all . . .

Mary Grace Swift O.S.U.
New York, October 28, 1975

ST. JOHN, with symbol of Holy Spirit inspiring his writing of Scripture. Eleventh century manuscript of Four Gospels, illuminated in East Anglia, using Irish prototype. The Pierpont Morgan Library.

Chapter I

THE HOLY SPIRIT IN SCRIPTURE

. . . the first thing we must do is listen simply to what Scripture tells us about the Spirit. *That* accepted, believed, lived, embraced, and loved in the depths of one's being . . . that is the Holy Spirit!

Karl Rahner

Introduction

In the Old Testament, the Hebrew word *ruah* is used to refer to the very spirit, the breath of God. It signifies a movement of traveling air—sometimes a violent tempest and other times merely a gentle breeze. In creation, this Spirit of God hovered over the primordial waters, impregnating primal matter with the seeds of life. When God sent His *ruah* upon the chosen leaders of the children of Israel in the pre-Christian era, they accomplished amazing feats of physical strength; they prophesied; they led armies to victory; they turned the hardened hearts of men from sin toward Yahweh, their God.

In the New Testament, the Spirit of God emerges as the very Person who impregnated the Mother of God with the seed of the life-giving Godhead. When God sent his Spirit at Pentecost upon the chosen leaders of the Church of the New Covenant, they, too, performed inordinate feats of endurance; they healed; they brought thousands to acknowledge that Jesus was Lord.

In his initial appearance in the New Testament, the Spirit of God brought sanctification to John the Baptist in his mother's womb as well as a promise to his parents of joy and delight with this child of the Spirit. Those charismatic individuals who were themselves possessed by the Spirit of God—Elizabeth, Simeon, and John the Baptist—were able to recognize the humble Jesus of Nazareth as the Son of God, for as St. Paul pointed out much later, spiritual vision comes only to those who are truly one with the Spirit of God.

After submitting to baptism Himself, Christ never ceased to proclaim to His followers that they, too, must be born again of water and the Spirit. To those who would drink of this living water, He promised the loving assistance of the Spirit as their inner, abiding light when called before sanhedrins and synagogues. His chosen apostles were bestowed with the grace of the Spirit in a special way to enable them to baptize and forgive sins. To His close companions, disconsolate at the thought that He was leaving them, the loving Christ promised the Gift of God Himself to be with them forever.

The frightened, disheartened group of followers upon whom the Spirit descended at Pentecost were forever changed by His coming, and they went forth boldly charged to preach the Good News in spite of prison, fire and sword. The coming of the Spirit had another result: a community of Christians was created who were willing to surrender not only their lives to the Church but also their fortunes and property.

When Saul of Tarsus made his dramatic surrender to the Spirit of God, the die-hard persecutor of Christians was converted into the most zealous of missionaries. He made no concessions to vice; impurity, foul talk and drunkenness were never to be tolerated in souls that were temples of the Spirit. Yet for all his adamancy, Paul was molded by the Spirit of God into a most loving evangelist whose converts weepingly kissed him farewell when they sensed he would never return to them again.

As the New Testament closes, the beloved disciple John, who in his long life had never ceased to preach the love of God, as an old man on Patmos delivers a final message to the Christian community in his allegorical Book of Revelation: "Listen to what the Spirit is saying to the Church."

THE OLD TESTAMENT

God's Spirit Hovers over the Waters

In the beginning God created the heavens and the earth. Now the earth was a formless void, there was darkness over the deep, and God's spirit hovered over the water *(Genesis 1:1-2)*.

The Spirit Possesses the Prophets

Gideon

Then all Midian and Amalek and the sons of the East joined forces, crossed the Jordan and encamped in the plain of Jezreel. And the spirit of Yahweh came on Gideon; he sounded the horn and Abiezer rallied behind him. He sent messengers throughout Manasseh, and Manasseh too rallied behind him; he sent messengers to Asher, Zebulun and Naphtali, and they too marched out to meet him *(Judges 6:33-35)*.

Samson

. . . . . His wife answered him, "If Yahweh had meant to kill us, he would not have accepted a holocaust and oblation from our hands; he would not have told us all these things." The woman gave birth to a son and called him Samson. The child grew, and Yahweh blessed him; and the spirit of Yahweh began to move him in the Camp of Dan, between Zorah and Eshtaol *(Judges 13:23-25)*.

Samson went down to Timnah, and as he reached the vineyards of Timnah he saw a young lion coming roaring towards him. The spirit of Yahweh seized on him, and though he had no weapon in his hand he tore the lion in pieces as a man tears a kid; but he did not tell his father or mother what he had done *(Judges 14:5-6)*.

Then the spirit of Yahweh seized on him. He went down to Ashkelon, killed thirty men there, took what they wore and gave the festal robes to those who had answered the riddle, then burning with rage returned to his father's house.

. . . . . Then they (three thousand men of Juda) bound him with two new ropes and brought him up from the Rock.

As he approached Lehi, and the Philistines came running towards him with triumphant shouts, the spirit of Yahweh seized on Samson; the ropes on his arms became like burnt strands of flax and the bonds melted off his hands. Catching sight of the fresh jawbone of a donkey, he reached out and snatched it up; then with it he struck down a thousand men *(Judges 14:19; 15:13-15)*.

Saul and the Prophets

"After this you will go to Gibeah of God (where the Philistine pillar is) and as you come to the town you will meet a group of prophets coming down from the high place, headed by harp, tambourine, flute and lyre; they will be in an ecstasy. Then the spirit of Yahweh will seize on you and you will go into an ecstasy with them, and be changed into another man. When these signs are fulfilled for you, act as occasion serves, for God is with you. . . ."

As soon as Saul had turned his back to leave Samuel, God changed his heart and all these signs were accomplished that same day. From there they came to Gibeah, and there was a group of prophets coming to meet him; the spirit of God seized on him and he fell into ecstasy in their midst. When all who knew him previously saw him prophesying with the prophets, the people said to each other, "What has happened to the son of Kish? Is Saul one of the prophets too?" One of the group retorted, "And who is their father?" And this is the origin of the proverb: Is Saul one of the prophets too? *(1 Samuel 10:5-7, 9-11)*.

David

. . . . . He then asked Jesse, "Are these all the sons you have?" He answered, "There is still one left, the youngest; he is out looking after the sheep." Then Samuel said to Jesse, "Send for him; we will not sit down to eat until he comes." Jesse had him sent for, a boy of fresh complexion, with fine eyes and pleasant bearing. Yahweh said, "Come, anoint him, for this is the one." At this, Samuel took the horn of oil and anointed him where he stood with his brothers; and the spirit of Yahweh seized on David and stayed with him from that day on. As for Samuel, he rose and went to Ramah.

Now the spirit of Yahweh had left Saul and an evil spirit from Yahweh filled him with terror *(1 Samuel 16:11-14)*.

These are the last words of David:

Oracle of David son of Jesse,
oracle of the man raised to eminence,
the anointed of the God of Jacob,
the singer of the songs of Israel.

The spirit of Yahweh speaks through me,
his word is on my tongue;
the God of Jacob has spoken,
the Rock of Israel has said to me:

He who rules men with justice,
who rules in the fear of God,
is like morning light at sunrise
(on a cloudless morning)
making the grass of the earth sparkle after rain.

(2 Samuel 23:1-4)

Azariah

The spirit of God came on Azariah son of Oded; he went out to meet Asa and said, "Listen to me, Asa, and all you of Judah and of Benjamin. Yahweh is with you so long as you are with him. When you seek him, he lets you find him; when you desert him, he deserts you. Many a day Israel will spend without a faithful God, without priest to teach, without law; but in their distress they will return to Yahweh, the God of Israel; they will seek him, and he will let them find him" *(2 Chronicles 15:1-4)*.

The Psalmist Sings of the Spirit

God, create a clean heart in me,
put into me a new and constant spirit,
do not banish me from your presence,
do not deprive me of your holy spirit.

(Psalms 51:10-12)

Yahweh, rescue me from my enemies,
I have fled to you for shelter;
teach me to obey you,
since you are my God;
may your good spirit guide me
on to level ground.

(Psalms 143:9-10)

Isaiah Prophesies in the Spirit

A shoot springs from the stock of Jesse,
a scion thrusts from his roots:
on him the spirit of Yahweh rests,
a spirit of wisdom and insight,
a spirit of counsel and power,
a spirit of knowledge and of the fear of Yahweh.

(Isaiah 11:1-2)

Once more there will be poured on us
the spirit from above;
then shall the wilderness be fertile land
and fertile land become forest.

(Isaiah 32:15)

The spirit of the Lord Yahweh has been given to me,
for Yahweh has anointed me.
He has sent me to bring good news to the poor.
to bind up hearts that are broken;

to proclaim liberty to captives,
freedom to those in prison;
to proclaim a year of favour from Yahweh!
a day of vengeance for our God,

to comfort all those who mourn . . .

(Isaiah 61:1-3)

Yahweh Speaks to Ezechiel

"I shall give you a new heart, and put a new spirit in you; I shall remove the heart of stone from your bodies and give you a heart of flesh instead. I shall put my spirit in you, and make you keep my laws and sincerely respect my observances. You will live in the land which I gave your ancestors. You shall be my people and I will be your God." . . .

The hand of Yahweh was laid on me, and he carried me away by the spirit of Yahweh and set me down in the middle of a valley, a valley full of bones. He made me walk up and down among them. There were vast quantities of these bones on the ground the whole length of the valley; and they were quite dried up. He said to me, "Son of man, can these bones live?" I said, "You know, Lord Yahweh." He said, "Prophesy over these bones. Say, 'Dry bones, hear the word of Yahweh. The Lord Yahweh says this to these bones: I am now going to make the breath enter you, and you will live. I shall put sinews on you, I shall make flesh grow on you. I shall cover you with skin and give you breath, and you will live; and you will learn that I am Yahweh.' " . . .

I prophesied as he had ordered me, and the breath entered them; they came to life again and stood up on their feet, a great, an immense army.

Then he said, "Son of man, these bones are the whole House of Israel. They keep saying, 'Our bones are dried up, our hope has gone; we are as good as dead.' So prophesy. Say to them, 'The Lord Yahweh says this: I am now going to open your graves; I mean to raise you from your graves, my people, and lead you back to the soil of Israel. And you will know that I am Yahweh, when I open your graves and raise you from your graves, my people. And I shall put my spirit in you, and you will live, and I shall resettle you on your own soil; and you will know that I, Yahweh, have said and done this—it is the Lord Yahweh who speaks' " *(Ezechiel 36:26-28; 37:1-6, 10-14).*

Daniel

Since they were elders of the people, and judges, the assembly took their word: Susanna was condemned to death. She cried out as loud as she could, "Eternal God, you know all secrets and everything before it happens; you know that they have given false evidence against me. And now have I to die, innocent as I am of everything their malice has invented against me?"

The Lord heard her cry and, as she was being led away to die, he roused the holy spirit residing in a young boy named Daniel who began to shout, "I am innocent of this woman's death!" At which all the people turned to him and asked, "What do you mean by these words?" Standing in the middle of the crowd he replied, "Are you so stupid, sons of Israel, as to condemn a daughter of Israel unheard, and without troubling to find out the truth? Go back to the scene of the trial: these men have given false evidence against her. . . ."

Then the whole assembly shouted, blessing God, the saviour of those who trust in him . . .

From that day onwards Daniel's reputation stood high with the people *(Daniel 13:41-49; 60-64)*.

Joel

"After this
I will pour out my spirit on all mankind.
Your sons and daughters shall prophesy,
your old men shall dream dreams,
and your young men see visions.
Even on the slaves, men and women,
will I pour out my spirit in those days."

(Joel 3:1-2)

Zechariah

"This is the word of Yahweh with regard to Zerubbabel, 'Not by might and not by power, but by my spirit, says Yahweh Sabaoth . . .' " *(Zechariah 4:6b)*.

THE NEW TESTAMENT

John the Baptist Lives in the Spirit

Then there appeared to him the angel of the Lord, standing on the right of the altar of incense. The sight disturbed Zechariah and he was overcome with fear. But the angel said to him, "Zechariah, do not be afraid, your prayer has been heard. Your wife Elizabeth is to bear you a son and you must name him John. He will be your joy and delight and many will rejoice at his birth, for he will be great in the sight of the Lord; he must drink no wine, no strong drink. Even from his mother's womb he will be filled with the Holy Spirit, and he will bring back many of the sons of Israel to the Lord their God" *(Luke 1:11-16)*.

Mary Conceives by the Spirit

In the sixth month the angel Gabriel was sent by God to a town in Galilee called Nazareth, to a virgin betrothed to a man named Joseph, of the House of David; and the virgin's name was Mary. He went in and said to her, "Rejoice, so highly favoured! The Lord is with you." She was deeply disturbed by these words and asked herself what this greeting could mean, but the angel said to her, "Mary, do not be afraid; you have won God's favour. Listen! You are to conceive and bear a son, and you must name him Jesus. He will be great and will be called Son of the Most High. The Lord God will give him the throne of his ancestor David; he will rule over the House of Jacob for ever and his reign will have no end." Mary said to the angel, "But how can this come about, since I am a virgin?"

"The Holy Spirit will come upon you" the angel answered "and the power of the Most High will cover you with its shadow. And so the child will be holy and will be called Son of God. . . ." *(Luke 1:26-35).*

Mary set out at that time and went as quickly as she could to a town in the hill country of Judah. She went into Zechariah's house and greeted Elizabeth. Now as soon as Elizabeth heard Mary's greeting, the child leapt in her womb and Elizabeth was filled with the Holy Spirit. She gave a loud cry and said, "Of all women you are the most blessed, and blessed is the fruit of your womb. Why should I be honoured with a visit from the mother of my Lord? For the moment your greeting reached my ears, the child in my womb leapt for joy. Yes, blessed is she who believed that the promise made her by the Lord would be fulfilled."

And Mary said:
"My soul proclaims the greatness of the Lord
and my spirit exults in God my saviour;
because he has looked upon his lowly handmaid . . ." *(Luke 1:39-48).*

This is how Jesus Christ came to be born. His mother Mary was betrothed to Joseph; but before they came to live together she was found to be with child through the Holy Spirit. Her husband Joseph, being a man of honour and wanting to spare her publicity, decided to divorce her informally. He had made up his mind to do this when the angel of the Lord appeared to him in a dream and said, "Joseph son of David, do not be afraid to take Mary home as your wife, because she has conceived what is in her by the Holy Spirit. She will give birth to a son and you must name him Jesus, because he is the one who is to save his people from their sins" *(Matthew 1:18-21).*

Enlightened by the Spirit, Simeon Recognizes Christ

Now in Jerusalem there was a man named Simeon. He was an upright and devout man; he looked forward to Israel's comforting and the Holy Spirit rested on him. It had been revealed to him by the Holy Spirit that he would not see death until he had set eyes on the Christ of the Lord. Prompted by the Spirit he came to the Temple; and when the

parents brought in the child Jesus to do for him what the Law required, he took him into his arms and blessed God; and he said:
"Now, Master, you can let your servant go in peace,
just as you promised;
because my eyes have seen the salvation
which you have prepared for all the nations to see,
a light to enlighten the pagans
and the glory of your people Israel."

(Luke 2:25-32)

John the Baptist Recognizes Christ

. . . Seeing Jesus coming towards him, John said, "Look, there is the lamb of God that takes away the sin of the world. This is the one I spoke of when I said: A man is coming after me who ranks before me because he existed before me. I did not know him myself, and yet it was to reveal him to Israel that I came baptising with water." John also declared, "I saw the Spirit coming down on him from heaven like a dove and resting on him. I did not know him myself, but he who sent me to baptise with water had said to me, 'The man on whom you see the Spirit come down and rest is the one who is going to baptise with the Holy Spirit.' Yes, I have seen and I am the witness that he is the Chosen One of God" *(John 1:29-34)*.

Manifestation of the Spirit at Christ's Baptism

Then Jerusalem and all Judaea and the whole Jordan district made their way to him, and as they were baptised by him in the river Jordan they confessed their sins. . . . He said to them. . . . I baptise you in water for repentance, but the one who follows me is more powerful than I am, and I am not fit to carry his sandals; he will baptise you with the Holy Spirit and fire. . . .

Then Jesus appeared; he came from Galilee to the Jordan to be baptised by John. John tried to dissuade him. "It is I who need baptism from you," he said "and yet you come to me!" But Jesus replied, "Leave it like this for the time being; it is fitting that we should, in this way, do all that righteousness demands." At this, John gave in to him.

As soon as Jesus was baptised he came up from the water, and suddenly the heavens opened and he saw the Spirit of God descending like a dove and coming down on him. And a voice spoke from heaven, "This is my Son, the Beloved; my favour rests on him."

Then Jesus was led by the Spirit out into the wilderness to be tempted by the devil *(Matthew 3:5-7, 11, 13-17; 4:1)*.

Re-birth through Water and the Spirit Necessary for Salvation

There was one of the Pharisees called Nicodemus, a leading Jew, who came to Jesus by night and said, "Rabbi, we know that you are a teacher who comes from God; for no one could perform the signs that you do unless God were with him." Jesus answered:

"I tell you most solemnly,
unless a man is born from above,
he cannot see the kingdom of God."

Nicodemus said, "How can a grown man be born? Can he go back into his mother's womb and be born again?" Jesus replied:

"I tell you most solemnly,
unless a man is born through water and the Spirit,
he cannot enter the kingdom of God:
what is born of the flesh is flesh;
what is born of the Spirit is spirit.
Do not be surprised when I say:
You must be born from above.
The wind blows wherever it pleases;
you hear its sound,
but you cannot tell where it comes from or where it is going.
That is how it is with all who are born of the Spirit" *(John 3:1-8)*.

On the last day and greatest day of the festival, Jesus stood there and cried out:

"If any man is thirsty, let him come to me!
Let the man come and drink who believes in me!"

As scripture says: From his breast shall flow fountains of living water.

He was speaking of the Spirit which those who believed in him were to receive; for there was no Spirit as yet because Jesus had not yet been glorified *(John 7:37-39)*.

Christ Promises the Spirit to Those Who Ask

So I say to you: Ask, and it will be given to you; search, and you will find; knock, and the door will be opened to you. For the one who asks always receives; the one who searches always finds; the one who knocks will always have the door opened to him. What father among you would hand his son a stone when he asked for bread? Or hand him a snake instead of a fish? Or hand him a scorpion if he asked for an egg? If you then, who are evil, know how to give your children what is good, how much more will the heavenly Father give the Holy Spirit to those who ask him! *(Luke 11:9-13).*

Christ Urges Trust in the Spirit

"Be on your guard: they will hand you over to sanhedrins; you will be beaten in synagogues; and you will stand before governors and kings for my sake, to bear witness before them, since the Good News must first be proclaimed to all the nations.

"And when they lead you away to hand you over, do not worry beforehand about what to say; no, say whatever is given to you when the time comes, because it is not you who will be speaking: it will be the Holy Spirit. Brother will betray brother to death, and the father his child; children will rise against their parents and have them put to death. You will be put to death. You will be hated by all men on account of my name; but the man who stands firm to the end will be saved" *(Mark 13:9-13).*

Devils Are Cast out through the Power of the Spirit

. . . . All the people were astounded and said, "Can this be the Son of David?" But when the Pharisees heard this they said, "The man casts out devils only through Beelzebul, the prince of devils."

Knowing what was in their minds he said to them, "Every kingdom divided against itself is heading for ruin; and no town, no household divided against itself can stand. Now if Satan casts out Satan, he is divided against himself; so how can his kingdom stand? And if it is through Beelzebul that I cast out devils, through whom do your own experts cast them out? Let them be your judges, then. But if it is through the Spirit of God that I cast devils out, then know that the kingdom of God has overtaken you" *(Matthew 12:23-28).*

Christ's Testament to His Followers: the Holy Spirit Himself

If you love me you will keep my commandments.
I shall ask the Father,
and he will give you another Advocate
to be with you for ever,
that Spirit of truth
whom the world can never receive
since it neither sees nor knows him;

but you know him,
because he is with you, he is in you. . . .
I have said these things to you
while still with you;
but the Advocate, the Holy Spirit,
whom the Father will send in my name,
will teach you everything
and remind you of all I have said to you.

(John 14:15-17, 25-26)

When the Advocate comes,
whom I shall send to you from the Father,
the Spirit of truth who issues from the Father,
he will be my witness.
And you too will be witnesses,
because you have been with me from the outset.

(John 15:26-27)

But now I am going to the one who sent me.
Not one of you has asked, "Where are you going?"
Yet you are sad at heart because I have told you this.
Still, I must tell you the truth:
it is for your own good that I am going
because unless I go,
the Advocate will not come to you;
but if I do go,
I will send him to you.
And when he comes,
he will show the world how wrong it was,
about sin:
and about who was in the right,
and about judgement:
about sin:
proved by their refusal to believe in me;
about who was in the right:
proved by my going to the Father
and your seeing me no more;
about judgement:
proved by the prince of this world being already condemned.
I still have many things to say to you
but they would be too much for you now.
But when the Spirit of truth comes
he will lead you to the complete truth,

since he will not be speaking as from himself
but will say only what he has learnt;
and he will tell you of the things to come.
He will glorify me,
since all he tells you
will be taken from what is mine.
Everything the Father has is mine;
that is why I said:
All he tells you
will be taken from what is mine.

(John 16:5-15)

Christ Bestows the Power of Forgiveness in the Spirit

The disciples were filled with joy when they saw the Lord, and he said to them again, "Peace be with you.

As the Father sent me,
so am I sending you."

After saying this he breathed on them and said:

"Receive the Holy Spirit.
For those whose sins you forgive,
they are forgiven;
for those whose sins you retain,
they are retained."

(John 20:20-23)

Christ Commissions His Disciples to Baptize

Meanwhile the eleven disciples set out for Galilee, to the mountain where Jesus had arranged to meet them. When they saw him they fell down before him, though some hesitated. Jesus came up and spoke to them. He said, "All authority in heaven and on earth has been given to me. Go, therefore, make disciples of all the nations; baptise them in the name of the Father and of the Son and of the Holy Spirit, and teach them to observe all the commands I gave you. And know that I am with you always; yes, to the end of time" *(Matthew 28:16-20).*

THE ACTS OF THE APOSTLES

Christ Promises the Coming of the Spirit

When he had been at table with them, he had told them not to leave Jerusalem, but to wait there for what the Father had promised. "It is," he had said, "what you have heard me speak about: John baptised with water but you, not many days from now, will be baptized with the Holy Spirit" *(Acts 1:4-5)*.

Pentecost

When Pentecost day came round, they had all met in one room, when suddenly they heard what sounded like a powerful wind from heaven, the noise of which filled the entire house in which they were sitting; and something appeared to them that seemed like tongues of fire; these separated and came to rest on the head of each of them. They were all filled with the Holy Spirit, and began to speak foreign languages as the Spirit gave them the gift of speech.

Now there were devout men living in Jerusalem from every nation under heaven, and at this sound they all assembled, each one bewildered to hear these men speaking his own language. They were amazed and astonished. "Surely," they said, "all these men speaking are Galileans? How does it happen that each of us hears them in his own native language? Parthians, Medes and Elamites; people from Mesopotamia, Judaea and Cappadocia, Pontus and Asia, Phrygia and Pamphylia, Egypt and the parts of Libya round Cyrene; as well as visitors from Rome—Jews and proselytes alike—Cretans and Arabs; we hear them preaching in our own language about the marvels of God." Everyone was amazed and unable to explain it; they asked one another what it all meant. Some, however, laughed it off. "They have been drinking too much new wine," they said.

Then Peter stood up with the Eleven and addressed them in a loud voice:

"Men of Judaea, and all you who live in Jerusalem, make no mistake about this, but listen carefully to what I say. These men are not drunk, as you imagine; why, it is only the third hour of the day. On the contrary, this is what the prophet spoke of:

In the days to come—it is the Lord who speaks—
I will pour out my spirit on all mankind.
Their sons and daughters shall prophesy,
your young men shall see visions,
your old men shall dream dreams.
Even on my slaves, men and women,
in those days, I will pour out my spirit.
I will display portents in heaven above
and signs on earth below.

The sun will be turned into darkness
and the moon into blood
before the great Day of the Lord dawns.
All who call on the name of the Lord will be saved.

"Men of Israel, listen to what I am going to say: Jesus the Nazarene was a man commended to you by God by the miracles and portents and signs that God worked through him when he was among you, as you all know. This man, who was put into your power by the deliberate intention and foreknowledge of God, you took and had crucified by men outside the Law. You killed him, but God raised him to life, freeing him from the pangs of Hades; for it was impossible for him to be held in its power . . . *(Acts 2:1-24).*

. . . . . God raised this man Jesus to life, and all of us are witnesses to that. Now raised to the heights by God's right hand, he has received from the Father the Holy Spirit, who was promised, and what you see and hear is the outpouring of that Spirit. . . .

Hearing this, they were cut to the heart and said to Peter and the apostles, "What must we do, brothers?" "You must repent," Peter answered "and every one of you must be baptised in the name of Jesus Christ for the forgiveness of your sins, and you will receive the gift of the Holy Spirit. The promise that was made is for you and your children, and for all those who are far away, for all those whom the Lord our God will call to himself." He spoke to them for a long time using many arguments, and he urged them, "Save yourselves from this perverse generation." They were convinced by his arguments, and they accepted what he said and were baptised. That very day about three thousand were added to their number *(Acts 2:32-33, 37-41).*

Anointing of Deacons in the Spirit

About this time, when the number of disciples was increasing, the Hellenists made a complaint against the Hebrews: in the daily distribution their own widows were being overlooked. So the Twelve called a full meeting of the disciples and addressed them, "It would not be right for us to neglect the word of God so as to give out food; you, brothers, must select from among yourselves seven men of good reputation, filled with the Spirit and with wisdom; we will hand over this duty to them, and continue to devote ourselves to prayer and to the service of the word." The whole assembly approved of this proposal and elected Stephen, a man full of faith and of the Holy Spirit, together with Philip, Prochorus, Nicanor, Timon, Parmenas, and Nicolaus of Antioch, a convert to Judaism. They presented these to the apostles, who prayed and laid their hands on them *(Acts 6:1-6).*

Deacon Stephen Speaks to the Sanhedrin

"You stubborn people, with your pagan hearts and pagan ears. You are always resisting the Holy Spirit, just as your ancestors used to do. Can you name a single prophet your ancestors never persecuted? In the past they killed those who foretold the coming of the Just One, and now you have become his betrayers, his murderers. You who had the Law brought to you by angels are the very ones who have not kept it."

They were infuriated when they heard this, and ground their teeth at him.

But Stephen, filled with the Holy Spirit, gazed into heaven and saw the glory of God, and Jesus standing at God's right hand. "I can see heaven thrown open," he said, "and the Son of Man standing at the right hand of God." At this all the members of the council shouted out and stopped their ears with their hands; then they all rushed at him, sent him out of the city and stoned him. The witnesses put down their clothes at the feet of a young man called Saul. As they were stoning him, Stephen said in invocation, "Lord Jesus, receive my spirit." Then he knelt down and said aloud, "Lord, do not hold this sin against them"; and with these words he fell asleep *(Acts 7:51-60).*

Simon the Magician Tries to Purchase the Spirit's Power

When Simon saw that the Spirit was given through the imposition of hands by the apostles, he offered them some money. "Give me the same power," he said, "so that anyone I lay my hands on will receive the Holy Spirit." Peter answered, "May your silver be lost forever, and you with it, for thinking that money could buy what God has given for nothing! You have no share, no rights, in this: God can see how your heart is warped. Repent of this wickedness of yours, and pray to the Lord; you may still be forgiven for thinking as you did; it is plain to see that you are trapped in the bitterness of gall and the chains of sin." "Pray to the Lord for me yourselves," Simon replied, "so that none of the things you have spoken about may happen to me" *(Acts 8:18-24).*

Philip Baptizes the Ethopian Eunuch

The angel of the Lord spoke to Philip saying, "Be ready to set out at noon along the road that goes from Jerusalem down to Gaza, the desert road." So he set off on his journey. Now it happened that an

Ethopian had been on pilgrimage to Jerusalem; he was a eunuch and an officer at the court of the kandake, or queen, of Ethiopia, and was in fact her chief treasurer. He was now on his way home; and as he sat in his chariot he was reading the prophet Isaiah. The Spirit said to Philip, "Go up and meet that chariot." When Philip ran up, he heard him reading Isaiah the prophet and asked, "Do you understand what you are reading?" "How can I," he replied, "unless I have someone to guide me?" So he invited Philip to get in and sit by his side. . . .

Further along the road they came to some water, and the eunuch said, "Look, there is some water here; is there anything to stop me being baptized?" He ordered the chariot to stop, then Philip and the eunuch both went down into the water and Philip baptized him. But after they had come up out of the water again Philip was taken away by the Spirit of the Lord, and the eunuch never saw him again but went on his way rejoicing *(Acts 8:26-31; 36-39).*

The Spirit Descends upon Both Jew and Gentile at Caesarea

While Peter was still speaking the Holy Spirit came down on all the listeners. Jewish believers who had accompanied Peter were all astonished that the gift of the Holy Spirit should be poured out on the pagans too, since they could hear them speaking strange languages and proclaiming the greatness of God. Peter himself then said, "Could anyone refuse the water of baptism to these people, now they have received the Holy Spirit just as much as we have?" He then gave orders for them to be baptized in the name of Jesus Christ *(Acts 10:44-48).*

The apostles and the brothers in Judaea heard that the pagans too had accepted the word of God, and when Peter came up to Jerusalem the Jews criticized him and said, "So you have been visiting the uncircumcised and eating with them, have you?" Peter in reply gave them the details point by point, [then concluded] "The Spirit told me to have no hesitation about going back with them. The six brothers here came with me as well, and we entered the man's house. He told us he had seen an angel standing in his house who said, 'Send to Jaffa and fetch Simon known as Peter; he has a message for you that will save you and your entire household!'

"I had scarcely begun to speak when the Holy Spirit came down on them in the same way as it came on us at the beginning, and I remembered that the Lord had said, 'John baptized with water, but you will be baptized with the Holy Spirit.' I realized then that God was giving them the identical thing he gave to us when we believed in the Lord Jesus Christ; and who was I to stand in God's way?"

This account satisfied them, and they gave glory to God. "God," they said, "can evidently grant even the pagans the repentance that leads to life" *(Acts 11:1-4, 12-18).*

Paul Baptizes the Ephesians in the Spirit

While Apollos was in Corinth, Paul made his way overland as far as Ephesus, where he found a number of disciples. When he asked, "Did you receive the Holy Spirit when you became believers?" they answered, "No, we were never even told there was such a thing as a Holy Spirit." "Then how were you baptized?" he asked. "With John's baptism," they replied. "John's baptism," said Paul, "was a baptism of repentance; but he insisted that the people should believe in the one who was to come after him—in other words Jesus." When they heard this, they were baptized in the name of the Lord Jesus, and the moment Paul had laid hands on them the Holy Spirit came down on them, and they began to speak with tongues and to prophesy. There were about twelve of these men *(Acts 19:1-7).*

THE EPISTLES OF PAUL

The Love of God Poured Forth by the Spirit

So far then we have seen that, through our Lord Jesus Christ, by faith we are judged righteous and at peace with God, since it is by faith and through Jesus that we have entered this state of grace in which we can boast about looking forward to God's glory. But that is not all we can boast about; we can boast about our sufferings. These sufferings bring patience, as we know, and patience brings perseverance, and perseverance brings hope, and this hope is not deceptive, because the love of God has been poured into our hearts by the Holy Spirit which has been given us *(Romans 5:1-5).*

In the Spirit We Can Call God "Father"

Though your body may be dead it is because of sin, but if Christ is in you then your spirit is life itself because you have been justified; and if the Spirit of him who raised Jesus from the dead is living in you, then he who raised Jesus from the dead will give life to your own mortal bodies through his Spirit living in you.

So then, my brothers, there is no necessity for us to obey our unspiritual selves or to live unspiritual lives. If you do live in that way, you are doomed to die; but if by the Spirit you put an end to the misdeeds of the body you will live.

Everyone moved by the Spirit is a son of God. The spirit you received is not the spirit of slaves bringing fear into your lives again; it is the spirit of sons, and it makes us cry out, "Abba, Father!" The Spirit himself and our spirit bear united witness that we are children of God. And if we are children we are heirs as well: heirs of God and coheirs with Christ, sharing his sufferings so as to share his glory *(Romans 8:10-17)*.

. . . But when the appointed time came, God sent his Son, born of a woman, born a subject of the Law, to redeem the subjects of the Law and to enable us to be adopted as sons. The proof that you are sons is that God has sent the Spirit of his Son into our hearts: the Spirit that cries, "Abba, Father" . . . *(Galatians 4:4-6)*.

The Spirit Prays in Us

From the beginning till now the entire creation, as we know, has been groaning in one great act of giving birth; and not only creation, but all of us who possess the first-fruits of the Spirit, we too groan inwardly as we wait for our bodies to be set free. . . .

The Spirit too comes to help us in our weakness. For when we cannot choose words in order to pray properly, the Spirit himself expresses our plea in a way that could never be put into words, and God who knows everything in our hearts knows perfectly well what he means, and that the pleas of the saints expressed by the Spirit are according to the mind of God *(Romans 8:22-23, 26-27)*.

Only the Spirit of God Grants True Spiritual Vision

As for me, brothers, when I came to you, it was not with any show of oratory or philosophy, but simply to tell you what God had guaranteed. During my stay with you, the only knowledge I claimed to have was about Jesus, and only about him as the crucified Christ. Far from relying on any power of my own, I came among you in great "fear and trembling" and in my speeches and the sermons that I gave, there were none of the arguments that belong to philosophy; only a demonstration of the power of the Spirit. And I did this so that your faith should not depend on human philosophy but on the power of God. . . .

The hidden wisdom of God which we teach in our mysteries is the wisdom that God predestined to be for our glory before the ages began.

It is a wisdom that none of the masters of this age have ever known, or they would not have crucified the Lord of Glory. . . .

These are the very things that God has revealed to us through the Spirit, for the Spirit reaches the depths of everything, even the depths of God. After all, the depths of a man can only be known by his own spirit, not by the Spirit of God. Now instead of the spirit of the world, we have received the Spirit that comes from God, to teach us to understand the gifts that he has given us. Therefore we teach, not in the way in which philosophy is taught, but in the way that the Spirit teaches us: we teach spiritual things spiritually. An unspiritual person is one who does not accept anything of the Spirit of God; he sees it all as nonsense; it is beyond his understanding because it can only be understood by means of the Spirit. A spiritual man, on the other hand, is able to judge the value of everything and his own value is not to be judged by other men *(1 Corinthians 2:1-5, 7-8, 10-15)*.

The Spirit Lives in Man, His Temple

Didn't you realise that you were God's temple and that the Spirit of God was living among you? If anybody should destroy the temple of God, God will destroy him, because the temple of God is sacred; and you are that temple *(1 Corinthians 3:16-17)*.

You know perfectly well that people who do wrong will not inherit the kingdom of God; people of immoral lives, idolators, adulterers, catamites, sodomites, thieves, usurers, drunkards, slanderers and swindlers will never inherit the kingdom of God. There are the sort of people some of you were once, but now you have been washed clean, and sanctified, and justified through the name of the Lord Jesus Christ and through the Spirit of our God . . .

Your body you know, is the temple of the Holy Spirit, who is in you since you received him from God. You are not your own property; you have been bought and paid for. That is why you should use your body for the glory of God *(1 Corinthians 6:9-11, 19-20)*.

In the meantime, brothers, we wish you happiness; try to grow perfect; help one another. Be united; live in peace, and the God of love and peace will be with you.

Greet one another with the holy kiss. All the saints send you greetings.

The grace of the Lord Jesus Christ, the love of God and the fellowship of the Holy Spirit be with you all *(2 Corinthians 13:11-13)*.

Those Stamped with the Seal of the Spirit Possess Freedom

Now you too, in him,
have heard the message of the truth and the good news
of your salvation,
and have believed it;
and you too have been stamped with the seal of the
Holy Spirit of the Promise,
the pledge of our inheritance
which brings freedom for those whom God has taken
for his own,
to make his glory praised *(Ephesians 1:13-14)*.

Paul's Loving Blessings to His Followers

This, then, is what I pray, kneeling before the Father, from whom every family, whether spiritual or natural, takes its name:

Out of his infinite glory, may he give you the power through his Spirit for your hidden self to grow strong, so that Christ may live in your hearts through faith, and then, planted in love and built on love, you will with all the saints have strength to grasp the breadth and the length, the height and the depth; until, knowing the love of Christ, which is beyond all knowledge, you are filled with the utter fullness of God *(Ephesians 3:14-19)*.

Guard against foul talk; let your words be for the improvement of others, as occasion offers, and do good to your listeners, otherwise you will only be grieving the Holy Spirit of God who has marked you with his seal for you to be set free when the day comes *(Ephesians 4:29-30)*.

Those Who Would Live in the Spirit Must Abstain from Immorality

Be very careful about the sort of lives you lead, like intelligent and not like senseless people. This may be a wicked age, but your lives should redeem it. And do not be thoughtless but recognise what is the will of the Lord. Do not drug yourselves with wine, this is simply dissipation; be filled with the Spirit. Sing the words and tunes of the psalms and hymns when you are together, and go on singing and chanting to the Lord in your hearts, so that always and everywhere you are giving thanks to God who is our Father in the name of our Lord Jesus Christ *(Ephesians 5:15-20)*.

Paul Urges Courage and Constancy while Promising the Strength of the Spirit

So stand your ground, with truth buckled round your waist, and integrity for a breastplate, wearing for shoes on your feet the eagerness to spread the gospel of peace and always carrying the shield of faith so that you can use it to put out the burning arrows of the evil one. And then you must accept salvation from God to be your helmet and receive the word of God from the Spirit to use as a sword.

Pray all the time, asking for what you need, praying in the Spirit on every possible occasion *(Ephesians 6:14-18).*

If our life in Christ means anything to you, if love can persuade at all, or the Spirit that we have in common, or any tenderness and sympathy, then be united in your convictions and united in your love, with a common purpose and a common mind *(Philippians 2:1-2).*

We know, brothers, that God loves you and that you have been chosen, because when we brought the Good News to you, it came to you not only as words, but as power and as the Holy Spirit and as conviction. And you observed the sort of life we lived when we were with you, which was for your instruction, and you were led to become imitators of us, and of the Lord; and it was with the joy of the Holy Spirit that you took to the gospel, in spite of the great opposition all round you *(1 Thessalonians 1:4-7).*

What God wants is for all to be holy. He wants you to keep away from fornication, and each one of you to know how to use the body that belongs to him in a way that is holy and honourable, not giving way to selfish lust like the pagans who do not know God. He wants nobody at all ever to sin by taking advantage of a brother in these matters; the Lord always punishes sins of that sort, as we told you before and assured you. We have been called by God to be Holy, not to be immoral; in other words, anyone who objects is not objecting to a human authority, but to God, who gives you his Holy Spirit *(1 Thessalonians 4:3-8).*

FIRST EPISTLE OF ST. JOHN

My dear people,
since God has loved us so much,
we too should love one another.
No one has ever seen God;
but as long as we love one another

God will live in us
and his love will be complete in us.
We can know that we are living in him
and he is living in us
because he lets us share his Spirit.
We ourselves saw and we testify
that the Father sent his Son
as savior of the world.
If anyone acknowledges that Jesus is the Son of God,
God lives in him, and he in God.
We ourselves have known and put our faith in
God's love towards ourselves.
God is love
and anyone who lives in love lives in God,
and God lives in him *(1 John 4:11-16)*.

THE BOOK OF REVELATION

John Exhorts the Church to Listen to the Spirit

My name is John, and through our union in Jesus I am your brother and share your sufferings, your kingdom, and all you endure. I was on the island of Patmos for having preached God's word and witnessed for Jesus; it was the Lord's day and the Spirit possessed me, and I heard a voice behind me, shouting like a trumpet, "Write down all that you see in a book, and send it to the seven churches. . . ."

If anyone has ears to hear, let him listen to what the Spirit is saying to the churches: those who prove victorious I will feed from the tree of life set in God's paradise. . . .

To those who prove victorious, and keep working for me until the end, I will give the authority over the pagans which I myself have been given by my Father, to rule them with an iron sceptre and shatter them like earthenware. And I will give him the Morning Star. If anyone has ears to hear, let him listen to what the Spirit is saying to the churches. . . .

The Spirit and the Bride say, "Come." Let everyone who listens answer, "Come."

(Revelation 1:9-11; 2:7; 2:26-29; 22:17)

Abraham Bloemaert, THE FOUR DOCTORS OF THE CHURCH. Former collection of Bishop of Durham. Photograph: Courtauld Institute, University of London.

Chapter II

THE HOLY SPIRIT IN MAGISTERIAL ACTS OF THE CHURCH

Introduction

In the very early centuries of the Church's history, there was little time spent in formulating a theology of the Holy Spirit. The paramount problem which diverted the energies of the early pastors and theologians was that of the divinity of Christ—a belief formidably challenged by Arius. The Nicene Creed, which expressed the mind of the Church at the close of this struggle (325), merely *mentions* the Spirit.

However, in the middle of the fourth century, some Christians denied the divinity of the Spirit, placing Him in a category a bit higher than the angels, but a bit less than God. Nicknamed the "Pneumatomachians" (adversaries of the Spirit), the adherents of this belief stirred up such controversy that Emperor Theodosius called a council at Constantinople to deal with the question. Under the guidance of Gregory of Nazianzus, the council accepted the proposition that "we believe in the Holy Spirit, the Lord, the giver of life, who proceeds from the Father. With the Father and the Son he is worshiped and glorified." In 451, a council at Chalcedon confirmed the acceptance of the Nicene Creed with the addition of the clause from Constantinople as the basic doctrine of the Church in regard to the Holy Spirit's divinity.

The question of the *relationship* of the Spirit to the Father and the Son became the focus of the next controversy—which was rending the very fabric of Christendom itself. At a council held in Toledo, Spain (675), seventeen bishops of the Western Church articulated the idea that the Spirit *proceeded from both the Father and the Son*. Though the clause was used subsequently in France and Germany, it remained for Pope Benedict VIII (1012-1024) to accept the addition of this "Filioque clause" into the Creed. Eastern churchmen felt that this addition to the creed was heresy; they believed that the Holy Spirit proceeded from the Father *through* the Son. With this dogma as a focal point, ultimately a schism took place between the Eastern Church at Constantinople and the Western Church of Rome.

In the thirteenth century a group of heretics, the Albigenses, posed a serious threat to the Western Church in southern France by their denial of belief in the Trinity as well as of other basic Christian doctrines. In this age, the Fourth Lateran Council (1215) reaffirmed many of the traditional beliefs. At a second Council of Lyons, France (1274), reunion between the Eastern and Western Churches was formally effected. Though Greek representatives of the emperor acceded at the gathering to the very explicit decree promulgated by the council, the union proved unpopular in the East and was later repudiated. An attempt was made again at reconciliation at the Council of Ferrara-Florence in 1439. After fourteen sessions over the "Filioque clause," union was achieved, with the delegates accepting the resulting decree. Again, however, their action was repudiated at home by the Eastern Church.

After the Western Church was rent in the sixteenth century by the Protestant Revolt, the Council of Trent reminded the Church that the Spirit proceeded from the divine will inflamed with love. Many centuries later, Pope Leo XIII reaffirmed the Tridentine injunctions that pastors should instruct their flocks about the Spirit of Love, likewise urging that love should "run forward toward action." Pius XI called upon the Spirit of God in prayer to effect unity once more between East and West. Pius XII in *Mystici Corporis* reminded mankind that the Spirit of Christ unites all the members of his Body, and in *Haurietis Aqua* he emphasized the idea that the Paraclete was "the personified mutual love of the Father."

With humble boldness, upon invoking the Second Vatican Council, John XXIII prayed: "Renew in your own days your miracles as of a second Pentecost." In continuing the work of the Council, Paul VI urged the participants to be docile to the Spirit while asserting his firm belief that "the Spirit is here." Subsequent decrees of the Council reminded the faithful that the Spirit has called all members of the Church to unity of fellowship and service. By bestowing a variety of hierarchical and charismatic gifts, the Spirit calls *all* to become associated in the work of salvation. While acknowledging the call of the Council toward the human dimension, in *Fate Attenzione* Paul VI expressed a hope that the vertical dimension would not be neglected; he reminded the Church that the interior life was absolutely necessary for the fruition of the works of the Spirit.

In 1967, Paul VI communicated to Patriarch Athenagoras his feeling that the Spirit was urging the Church, as part of the renewal effort, to heal the ancient schism between East and West. A historic meeting resulted between Pope and Patriarch permeated with the *fellowship* of the Spirit. Hopefully for the future, the *unity* of the Spirit may yet prevail.

THE APOSTLES' CREED

(Roman form: ca. Middle of the 2nd Century)

. . . . I believe in the Holy Ghost. . . . . .[1]

THE PROFESSION OF FAITH OF THE COUNCIL OF NICAEA (325)

We believe in one God, the Father almighty, maker of all things visible and invisible. And in one Lord Jesus Christ, . . . And in the Holy Ghost.

THE NICAEO-CONSTANTINOPOLITAN PROFESSION OF FAITH KNOWN AS THE NICENE CREED (381)

. . . And *(I believe)* in the Holy Ghost, the Lord and giver of life; who proceeds from the Father (and the Son). Who together with the Father and the Son is adored and glorified: who spoke through the prophets. . . . [and the Son: This *Filioque* clause was only officially introduced into the Creed by Benedict VIII: Ed.]

THE CREED OF EPIPHANIUS, BISHOP OF CYPRUS (*ca.* 374)

An Elaboration of the Nicene Profession of Faith

We believe also in the Holy Spirit, who spoke in the Law and preached through the prophets, and descended to Jordan, and spoke through the Apostles and lives in the faithful. Thus then we believe in him, that he is the Holy Spirit, the Spirit of God, the perfect Spirit, the Paraclete, uncreated, proceeding from the Father and receiving from the Son, in whom we believe.

ST. DAMASUS I (366-384)

COUNCIL OF ROME (382)

We anathematize those who do not wholly freely proclaim that he (*the Holy Spirit*) is of one power and substance with the Father and the Son . . .

Any one who does not say that the Holy Spirit, like the Son, is really and truly from the Father, of the divine substance, and true God, is heretical.[1]

Any one who does not say that the Holy Spirit can do all things, and knows all things, and is everywhere present, is heretical.

Any one who says that the Holy Spirit is a creature, or created through the Son, is heretical . . .

Any one who does not say that the Holy Spirit is to be adored, as the Father and Son (*are adored*) is heretical.

FORMULA CALLED "FIDES DAMASI" (*Gaul, ca.* 500)

We believe in one God, the Father all powerful, and in our one Lord Jesus Christ, Son of God, and in one Holy Spirit, who is God. There are not three gods we honor and acknowledge, but one only God, the Father, Son and Holy Spirit . . . truly a holy Spirit who is neither begotten nor unbegotten, who is neither created nor produced, who proceeds from the Father and the Son, coeternal with the Father and the Son, their equal and their cooperator. . . .[2]

FORMULA "CLEMENS TRINITAS" (*Gaul, ca.* 500)

The merciful Trinity is one divinity. Thus the Father as well as the Son and the Holy Spirit are one principle, one substance, one force, one power. The Father is God, the Son is God and the Holy Spirit is God. We do not say that they are three gods, but they are confessed very filially by us to be one. . . . The three are not confounded, nor divided, but conjoined, united in substance, but distinguished by their names. They are conjoint by their nature, distinct by their persons, equal in their divinity, entirely the same by their majesty, in accord as a trinity, participants in the glory of it. They are one in such a way that we doubt no more that they are three; they are three in such a way that we confess that they are not separable.

THE ATHANASIAN CREED *(4th-5th Century)*

(Of uncertain authorship, this creed is one of the clearest statements of Trinitarian belief.)

Whoever wishes to be saved must first of all hold the Catholic faith, for anyone who does not maintain this whole and inviolate will surely be lost eternally.

And the Catholic faith is this, that we worship one God in Trinity, and Trinity in Unity, neither confounding the Persons nor dividing the substance.

For there is one person of the Father, another of the Son, and another of the Holy Spirit. But the godhead of the Father, of the Son and of the Holy Spirit is all one, the glory equal, the majesty co-eternal. As the Father is, so is the Son, and so is the Holy Spirit.

Uncreated the Father, the Son uncreated, and the Holy Spirit uncreated.

The Father immeasurable, the Son immcasurable, and the Holy Spirit immeasurable.

The Father eternal, the Son eternal, and the Holy Spirit eternal. And yet there are not three eternals but one eternal. Just as there are not three uncreated nor three immeasurables, but one uncreated and one immeasurable.

Likewise the Father is almighty, the Son is almighty, and the Holy Spirit is almighty; yet not three almighties, but one almighty.

Thus God the Father, God the Son, and God the Holy Spirit; yet not three Gods but one God. Thus the Father is Lord, the Son is Lord, and the Holy Spirit is Lord; yet there are not three Lords, but one Lord. For as we are compelled by Christian truth to acknowledge that each Person by himself is God and Lord, we are forbidden by the true Catholic religion to say that there are three Gods or Lords.

The Father is made by none, nor created nor begotten. The Son is from the Father alone, not made nor created but begotten. The Holy Spirit is from the Father and the Son, not made nor created nor begotten, but proceeding.

So there is one Father, not three Fathers; one Son, not three Sons; and one Holy Spirit, not three Holy Spirits. And in this Trinity none is before or after another, none is greater or less, but all three Persons are co-eternal with one another and co-equal. So that in all things . . . both Unity in Trinity and Trinity in Unity are to be adored. Therefore whoever will be saved must believe this of the Trinity . . .[3]

CREED (SYMBOL) OF THE COUNCIL OF TOLEDO (675)

We confess and believe that the holy and ineffable Trinity, Father, Son, and Holy Spirit, one God, is by nature of one substance, one nature, one majesty and power. . . .

We also believe that the *Holy Spirit*, who is the third Person of the Trinity, is one and the same God with God the Father and the Son, of one substance and one nature, not, however, born or created by proceeding, and that he is the Spirit of them both. In our belief, therefore, this Holy Spirit is neither unbegotten nor begotten, for if we were to say unbegotten we should assume two Fathers, or if begotten we should be shown to teach two Sons. And he is called the Spirit not of the Father alone, nor of the Son alone, but of both Father and Son. For he does not proceed from the Father to the Son, nor from the Son to the sanctification of creation, but he is shown to have proceeded at the same time from both, for he is to be acknowledged as the love or the sanctity of both. Hence we believe that the Holy Spirit is sent by both, as the Son is sent by the Father. But he is not less than the Father and the Son, as the Son acknowledges that on account of taking a body he is less than the Father and the Holy Spirit.[4]

Profession of Faith of the IV Lateran Council (1215)

We firmly believe and simply confess that there is only one true God, eternal, immense, unchangeable, incomprehensible, omnipotent and ineffable, the Father, the Son and the Holy Spirit: three Persons, but one essence, substance or wholly simple nature: the Father from no one, the Son from the Father alone, and the Holy Spirit equally from both: and from the beginning, always, and without end: the Father begetting, the Son being born, and the Holy Spirit proceeding: of the same substance, equal, equally omnipotent and equally eternal: one origin of all things. . . .[5]

GREGORY X (1271-1276)

Constitution of the II Council of Lyons (1274)

Declaration concerning the Procession of the Spirit of God

We profess, with fidelity and devotion, that the Holy Spirit proceeds eternally from the Father and the Son, not as if from two principles, but as from one principle; not as from a double spiration, but from one unique spiration. This, up to now, the sacrosanct Roman Church mother and mistress of all the faithful has professed, preached and taught; this she holds firmly, preaches, professes and teaches. This is the unchangeable and truthful thought of the orthodox fathers and doctors, Latin as well as Greek.[6]

Profession of Faith of Michael Paleologue (1274)

We believe also in the Holy Spirit, fully, perfectly and truly God, proceeding from the Father and the Son, coequal and consubstantial and co-omnipotent and coeternal in all things with the Father and the Son. We believe that this holy Trinity is not three Gods, but one God, almighty, eternal, invisible and immutable.[7]

EUGENE IV (1431-1447)

Council of Florence (*Laetentur Coeli*, 1439)

In the name, therefore, of the Holy Trinity, Father, Son and Holy Spirit, with the approbation of this holy general Council of Florence we define that this truth of faith be believed and accepted by all Christians, and that all likewise profess that the Holy Spirit is eternally from the Father and the Son . . . and proceeds eternally from both as from one principle and a single spiration; we declare that what the holy Doctors and Fathers say, namely that the Holy Spirit proceeds from the Father through the Son tends to this meaning, that by it is signified that the Son like the Father is, according to the Greeks the cause, but according to the Latins the principle of the subsistence of the Holy Spirit . . .[8]

General Council of Florence
Decree for the Armenians (1439)

The Sacrament of Confirmation

. . . The *effect* of this sacrament is that the Holy Spirit is given for strength, as he was given to the Apostles on the day of Pentecost, so that the Christian may courageously confess the name of Christ. Therefore the confirmand is anointed on the forehead which is the seat of shame so that he may not blush for the name of Christ and especially his cross, which is a stumbling block for the Jews and foolishness for the Gentiles according to the Apostle; wherefore he is signed with the sign of the Cross . . .[9]

Catechism of the Council of Trent (1566)

Article VIII

"I Believe in the Holy Ghost"

The third person of the Trinity is called by the common name of "Holy Ghost," a name which is peculiarly appropriate to him, as we must acknowledge, seeing that he infuses into us spiritual life, and without his most holy inspiration we can do nothing deserving of eternal life.

The import of the name being explained, the people should first of all be taught, that the Holy Ghost is equally God with the Father and the Son, equal to them, equally omnipotent, eternal, and of infinite perfection, the supreme good, and infinitely wise, and of the same nature with the Father and the Son . . .

The pastor must also accurately explain to the faithful that the Holy Ghost is God . . . confessedly the third person in the divine nature, distinct from the Father and the Son, and produced by their will . . .

"The Lord"

By confessing the Holy Ghost to be Lord, they declare how far he excels the angels, who, however, are the noblest spirits created by God . . .

"The Giver of Life"

The Holy Ghost they designate The Giver of life, because the soul lives more by its union with God, than the body is nourished and sustained by its union with the soul. . . .

"Who Proceedeth from the Father and the Son"

The faithful are to be taught that the Holy Ghost proceeds, by eternal procession, from the Father and the Son, as from one beginning. For this truth is propounded to us by the Church's rule of faith, from which it is not lawful for a Christian to deviate, and which is confirmed by the authority of the Sacred Scriptures and Councils.

Certain Divine Works Are Appropriated to the Holy Ghost

The pastor must also teach, that there are certain admirable effects, and certain most exalted gifts of the Holy Ghost, which are said to originate and emanate from him, as from a perennial fountain of goodness. For although the extrinsic works of the most Holy Trinity are common to the three persons, yet many of them are attributed especially to the Holy Ghost, to the end that we may understand that they proceed from the boundless love of God towards us; for seeing that the Holy Ghost proceeds from the divine will, inflamed as it were with love, it may be comprehended that these effects, which are referred particularly to the Holy Ghost, arise from extreme love of God towards us. Hence it is that the Holy Ghost is called *a gift*; for by the term gift we understand that which is kindly and gratuitously bestowed, no anticipation of remuneration being entertained. Whatever blessings and benefits therefore have been bestowed on us by God . . . those we should with a pious and grateful mind acknowledge to be bestowed by the bounty and gift of the Holy Ghost.

Effects of the Spirit

The effects of the Spirit are numerous; for, not to mention the creation of the world, the propagation and government of created things, of which we have made mention . . . it was shown a little before that to the Holy Ghost is particularly attributed the giving of life; and this is further confirmed by the testimony of Ezekiel: *I am now going to make the breath* [ruah] *enter you, and you will live (Ezekiel 37:6).* The prophet Isaias enumerates the principal effects, peculiarly attributed to the Holy Ghost: The spirit of wisdom and understanding, the spirit of counsel and might, the spirit of knowledge and piety, and the spirit of the fear of the Lord; effects which are called the gifts of the Holy Ghost, and sometimes by the name of the Holy Ghost. Wisely therefore does St. Augustine admonish us, that, whenever we meet the word Holy Ghost in Scripture, we distinguish whether it means the third person of the Trinity, or his effects and operations; for they are equally as distinct from one another as is the Creator from things created. And these matters should the more diligently be explained, as from these gifts of the Holy Ghost we derive rules of a Christian life, and are enabled to perceive whether the Holy Ghost dwells within us. But that grace of justification, which seals us with the holy Spirit of promise, who is the earnest of our inheritance, is to be proclaimed by us above his other most exalted gifts, for this it is that unites our hearts to God in the closest bonds of love; whence it comes to pass, that, inflamed with a supreme desire of piety, we begin a new life, and being made partakers of the divine nature, are called and really *are* sons of God.[10]

LEO XIII (1810-1903)

Encyclical Letter Divinum Illud: *The Holy Spirit, 1897*

. . . Now that We are looking forward to the approach of the closing days of Our life, Our soul is deeply moved to dedicate to the Holy Ghost, who is the life-giving Love, all the Work We have done during Our pontificate, that He may bring it to maturity and fruitfulness. . . .

The fullness of divine gifts is in many ways a consequence of the indwelling of the Holy Ghost in the souls of the just. . . . Among these gifts are those secret warnings and invitations which from time to time are excited in our minds and hearts by the inspiration of the Holy Ghost. Without these there is no beginning of a good life, no progress, no arriving at eternal salvation. . . .

Perchance there are still to be found . . . even nowadays, some who, if asked, as were those of old by St. Paul the Apostle, whether they have received the Holy Ghost, might answer in like manner: We have not so much as heard whether there be a Holy Ghost. At least there are certainly many who are very deficient in their knowledge of Him. They frequently use His name in their religious practices, but their faith is involved in much darkness. Wherefore all preachers and those having care of souls should remember that it is their duty to instruct their people more diligently and more fully about the Holy Ghost. . . . What should be chiefly dwelt upon and clearly explained is the multitude and greatness of the benefits which have been bestowed, and are constantly bestowed, upon us by this divine Giver, so that errors and ignorance concerning matters of such moment may be entirely dispelled, as unworthy of "the children of light." We urge this not only because it effects a mystery by which we are directly guided to eternal life, and which must therefore be firmly believed, but also because the more clearly and fully the good is known the more earnestly it is loved. . . . Yet we must strive that this love should be of such a nature as not to consist merely in dry speculations or external observances, but rather to run forward towards action, and especially to fly from sin, which is in a more special manner offensive to the Holy Spirit. For whatsoever we are, that we are by the divine goodness; and this goodness is specially attributed to the Holy Ghost. . . .

We ought to pray to and invoke the Holy Spirit for each one of us greatly needs His protection and His help. The more a man is deficient in wisdom, weak in strength, borne down with trouble, prone to sin, so ought he the more to fly to Him who is the never-ceasing fount of light, strength, consolation and holiness. . . .

Unite . . . Venerable Brethren, your prayers with Ours, and at your exhortation let all Christian peoples add their prayers also, invoking the powerful and ever-acceptable intercession of the Blessed Virgin. You know well the intimate and wonderful relations existing between her and the Holy Ghost, so that she is justly called His spouse. The intercession of the Blessed Virgin was of great avail both in the mystery of the incarnation and in the coming of the Holy Ghost upon the apostles. May she continue to strengthen our prayers with her suffrages, that in the midst of all the stress and trouble of nations, those divine prodigies may be happily revived by the Holy Ghost which were foretold in the words of David: Send forth Thy Spirit and they shall be created, and Thou shalt renew the face of the earth.[11]

PIUS XI (1857-1939)

Pentecost, May 31, 1925

Venerable Brothers, Dear Sons:

Both for Us and for all the faithful, it is a very special cause of joy that the venerable solemnity of this day brings: We see again the marvellous birth of the Church, which adorned with all the gifts of the Holy Spirit, came out of the silence of the Cenacle retreat, and for the first time appeared on that great day and manifested itself to the crowds. From that hour, there was an incessant flux of life and spiritual vigour which began to course through the veins of the immaculate Spouse of Christ . . . By the help always assured by the Spirit, not only has the Church remained sheltered from error, but never has she ceased to sow and cultivate with the greatest zeal the seeds of holy doctrine and of charity among all people. Was she not born for the health of all people?

That divine power of the Spirit Consoler, deployed to shield the Church from the contagion of error, was assuredly manifested with the liveliest renown, in the celebration of the Council of Nicea, six centuries ago. On these commemorative feasts We call from on high upon hearts and souls the graces of light and enthusiasm which hasten the realization of our most dear prayers for union to be effected finally between the dissident churches and the Apostolic See.

The work accomplished by the Apostles after Pentecost, and so to speak sealed with their blood—this work which snatched the world from pagan depravation to lead it to the new religion—is in some way continued and perpetuated by all those who, renouncing the comforts of home and of life go forth, at the cost of immense fatigue, at the risk even of their life, to carry to the uncivilized nations both the light of the Gospel and of civilization. . . .

We address ourselves to the Spirit of Truth, who is also the principle of all sanctity; and join your prayers, Venerable Brothers and Dear Sons to ours, and do not cease soliciting his favor for Catholic interests. . . . It is He who, at the Council of Nicea and in all the councils in the course of the ages, has directed the thought of the Fathers.

O let Him still assist the Church from day to day by the abundance of his gifts. Let Him still pray for us "with ineffable sighs," and by that prayer, renew the face of the earth and hasten Christian unity, He who lives and reigns with the Father and Son, from century to century.[12]

PIUS XII (1876-1958)

Prayer to the Holy Spirit for the Church, 1942

O Creator Spirit, by hovering above the waters of the created universe You renewed the face of the earth. You first announced truth and salvation to the Romans when they listened to Peter's sermon at Jerusalem. Turn Your face to the sons of this Rome, the heart of the world, to which Peter by his apostolic life and martyrdom was later to show the strength of his faith, the firmness of his hope, and the extent of his love. . . .

Come down, O Creator Spirit! Indeed, You have already come down; You are with us. You are with the Spouse of Christ; You are her life, her soul, her comfort, her protector at all times, but especially in times of distress and sorrow. Shower from on high such an abundance of Your gifts that all, both Shepherd and flock, may diffuse in the world the light of their faith, the support of their hope, and the power of their love.

Spirit of understanding, Spirit of counsel and fortitude, make all Christian minds, whether exalted or humble, understand and feel not only the extraordinary seriousness, but also the grave responsibility of the present moment, when an old world in its last throes is bringing forth a new one. Point out to all who carry on their foreheads the name of Christ the narrow road of virtue which alone leads to salvation, so that they may shake off the stupor of indifference, lukewarmness and indecision and make every effort to leave behind all inordinate attachments to things of the world.

Spirit of consolation, graciously restore not only the solace of resignation, but above all the strength of confidence to the numberless hearts who are sighing and on the point of breaking, burdened with the weight of worry and want, of sacrifices and injustices, of oppression and discouragement. Be their rest in time of weariness, their shade in time of heat, their warmth in time of cold, their comfort in time of tears. Be father to orphans, protector to widows, food to the poor, support to the abandoned, roof to refugees, guardian to the persecuted, fortification to soldiers, freedom to prisoners, balm to the wounded, medicine to the sick, refuge to sinners, help to the dying. Console and unite those who love each other with a pure heart but whom difficult circumstances have separated. Grant that the smile and the helping hand of Christian charity may speak where the voice of human comfort has become silent.

Spirit and Teacher of Truth, may there be inspired through You, and diffused among the hearts and minds of men, not because of the fear of sacrifice but because of a moral reawakening, an intense desire for peace, a peace of justice, of moderation and wisdom; a peace which in its extent, depth, and realization, will never belie Your admonishing word: "There is no wisdom, no understanding, no counsel against the Lord." At the same time infuse in them so ardent a desire for such a peace that they will not refuse its indispensable prerequisites, its basic traits, and its necessary consequences. Grant that the rulers of the nations may elevate and direct their thought to the grandeur, the dignity, the benefits, and the merits of such a happy peace, and that they may formulate the vital rights of their countries not according to the length of their swords, nor according to the extension of ambitious interests, but according to the norms of your holy will and the divine law.

O Spirit Creator, visit the minds of Your people and fill their hearts with Your grace; and during the time that this trial will continue, by the omnipotence of Your gifts give Us,—the Shepherd of Christ's flock and all who hear Our voice,—the ability to fulfill and to promote with a firm faith, a joyous hope, and an ardent charity, the saving mission left to His disciples by the Redeemer: "You shall be my witnesses."[13]

Mystici Corporis: (The Mystical Body, 1943)
The Spirit Unites the Mystical Body

Christ our Lord bids the Church live by His own supernatural life, makes His divine power pervade the whole of His Body, and feeds and sustains each member according to the place which it occupies in the Body, in much the same way as the vine-stock nourishes and fecundates the branches united with it.

If, now, we carefully consider this divine principle of life and power given by Christ inasmuch as it constitutes the very well-spring of every created gift and grace, we shall easily understand that it is none other than the Paraclete, the Spirit who proceeds from the Father and the Son, and who in a special manner is called the "Spirit of Christ" or the "Spirit of the Son." For it was with this Spirit of grace and truth that the Son of God adorned His soul in the Virgin's immaculate womb; He is the Spirit who delights to dwell in the Redeemer's pure soul as in His favourite temple; He is the Spirit whom Christ merited for us on the Cross with the shedding of His own blood, the Spirit whom He bestowed upon the Church for the remission of sins, breathing Him upon the Apostles. And while Christ alone received this Spirit without measure, it is only according to the measure of the giving of Christ and from the fullness of Christ Himself that He is bestowed upon the members of the mystical Body. And since Christ has been glorified on the Cross His Spirit is communicated to the Church in abundant outpouring, in order that she and each of her members may grow daily in likeness to our Saviour. It is the Spirit of Christ who has made us adopted sons of God, so that one day "we all, beholding the glory of the Lord with open face, may be transformed into the same image from glory to glory."

This Spirit of Christ is the invisible principle to which we must also attribute the union of all parts of the Body with one another and with their exalted Head, dwelling as He does whole in the Head, whole in the Body, and whole in each of its members, and assisting these with His presence in divers manners according to their various functions and duties and their higher or lower degree of spiritual perfection. He, with His heavenly breath of life, is the source from which proceeds every single vital and effectively salutary action in all the parts of the Body. It is He Himself who is present in all the members and divinely acts in each, though He also acts in the lower members through the ministry of the higher. And, finally, it is He who, while by the inspiration of His grace giving ever new increase to the Church, refuses to dwell by sanctifying grace in members which are completely severed from the Body. This presence and operation of the Spirit of Jesus Christ has been vigorously and compendiously described by Our wise Predecessor of immortal Memory, Leo XIII, in the following words: "It is enough to state that, since Christ is the Head of the Church, the Holy Spirit is her soul."[14]

Haurietis Aquas: On the Devotion to the Sacred Heart, 1956
The Spirit: The Personalized Mutual Love of the Father and Son

The gift of the Holy Spirit to His disciples is the first clear sign of His munificent charity after His triumphal ascent to the right hand of the Father. Indeed after ten days the Spirit, the Paraclete, given by the Heavenly Father, descended upon them gathered in the Cenacle, as He had promised them at the Last Supper. . . .

This Spirit, the Paraclete, since He is the personified mutual love of the Father for the Son and of the Son for the Father, is sent indeed by both. Assuming the appearance of tongues of fire, He poured the abundance of divine love and other heavenly gifts into their souls. The infusion of this divine love also sprang from the Heart of our Saviour "in whom are hidden all the treasures of wisdom and knowledge."

Indeed, this love is the gift of the Heart of Jesus and His Spirit, who is indeed the Spirit of the Father and the Son and from whom both the rise of the Church and its remarkable spread is unfolded for all the pagan nations which the worship of idols, hatred of brothers, and corruption of morals as well as violence had befouled.

This divine love is the most precious gift of the Heart of Christ and His Spirit. This love gave the apostles and martyrs that fortitude with which they were strengthened to fight even to the point of death, which they met with heroic spirit, to preach the truth of the gospel and to testify to it with their blood. This gave to the Doctors of the Church a most ardent desire to teach and defend the Catholic Faith.

It was this love which nourished the virtues of the confessors and urged them to accomplish eminently useful and marvellous deeds, profitable for their own eternal and temporal welfare and that of others. This was the love which persuaded virgins to abstain, willingly and joyfully, from sensual pleasures, and to consecrate themselves entirely to the love of their heavenly Spouse. This love, pouring forth from the Heart of the Incarnate Word, is infused by the Holy Spirit into the souls of all the faithful.[15]

JOHN XXIII (1881-1963)

Prayer for the Second Ecumenical Council
September 23, 1959

O divine Spirit, sent by the Father in the Name of Jesus, give your aid and infallible guidance to your Church and pour out on the Ecumenical Council the fullness of your gifts.

O gentle Teacher and Consoler, enlighten the hearts of our prelates who, eagerly responding to the call of the Supreme Roman Pontiff, will gather here in solemn conclave.

May this Council produce abundant fruits, may the light and power of the Gospel be more widely diffused in human society: may new vigor be imparted to the Catholic religion and its missionary function: may we all acquire a more profound knowledge of the Church's doctrine and a wholesome increase of Christian morality.

O gentle Guest of our souls, confirm our minds in truth and dispose our hearts to obedience, that the deliberations of the Council may find in us generous consent and prompt obedience.

We pray to you again for the lambs who are no longer part of the one fold of Jesus Christ, that they too, who still glory in the name of Christians, may at last be united under one Shepherd.

Renew in our own days your miracles as of a second Pentecost; and grant that Holy Church, reunited in one prayer, more fervent than before, around Mary the Mother of Jesus, and under the leadership of Peter, may extend the kingdom of the divine Saviour, a kingdom of truth, justice, love and peace. Amen.[16]

Prayer to the Holy Ghost
June 10, 1962

O Holy Ghost, Paraclete, perfect in us the work begun by Jesus;

enable us to continue to pray fervently in the name of the whole world: hasten in every one of us the growth of a profound interior life; give vigour to our apostolate so that it may reach all men and all peoples, all redeemed by the Blood of Christ and all belonging to him. Mortify in us our natural pride, and raise us to the realms of holy humility, of the real fear of God, of generous courage. Let no earthly bond prevent us from honouring our vocation, no cowardly considerations disturb the claims of justice, no meanness confine the immensity of charity within the narrow bounds of petty selfishness. Let everything in us be on a grand scale: the search for truth and the devotion to it, and readiness for self-sacrifice, even to the cross and death; and may everything finally be according to the last prayer of the Son to his heavenly Father, and according to your Spirit, O Holy Spirit of love, which the Father and the Son desired to be poured out over the Church and its institutions, over the souls of men and over nations. Amen. Amen. Alleluia, Alleluia![17]

Second Vatican Council

Prayer of the Council Fathers

We are here before You, O Holy Spirit, conscious of our innumerable sins, but united in a special way in Your Holy Name. Come and abide with us. Deign to penetrate our hearts.

Be the guide of our actions, indicate the path we should take, and show us what we must do so that, with Your help, our work may be in all things pleasing to You.

May you be our only inspiration and the overseer of our intentions for You alone possess a glorious name together with the Father and the Son.

May You, who are infinite justice, never permit that we be disturbers of justice. Let not our ignorance induce us to evil, nor flattery sway us, nor moral and material interest corrupt us. But unite our hearts to You alone, and do it strongly, so that, with the gift of Your grace, we may be one in You and may in nothing depart from the truth.

Thus, united in Your name, may we in our every action follow the dictates of Your mercy and justice, so that today and always our judgements may not be alien to You and in eternity we may obtain the unending reward of our actions. Amen.[18]

Toward a New Pentecost
Address at the Close of the Council's First Session

Even though the Ecumenical Council has not yet promulgated its decrees. . . . it is nonetheless consoling to look forward even at this stage to thc real benefits which will result from it. In God's providence, it will not merely be the sons of the Catholic Church who will reap these benefits, but all those brothers of ours who rejoice in the name of Christian, and those countless children of ancient and glorious civilizations on whom the light of Christianity has not yet dawned. . . . .

When that time comes, all the decisions of this Ecumenical Council will have to be implemented in every field of the Church's striving. . . . Then, doubtless, will dawn that new Pentecost which is the object of our yearning—a Pentecost that will increase the Church's wealth of spiritual strength and extend her maternal influence and saving power to every sphere of human endeavor. Then will we see the extension of Christ's kingdom on earth, and throughout the world will reecho more clearly, more eloquently, the good news of man's redemption; confirming the kingship of almighty God, strengthening the bonds of fraternal love among men, and establishing that peace which was promised in this world to men of good will.[19]

PAUL VI (1897-)

ALLOCUTION AT OPENING OF THIRD SESSION OF SECOND VATICAN COUNCIL

An Urge to the Episcopate for Docility to the Spirit
September 14, 1964

There are, as you know, two factors which Christ has promised and arranged in different ways to continue His mission, to extend in time and on earth the kingdom He founded and to make of redeemed mankind His Church, His Mystical Body, His fullness, in expectation of His definitive and triumphant return at the end of time.

These two factors are the apostolate and the Spirit.

The apostolate is the external and objective factor. It forms the material body, so to speak, of the Church and is the source of her visible and social structures.

The Holy Spirit is the internal factor who acts within each person, as well as on the whole community, animating, vivifying, sanctifying.

These two agents, the apostolate which is entrusted to the sacred hierarchy, and the Spirit of Jesus, which uses the hierarchy as its ordinary instrument in the ministry of the word and the sacraments, cooperate with one another. Pentecost shows them wonderfully linked at the beginning of the great work of Jesus, who although invisible remains ever present in His apostles and their successors, "whom He set over His Church as His shepherds and vicars." (Preface, Mass of Apostles). . . .

May we believe that the salvific plan, by which the redemption of Christ reaches and is fulfilled in us, is even now in action? Yes, brethren, we may believe indeed. . . . To doubt this would be an insult to Christ's faithfulness to His promises, a betrayal of our apostolic mandate, depriving the Church of her certainty, which the Divine Word has guaranteed and history has confirmed, and of her indefectibility.

The Spirit is here, not yet to confirm with sacramental grace the work which all of us, united in the council, are bringing to completion, but rather to illuminate and guide our labors to the benefit of the Church and all mankind. The Spirit is here. We call upon Him, wait for Him, follow Him. The Spirit is here.

Let us reflect on this doctrine and this present reality so that, above all, we may realize once more and in the fullest and most sublime degree possible our communion with the living Christ. It is the Spirit who joins us to Him. Let us reflect on this truth also that we may put ourselves before Him in trepidation, fully at His disposal; that we may become aware of the humiliating emptiness of our misery and the crying need we have of His help and mercy; that we may hear as if spoken in the secret recesses of our soul the words of the Apostle: "Discharging . . . this ministry in accordance with the mercy shown us, we do not lose heart."

The Council is for us a moment of deep interior docility, a moment of complete and filial adherence to the word of the Lord, a moment of fervent, earnest invocation and of love, a moment of spiritual exaltation. To this unique occasion the poetic words of St. Ambrose apply with a special aptness: "Let us drink in joy the sober inebriation of the Spirit." (Hymn at Lauds.) Such for us should be this blessed time of council.[20]

PAUL VI

SECOND VATICAN COUNCIL

Dogmatic Constitution on the Church

Lumen Gentium

When the work which the Father had given the Son to do on earth was accomplished, the Holy Spirit was sent on the day of Pentecost in order that He might forever sanctify the Church, and thus all believers would have access to the Father through Christ in the one Spirit. He is the Spirit of life, a fountain of water springing up to life eternal. Through Him the Father gives life to men who are dead from sin, till at last He revives in Christ even their mortal bodies.

The Spirit dwells in the Church and in the hearts of the faithful as in a temple. In them He prays and bears witness to the fact that they are adopted sons. The Spirit guides the Church into the fullness of truth and gives her a unity of fellowship and service. He furnishes and directs her with various gifts, both hierarchical and charismatic, and adorns her with the fruits of His grace. By the power of the gospel He makes the Church grow, perpetually renews her, and leads her to perfect union with her Spouse. The Spirit and the Bride both say to the Lord Jesus, "Come!"

Thus, the Church shines forth as "a people made one with the unity of the Father, the Son, and the Holy Spirit."[21]

Decree on the Missionary Activity of the Church

Ad Gentes

Now, before freely giving His life for the world, the Lord Jesus so arranged the ministry of the apostles and so promised to send the Holy Spirit, that both they and the Spirit were to be associated in effecting the work of salvation always and everywhere. Throughout all ages, the Holy Spirit gives the entire Church "unity in fellowship and in service; He furnishes her with various gifts, both hierarchical and charismatic." He vivifies ecclesiastical institutions as a kind of soul and instills into the hearts of the faithful the same mission spirit which motivated Christ Himself. Sometimes He visibly anticipates the apostles' action, just as He unceasingly accompanies and directs it in different ways.[22]

Pastoral Constitution on the Church in the Modern World

Gaudium et Spes

Christ is now at work in the hearts of men through the energy of His Spirit. He arouses not only a desire for the age to come, but by that very fact, He animates, purifies, and strengthens those noble longings too by which the human family strives to make its life more human and to render the whole earth submissive to this goal.

Now, the gifts of the Spirit are diverse. He calls some to give clear witness to the desire for a heavenly home and to keep that desire green among the human family. He summons others to dedicate themselves to the earthly service of men and to make ready the material of the celestial realm by this ministry of theirs. Yet He frees all of them so that by putting aside love of self and bringing all earthly resources into the service of human life they can devote themselves to that future when humanity itself will become an offering accepted by God.[23]

Fate Attenzione: The Holy Spirit and the Life of the Church, 1966

On what does the Church live? The question is addressed to that which is the internal principle of its life; the original principle which distinguishes the Church from every other society; an indispensable principle, just as breathing is for man's physical life; a divine principle which makes a son of earth a son of heaven and confers on the Church its mystical personality: the Holy Spirit. The Church lives on the Holy Spirit. The Church was truly born, you could say, on the day of Pentecost. The Church's first need is always to live Pentecost. . . .

It is in the Holy Spirit that the twofold union is perfected—that of the Church with Christ and with God, and that of the Church with all its members, the faithful. It is the Holy Spirit who gives life to the whole body of the Church and to its individual members by means of that intimate action which we call grace. We are all firmly convinced of this theological truth of our faith, even if it isn't easy for us to form an adequate concept of the ontological and psychological reality to which it corresponds.

But this is enough for us now, and we can say: If the Church lives on the illuminating and sanctifying inspiration of the Holy Spirit, then the Church has a need of the Holy Spirit: a basic need, an existential need, a need that cannot be satisfied with illusions, with substitutes . . . a universal need, a permanent need.

At this point, someone might raise the objection: But doesn't the Church already possess the Holy Spirit? Isn't this need already satisfied? Yes, of course, the Church already possesses the Holy Spirit. But first of all, His action admits of various degrees and circumstances, so that our action is needed too, if the activity of the Holy Spirit is to be free and full; and secondly, the Holy Spirit's presence in individual souls can diminish or be missing entirely. This is why the Word of God is preached and the sacraments of grace are distributed; this is why people pray and why each individual tries to merit the great "gift of God," the Holy Spirit, for himself and for the whole Church.

For this reason, if we really love the Church, the main thing we must do is to foster in it an outpouring of the divine Paraclete, the Holy Spirit. And if we accept the ecclesiology of the Council, which lays so much stress on the action of the Holy Spirit in the Church—as we likewise note in the traditional ecclesiology of Greek theology—then we should be glad to accept its guideline for fostering the Church's vitality and renewal, and for orientating our own personal Christian lives along these lines.

Where does this guideline lead us? Toward the Holy Spirit, We repeat—which means toward the mystery of the Church, toward the vital communion which the Father in His infinite and transcendent goodness wanted to establish through Christ, in the Spirit, with the human soul and with believing and redeemed mankind, the Church. In other words, it leads us toward the search for and the attainment of God; toward theological truth, toward faith which discloses to us the religious order of salvation.

Some people have preferred to see in the Council an orientation of the Church in what might be called a horizontal direction—toward the human community that makes up the Church; toward the brothers still separated from us who are the object of our longing and are called to the same perfect communion; toward the world around us, to which we must carry the message of our faith and the gift of our charity; toward earthly realities which must be recognized as good and worthy of being taken up in the light of the kingdom of God.

All this is very true and very beautiful; but we mustn't forget what we might call the vertical orientation, which the Council reaffirmed as primary for interpreting God's design for the destiny of mankind and for explaining the Church's mission in time. God—His mystery, His charity, His worship, His truth, the expectation of Him—always remains in first place. Christ, mediator between man and God, is the necessary Redeemer who binds together all of our capacity for love and dedication. The Spirit, who makes us Christians and raises us to supernatural life, is the true and profound principle of our interior life and of our external apostolic activity.

And if we follow this unmistakable orientation, where are we directed? Where are we led? We are guided and led to the interior life; to that interior life—of recollection, silence, meditation, absorption of God's word, spiritual exercise—which seems to annoy some people (we say with amazement and with sorrow), some beloved sons of the Church. They act as if the interior life were an outgrown phase, a pedagogy no longer needed for a Christian life, which should instead be projected outward in the secular and naturalistic experience, which the world offers us, as if—relying on this alone and deprived of the protective and strengthening force of interior grace—we could, with our poor forces, succeed in mastering and redeeming it.

No, if we want to be wise and give the Church what it needs most of all, the Holy Spirit, then we must be prompt and faithful in keeping the fixed appointment for a vivifying encounter with Him, which is the interior life.

May Our apostolic blessing guide and strengthen you for this.[24]

Address to Orthodox Patriarch Athenagoras of Constantinople
Oct. 26, 1967

The Spirit gives us to know Christ, to guard the truths entrusted to the Church, to penetrate the mystery of God and His truth, for He is life and inward transformation. And He demands with greater insistence than ever that we be one that the world may believe.

This request of the Holy Spirit we see manifested first of all in the movement of renewal that He is bringing about everywhere in the Church. This renewal, the desire to be more attentive and receptive in our faithfulness, is in fact the most fundamental prerequisite for our drawing closer to one another. . . .

If in our efforts for renewal we see a sign of the action of the Spirit urging us on to re-establish full communion with one another and preparing us for it, does not the contemporary world, filled with unbelief in many forms, also give us a peremptory reminder of our need for unity with one another?

If the unity of Christ's disciples was given as the great sign that was to call forth the faith of the world, is not the unbelief of many of our contemporaries also a way whereby the Spirit speaks to the Churches, causing a fresh awareness in them of the urgency there is to fulfill this precept of Christ who died "that he might gather into one the children of God who were scattered abroad?". . . .

We come now to the other aspect of the Spirit that We mentioned when We began, His action in each member of the Christian faithful, the fruits of holiness and generosity it produces, another fundamental prerequisite of our drawing closer to one another: change of heart. This enables us in our personal life to hear and carry out with ever greater docility the bidding of the Spirit. Without this effort—which must be unceasing—to be faithful to the Holy Spirit, who transforms us into the likeness of the Son, there can be no true lasting brotherhood.

It is only by becoming truly sons in the Son that we also truly become, in a mysterious manner, brothers of one another. . . .

United in a fraternal love that nothing must be allowed to lessen, and inspired only by the desire to carry out what the Spirit asks of the Church, we shall, in a hope stronger than all obstacles, go forward in the name of the Lord.[25]

NOTES

1. *The Teaching of the Catholic Church, as Contained in Her Documents*, originally prepared by Josef Neuner and Heinrich Roos, edited by Karl Rahner (Staten Island: Alba House, 1967), pp. 424-426; 90.

2. *Enchridion Symbolorum*. Ed. by Henrici Denzinger (Friburg: Herder, 1955), pp. 12-13.

3. Neuner and Roos, pp. 428-429.

4. *Ibid.*, pp. 93-94.

5. *Ibid.*, p. 430.

6. *Enchridion Symbolorum*, p. 214.

7. Neuner and Roos, p. 433.

8. Joseph Gill, *The Council of Florence* (Cambridge: University Press, 1959), p. 248 (with adaptation).

9. Neuner and Roos, p. 276.

10. *The Catechism of the Council of Trent*. Translated by Theodore A. Buckley (London: George Routledge, 1852), pp. 86-91.

11. *The Great Encyclical Letters of Pope Leo XIII* (New York: Benziger Brothers, 1903), pp. 423-440.

12. Homily given May 31, 1925, Feast of Pentecost, for the canonization of Saints John-Baptist-Marie Vianney and John Eudes. *Documentation Catholique*, XIV (November 28, 1925), pp. 970-973.

13. Homily given at St. Peter's, May 14, 1942, from *Prayers of Pope Pius XII* Translated by Martin W. Schoenberg (Westminster: Newman Press, 1957), pp. 11-13.

14. *Selected Letters and Addresses of Pius XII* (London: Catholic Truth Society, 1949), pp. 78-79.

15. *Selected Documents of His Holiness, Pope Pius XII* (Washington: National Catholic Welfare Conference, n.d.), pp. 22-23.

16. *Journal of a Soul*. Translated by Dorothy White (New York: The New American Library, 1965), p. 446.

17. *Ibid.*, p. 452.

18. Believed to be composed by St. Isidore of Seville, to be used during the Second Provincial Council of Seville, Spain in 619. It was also used during the Fourth Provincial Council of Toledo, Spain in 633. The prayer was used to open sessions of the First Vatican Council in 1869 as well as for an opening prayer at meetings of the preparatory commissions for Vatican II. *The Documents of Vatican II*. General Editor: Walter M. Abbott; translated and edited by Joseph Gallagher (New York: America Press, 1966), p. xxii.

19. *The Encyclicals and Other Messages of John XXIII*. Arranged and edited by the staff of *The Pope Speaks* Magazine (Washington D.C.: The Pope Speaks Press, 1964), pp. 444-445.

20. "The Role of the Episcopate," *Catholic Mind*, LXII (November, 1964), pp. 57-58.

21. *Documents of Vatican II* (cf. Note 18), pp. 16-17.

22. *Ibid.*, pp. 588-589.

23. *Ibid.*, p. 236.

24. *The Pope Speaks*, XII (No. 1, 1967), pp. 79-81. Translated by Austin Vaughan.

25. *The Pope Speaks*, XII (No. 4, 1967), pp. 343-346. Translation from NC News Service.

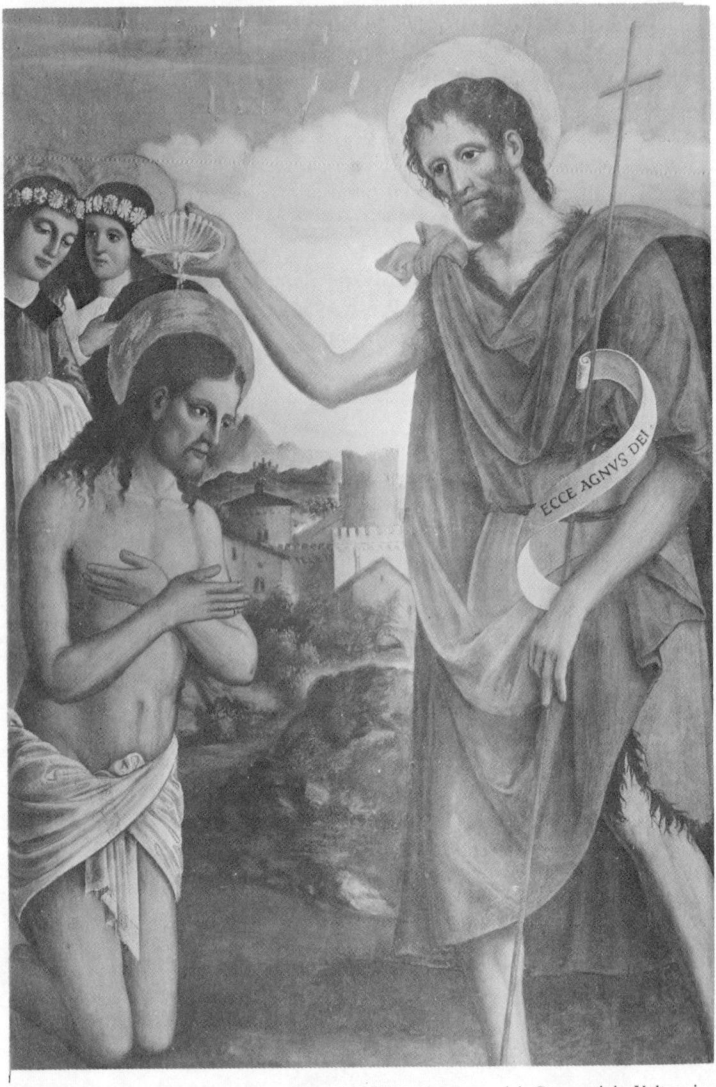

Lodovico Brea, THE BAPTISM OF CHRIST, Convento dei Cappuccini, Voltaggio.
Photo: Frick Art Reference Library.

Chapter III

THE HOLY SPIRIT IN THE LITURGY AND IN STANDARD PRAYERS

Introduction

The liturgy itself can be viewed as a school wherein the Christian may learn the role that the Spirit plays in the great drama of redemption. In the Mass, the Lord of all creation makes Himself present in the Church, under the species of bread and wine, but through the power of the Spirit of God. Before the Consecration, the priest prays:

That we might live no longer for ourselves
    but for Him who died and rose again for us.
    He sent the Holy Spirit from You, Father,
    as His *first gift* to those who believe,
to complete His work on earth
    and bring us the fullness of grace.
Father, may this Holy Spirit sanctify these offerings.
Let them become the body and blood
    of Jesus Christ, our Lord. . . .

It is indeed the Spirit of God who accomplishes the mystic sacrifice; we who partake of the same Bread and the same Chalice are united to one another in the communion of the one Holy Spirit.

Every sacrament in truth operates by the descent of the grace of the Holy Spirit. The very words of the rite of Baptism affirm that "through water and the Holy Spirit, we are reborn to everlasting life." The bishop, in extending his hands over those to be confirmed, beseeches heaven to send forth all the sevenfold gifts of the Spirit upon the assembled Christians. In Holy Orders, the *ordinandi* must declare that they are resolved, with the help of the Holy Spirit, to discharge their priestly offices. After beseeching God to renew the spirit of holiness within the candidate, the bishop anoints his hands and reminds him that "the Father anointed Jesus Christ as Lord through the power of the Holy Spirit."

In mutually ministering the Sacrament of Matrimony, a couple, in effect, call down upon each other a new pentecost for achieving true unity in the love of the Spirit. The Council of Trent declared that the effect of the Sacrament of the Sick was an outpouring of the grace of the Holy Spirit which heals even the body when this is expedient for the health of the soul.

What a source of hope it is to recall that each time the Christian invokes the Spirit either in private or liturgical prayer, he can be assured, as the great pastor Cyril of Jerusalem pointed out: "That which the Holy Spirit touches is *changed*."

Some of the loveliest gems of medieval Latin poetry are hymns to the Holy Spirit used in the breviary and liturgy. The *Veni, Sancte Spiritus* is so perfect in its original Latin that it has been styled "The Golden Sequence." One sixteenth-century commentator declared, "I well believe that the author . . . when he composed this piece, had his soul transfused by a certain heavenly sweetness, by which, the Holy Spirit being its author, he uttered so much sweetness in so few words." Mass prayers from non-Roman liturgical rites often reveal an intensity of devotion to the Holy Spirit that equals or even supersedes the Roman rite prayers.

THE SACRAMENT OF BAPTISM[1]

Prayer of Exorcism and Anointing before Baptism

Almighty and ever-living God,
you sent your only Son into the world
to cast out the power of Satan, spirit of evil,
to rescue man from the kingdom of darkness,
and bring him into the splendor of your kingdom of light.
We pray for this child:
set him (her) free from original sin,
make him (her) a temple of your glory,
and send your Holy Spirit to dwell with him (her).
(We ask this) through Christ our Lord.

When they come to the font, the celebrant questions the congregation with these or similar words:

My dear brothers and sisters, we now ask God to give this child new life in abundance through water and the Holy Spirit.

Blessing and Invocation of God over Baptismal Water

Father, you give us grace through sacramental signs, which tell us of the wonders of your unseen power.

In baptism we use your gift of water, which you have made a rich symbol of the grace you give us in this sacrament.

At the very dawn of creation your Spirit breathed on the waters, making them the wellspring of all holiness.

The waters of the great flood you made a sign of the waters of baptism, that make an end of sin and a new beginning of goodness.

Through the waters of the Red Sea you led Israel out of slavery, to be an image of God's holy people, set free from sin by baptism.

In the waters of the Jordan your Son was baptized by John and anointed with the Spirit.

Your Son willed that water and blood should flow from his side as he hung upon the cross.

After his resurrection he told his disciples: "Go out and teach all nations, baptizing them in the name of the Father, and of the Son, and of the Holy Spirit."

Father, look now with love upon your Church, and unseal for her the fountain of baptism.

By the power of the Spirit give to the water of this font the grace of your Son.

You created man in your own likeness: cleanse him from sin in a new birth to innocence by water and the Spirit.

The celebrant touches the water with his right hand and continues:

We ask you, Father, with your Son to send the Holy Spirit upon the water of this font. May all who are buried with Christ in the death of baptism rise also with him to newness of life.

The celebrant speaks to the parents and godparents in these words:

You have come here to present this child for baptism. By water and the Holy Spirit he is to receive the gift of new life from God, who is love. . . .

Do you believe in the Holy Spirit, the holy catholic Church, the communion of saints, the forgiveness of sins, the resurrection of the body, and life everlasting? . . .

The celebrant baptizes the child, saying:

I baptize you in the name of the Father, and of the Son and of the Holy Spirit.

Anointing with Chrism

God the Father of our Lord Jesus Christ has freed you from sin, given you a new birth by water and the Holy Spirit, and welcomed you into his holy people. He now anoints you with the chrism of salvation. As Christ was anointed Priest, Prophet, and King, so may you live always as a member of his body, sharing everlasting life.

Final Blessing

By God's gift, through water and the Holy Spirit, we are reborn to everlasting life. In his goodness, may he continue to pour out his blessings upon these sons and daughters of his. May he make them always, wherever they may be, faithful members of his holy people. May he send his peace upon all who are gathered here, in Christ Jesus our Lord. Amen.

May almighty God, the Father, and the Son, and the Holy Spirit bless you. Amen.

CONFIRMATION MASS (A)[2]

Opening Prayer

God of power and mercy,
send your Holy Spirit to live in our hearts
and make us temples of his glory.

We ask this through our Lord Jesus Christ, your Son,
who lives and reigns with you and the Holy Spirit,
one God, for ever and ever.

Or:

Lord,
fulfill your promise.
Send your Holy Spirit to make us witnesses before the world
to the good news proclaimed by Jesus Christ our Lord,
who lives and reigns with you and the Holy Spirit,
one God, for ever and ever.

Prayer over the Gifts

Lord,
we celebrate the memorial of our redemption
by which your Son won for us the gift of the Holy Spirit.
Accept our offerings,
and send us your Holy Spirit
to make us more like Christ
in bearing witness to the world.

Prayer after Communion

Lord,
help those you have anointed by your Spirit
and fed with the body and blood of your Son.
Support them through every trial
and by their works of love
build up the Church in holiness and joy.

Solemn Blessing

God our Father
made you his children by water and the Holy Spirit:
may he bless you
and watch over you with his fatherly love. Amen.

Jesus Christ the Son of God
promised that the Spirit of truth
would be with his Church for ever:
may he bless you and give you courage
in professing the true faith. Amen.

The Holy Spirit
came down upon the disciples
and set their hearts on fire with love:
may he bless you,
keep you one in faith and love
and bring you to the joy of God's kingdom. Amen.

Or:

Prayer over the People

God our Father,
complete the work you have begun
and keep the gifts of your Holy Spirit
active in the hearts of your people.
Make them ready to live his gospel
and eager to do his will.
May they never be ashamed
to proclaim to all the world Christ crucified
living and reigning for ever and ever. Amen.

CONFIRMATION MASS (B)

Opening Prayer

Lord,
send us your Holy Spirit
to help us walk in unity of faith
and grow in the strength of his love
to the full stature of Christ,
who lives and reigns with you and the Holy Spirit,
one God, for ever and ever.

PRAYER OVER THE GIFTS

Lord,
you have signed our brothers and sisters
with the cross of your Son
and anointed them with the oil of salvation.
As they offer themselves with Christ,
continue to fill their hearts with your Spirit.

PRAYER AFTER COMMUNION

Lord,
you give your Son as food
to those you anoint with your Spirit.
Help them to fulfill your law
by living in freedom as your children.
May they live in holiness
and be your witnesses to the world.

OTHER PRAYERS

OPENING PRAYER

Lord,
fulfill the promise given by your Son
and send the Holy Spirit
to enlighten our minds
and lead us to all truth.

Grant this through our Lord Jesus Christ, your Son,
who lives and reigns with you and the Holy Spirit,
one God, for ever and ever.

PRAYER OVER THE GIFTS

Lord,
accept the offering of your family
and help those who receive the gift of your Spirit
to keep him in their hearts
and come to the reward of eternal life.

PRAYER AFTER COMMUNION

Lord,
we have shared the one bread of life.
Send the Spirit of your love
to keep us one in faith and peace.

RITE OF CONFIRMATION

Renewal of Baptismal Promises

Do you believe in the Holy Spirit,
the Lord, the giver of life,
who came upon the apostles at Pentecost
and today is given to you sacramentally in confirmation?

Imposition of Hands

All-powerful God, Father of our Lord Jesus Christ,
by water and the Holy Spirit
you freed your sons and daughters from sin
and gave them new life.
Send your Holy Spirit upon them
to be their Helper and Guide.
Give them the spirit of wisdom and understanding,
the spirit of right judgment and courage,
the spirit of knowledge and reverence.
Fill them with the spirit of wonder and awe in your presence.
We ask this through Christ our Lord. Amen.

Anointing with Chrism

N., be sealed with the Gift of the Holy Spirit.

THE SACRAMENT OF HOLY ORDERS[3]

The bishop questions those being ordained:

Are you resolved, with the help of the Holy Spirit, to discharge without fail the office of priesthood in the rank of presbyters as the trusted partners of the bishops in caring for the Lord's flock? . . .

The bishop stands alone and, with his hands joined, sings or says in a loud voice:

Listen to us, we pray, Lord our God, and pour out upon these servants of yours the blessing of the Holy Spirit and the strength given to the priesthood. In your sight we offer these men to be set apart for a sacred office. In your unfailing generosity accept our decision, through Christ our Lord. . . .

The bishop sings the prayer of consecration or says it in a loud voice:

. . . . We ask you, all-powerful Father, give these servants of yours the dignity of the presbyterate. Renew the Spirit of holiness within them. . . .

Anointing of Hands: The bishop puts on the linen gremial and anoints with holy chrism the palms of each new priest before him. He says:

The Father anointed Jesus Christ as Lord through the power of the Holy Spirit. May Jesus keep you worthy of offering sacrifice to God and sanctifying the Christian assembly.

At the end, an appropriate song may be sung, or:

No longer do I call you servants, but my friends, because you know all that I have done among you (alleluia). Receive the Holy Spirit as an Advocate within you. . . .

PRAYERS OF THE ROMAN MISSAL

LITURGY FOR VIGIL OF PENTECOST

Opening Prayer

Let us pray
[that the Holy Spirit
may bring peace and unity to all mankind]

Almighty and ever-living God,
you fulfilled the Easter promise
by sending us your Holy Spirit.
May that Spirit unite the races and nations on earth
to proclaim your glory.

Grant this through our Lord Jesus Christ, your Son,
who lives and reigns with you and the Holy Spirit,
one God, for ever and ever.

Alternative Opening Prayer

Let us pray
[that the flame of the Spirit will descend upon us]

Father in heaven,
fifty days have celebrated the fullness
of the mystery of your revealed love.

See your people gathered in prayer,
open to receive the Spirit's flame.

May it come to rest in our hearts
and disperse the divisions of word and tongue.
With one voice and one song
may we praise your name in joy and thanksgiving.
Grant this through Christ our Lord.

Or:

God our Father,
you have given us new birth.
Strengthen us with your Holy Spirit
and fill us with your light.
Grant this through our Lord Jesus Christ, your Son,
who lives and reigns with you and the Holy Spirit,
one God, for ever and ever.

Prayer over the Gifts

Lord,
send your Spirit on these gifts
and through them help the Church you love
to show your salvation to all the world.

Prayer after Communion

Lord,
through this eucharist,
send the Holy Spirit of Pentecost into our hearts
to keep us always in your love.

LITURGY FOR PENTECOST

Opening Prayer

Let us pray
[that the Spirit will work through our lives
to bring Christ to the world]

God our Father,
let the Spirit you sent on your Church
to begin the teaching of the gospel
continue to work in the world
through the hearts of all who believe.
We ask this through our Lord Jesus Christ, your Son,
who lives and reigns with you and the Holy Spirit,
one God, for ever and ever.

Alternative Opening Prayer

Let us pray
[in the Spirit who dwells within us]

Father of light, from whom every good gift comes,
send your Spirit into our lives
with the power of a mighty wind,
and by the flame of your wisdom
open the horizons of our minds.

Loosen our tongues to sing your praise
in words beyond the power of speech,
for without your Spirit
man could never raise his voice in words of peace
or announce the truth that Jesus is Lord,
who lives and reigns with you and the Holy Spirit,
one God, for ever and ever.

Prayer over the Gifts

Lord,
may the Spirit you promised
lead us into all truth
and reveal to us the full meaning of this sacrifice.

Eucharistic Prayer

Father, all-powerful and ever-living God,
we do well always and everywhere to give you thanks.

Today you sent the Holy Spirit
on those marked out to be your children
by sharing the life of your only Son,
and so you brought the paschal mystery to its completion.

Today we celebrate the great beginning of your Church
when the Holy Spirit made known to all peoples the one true God
and created from the many languages of man
one voice to profess one faith.

The joy of the resurrection renews the whole world,
while the choirs of heaven sing for ever to your glory:

Holy, holy, holy. . . .

Prayer after Communion

Father,
may the food we receive in the eucharist
help our eternal redemption.
Keep within us the vigor of your Spirit
and protect the gifts you have given to your Church.

Solemn Blessing or Prayer over the People

This day the Father of light
has enlightened the minds of the disciples
by the outpouring of the Holy Spirit.
May he bless you
and give you the gifts of the Spirit for ever. Amen.

May that fire which hovered over the disciples
as tongues of flame
burn out all evil from your hearts
and make them glow with pure light. Amen.

God inspired speech in different tongues
to proclaim one faith.
May he strengthen your faith
and fulfill your hope to see him face to face. Amen.

VOTIVE MASSES OF THE HOLY SPIRIT (A)

Opening Prayer

Father,
you taught the hearts of your faithful people
by sending them the light of your Holy Spirit.
In that Spirit give us right judgment
and the joy of his comfort and guidance.
We ask this through our Lord Jesus Christ, your Son,
who lives and reigns with you and the Holy Spirit,
one God, for ever and ever.

Prayer over the Gifts

Pray, brethren . . .
Lord,
make this offering holy
and cleanse our hearts from sin.
Send the light of your Holy Spirit.

Prayer after Communion

Lord,
fill our hearts with your Holy Spirit
to free us from our sins
and make us rich in love for you and one another.

(B)

Opening Prayer

Lord,
may the Helper, the Spirit who comes from you,
fill our hearts with light
and lead us to all truth
as your Son promised,
for he lives and reigns with you and the Holy Spirit,
one God, for ever and ever.

Or:

God our Father,
no secret is hidden from you,
for every heart is open to you
and every wish is known.
Fill our hearts with the light of your Holy Spirit
to free our thoughts from sin,
that we may perfectly love you and fittingly praise you.
Grant this through our Lord Jesus Christ, your Son,
who lives and reigns with you and the Holy Spirit,
one God, for ever and ever.

Prayer after Communion

Lord our God,
you renew us with food from heaven;
fill our hearts with the gentle love of your Spirit.
May the gifts we have received in this life
lead us to the gift of eternal joy.

(C)

Opening Prayer

God our Father,
pour out the gifts of your Holy Spirit on the world.
You sent the Spirit on your Church

to begin the teaching of the gospel:
now let the Spirit continue to work in the world
through the hearts of all who believe.
We ask this through our Lord Jesus Christ, your Son,
who lives and reigns with you and the Holy Spirit,
one God, for ever and ever.

Or:

Father,
as your Spirit guides us and your loving care keeps us safe,
be close to us in your mercy and listen to those who call on you.
Strengthen and protect by your kindness
the faith of all who believe in you.
We ask this through our Lord Jesus Christ, your Son,
who lives and reigns with you and the Holy Spirit,
one God, for ever and ever.

Prayer over the Gifts

Lord,
may the fire of your Spirit,
which filled the hearts of the disciples of Jesus
with courage and love,
make holy the sacrifice we offer in your sight.

Eucharistic Prayer

Father, all-powerful and ever-living God,
we do well always and everywhere to give you thanks
through Jesus Christ our Lord.

He ascended above all the heavens,
and from his throne at your right hand
poured into the hearts of your adopted children
the Holy Spirit of your promise.

With steadfast love
we sing your unending praise;
we join with the hosts of heaven
in their triumphant song:

Holy, holy, holy. . . .

Or:

Father, all-powerful and ever-living God,

we do well always and everywhere to give you thanks.

You give your gifts of grace
for every time and season
as you guide the Church
in the marvelous ways of your providence.

You give us your Holy Spirit
to help us always by his power,
so that with loving trust
we may turn to you in all our troubles
and give you thanks in all our joys. . . .

Prayer after Communion

Lord,
through this eucharist,
send the Holy Spirit of Pentecost into our hearts
to keep us always in your love.

Sequence for Pentecost
Veni, Sancte Spiritus—The "Golden Sequence"

Holy Spirit, Lord of light!
From Thy clear celestial height,
Thy pure, beaming radiance give:

Come, Thou Father of the poor!
Come with treasures which endure!
Come, Thou Light of all that Live!

Thou, of all consolers best,
Visiting the troubled breast,
Dost refreshing peace bestow:

Thou in toil art comfort sweet;
Pleasant coolness in the heat;
Solace in the midst of woe.

Light immortal! Light divine!
Visit Thou these hearts of Thine,
And our inmost being fill;

If Thou take Thy grace away,
Nothing pure in man will stay;
All his good is turned to ill.

Heal our wounds—our strength renew;
On our dryness pour Thy dew;
Wash the stains of guilt away.

Bend the stubborn heart and will;
Melt the frozen, warm the chill;
Guide the steps that go astray.

Thou, on those who evermore,
Thee confess and Thee adore,
In Thy sevenfold gifts descend.

Give them comfort when they die;
Give them life with Thee on high;
Give them joys which never end. Amen.[5]

PRAYERS OF THE ROMAN BREVIARY

Come Holy Ghost, Creator, Come

Come Holy Ghost, Creator come,
From Thy bright, heavenly throne;
Come, take possession of our souls,
And make them all Thy own.

Thou who art called the Paraclete
Best gift of God above;
The living spring, the living fire,
Sweet unction and true love.

Thou who art sevenfold in Thy grace,
Finger of God's right hand;
His promise, teaching little ones
To speak and understand.

O! guide our minds with Thy blest light,
With love our hearts inflame;
And with Thy strength which ne'er decays
Confirm our mortal frame.

Far from us drive our hellish foe,
True peace unto us bring;
And through all perils lead us safe,
Beneath Thy sacred wing.

Through Thee may we the Father know;

Through Thee, th' eternal Son.
And Thee, the Spirit of them both;
Thrice blessed Three in One.

All glory to the Father be,
With His co-equal Son,
The like to Thee, great Paraclete,
While endless ages run. Amen.[6]

JAM CHRISTIS ASTRA ASCENDERAT

Above the starry spheres
To where He was before
Christ had gone up, soon from on high
The Father's Gift to pour;

And now had fully come,
On mystic circle borne
Of seven times seven revolving days,
The Pentecostal morn:

When, as the Apostles knelt
At the third hour in prayer,
A sudden rushing sound proclaimed
The God of glory near.

Forthwith a tongue of fire
Alights on every brow;
Each breast receives the Father's Light,
The Word's enkindling glow.

The Holy Ghost on all
Is mightily outpoured;
Who straight in divers tongues declare
The wonders of the Lord.

While strangers of all climes
Flock round from far and near,
And with amazement, each at once
Their native accents hear.

But Judah, faithless still
Denies the hand Divine;
And madly jeer the Saints of Christ
As drunk with new-made wine.

Till Peter in the midst
Stood up, and spake aloud;
And their perfidious falsity
By Joel's witness showed.

Praise to the Father be!
Praise to the Son Who rose;
Praise to the Holy Paraclete!
While age on ages flows. Amen.[7]

MATINS LESSONS

A HOMILY OF ST. AUGUSTINE, BISHOP

Treatise 74 on John, and 75

In saying "I will ask the Father and He will give you another Advocate," Jesus indicates that He Himself is our Advocate. (The Greek *Paraclitus* of our Gospel text can be rendered by the Latin *advocatus*.) It has also been said of Christ: "We have an Advocate with the Father, Jesus Christ the just." Our Lord said that the world is incapable of receiving the Holy Spirit, just as it was also said, "The wisdom of the flesh is hostile to God, for it is not subject to the law of God, nor can it be." It is as if we were to say that what is unjust cannot be just. When "World" is used in this context it denotes those who love the world: this love does not come from the Father. And so the love of this world, which we are busy lessening and eradicating in ourselves, is at odds with that love of God which "is poured forth in our hearts by the Holy Spirit who has been given to us."[8]

Lesson ii

And so "the world cannot receive" the Spirit, "because it neither sees Him nor knows Him." For worldly love does not have that interior vision by which the Holy Spirit can be seen, and the Spirit can be perceived in no other way. "But you," says Christ, "shall know Him, because He will dwell with you, and be in you." He will be in them in order to dwell, or stay, in them, not stay in them in order to be in them; for being somewhere is a prerequisite to staying there. And, lest they think that "He will dwell with you" should be taken as equivalent to the ordinary visible way a guest stays with a man, Christ explains what "He will dwell with you" means by adding, "He will be in you."

Lesson iii

The Spirit is perceived invisibly, therefore. Nor can we have any knowledge of Him if He Himself is not in us. For He is seen in us in the same way as we see our conscience in ourselves: we see another person's face, but we cannot see our own; when it comes to conscience, however, it is our own that we see, not anyone else's. Our conscience, however, never exists except within us, whereas the Holy Spirit is also able to exist without us. The reason for His being given is precisely that He may exist within us also; if He be not in us, we cannot see and know Him in the only way in which He can be seen and known. After the promise of the Holy Spirit some might think that our Lord meant to give the Spirit in place of Himself, so that He Himself would no longer be with them. To prevent this misconception, Christ expanded His statement, saying, "I will not leave you orphans; I will come to you." Thus, even though the Son of God chose us for adoption as sons by His own Father, wishing to have by grace the very same Father He had by nature, still He Himself also displays a kind of fatherly affection for us in saying, "I will not leave you orphans."

HOMILIES OF POPE ST. GREGORY

Homily 30 on the Gospels (i)

I would like, dearest brothers, to go through the words of the Gospel lesson rather briefly, so as to have more time left to linger in contemplation of this great feast. On this day the Holy Spirit came upon the disciples in a sudden rush, and transformed the fleshly love of their hearts into love of Him. Outwardly, tongues of fire appeared: inwardly, their hearts were set ablaze; for when the disciples received God under the appearance of fire, they began to burn with a sweet love. Indeed, the Holy Spirit is Himself love, as St. John says: "God is love." Whoever, then, desires God wholeheartedly is already in real possession of the One whom he loves. For no one could love God if he did not possess the Beloved.

Lesson ii

But now, if any one of you were asked whether he loved God, he would feel safe in answering with complete confidence, "Yes." At the very beginning of this Gospel reading, however, you heard what Truth Himself says: "If anyone love Me, he will keep My word." The proof of love, then, is shown in works. Hence the same Evangelist St. John says in one of his epistles, "If anyone says, 'I love God,' and does not keep His commandments, he is a liar." We certainly do love God, that is, we keep His commandments, if we keep our lusts in check. For whoever still lets himself go in sinful desires obviously does not love God, because his will decides against God.

Homily iii

"And My Father will love him, and We will come to him and make Our abode with him." Consider, dearest brothers, how great a privilege it is to have God come into one's heart as a guest. If a wealthy or influential friend were coming to your house, would you not hurry and tidy the house thoroughly, in order that there would be nothing offensive to his eyes when he entered? In the same way, if you are preparing the house of your mind to receive God, remove the filth of evil deeds. Now look closely at what Truth Himself said: "We will come and make Our abode with him." For God indeed enters certain hearts, but He does not dwell there; such persons, by contrition, gain God's attention, but in time of temptation they forget the very acts for which they were sorry. Accordingly, they continue to commit those sins as if they had never bewailed them.

PENTECOST

Beata nobis gaudia

Again the slowly circling year
    Brings round the blessed hour
When on the Saints the Comforter
    Came down in grace and power.

In fashion of a fiery tongue
    The mighty Godhead came;
Their lips with eloquence He strung,
    And filled their hearts with flame.

Straightway with divers tongues they speak,
    Instinct with grace divine;
While wondering crowds the cause mistake,
    And deem them drunk with wine.

These things were mystically wrought,—
    The Paschal time complete,
When Israel's Law remission brought
    Of every legal debt

God of all grace! To Thee we pray,
    To Thee adoring bend;
Into our hearts this sacred day
    Thy Spirit's fulness send.

Thou, who in ages past didst pour
Thy graces from above,—
Thy grace in us where lost restore
And 'stablish peace and love.

All glory to the Father be;
And to the Son who rose;
Glory, O Holy Ghost! To Thee,
While age on ages flows.[9]

Antiphon to the "Magnificat" on the second vespers of Pentecost

Today the feast of Pentecost has come, alleluia. Today the Holy Spirit appeared to the disciples in the form of fire and gave them charismatic gifts; He sent them into the whole world to preach and bear witness: "He who believes and is baptized shall be saved, alleluia!"

Monday in the Octave of Pentecost (Collect)

O God, You have given the Holy Spirit to Your Apostles. Grant Your people the grace they ask of You: since You have given us the faith, give us peace also. This we ask of You through our Lord . . . in the unity of the same.

Tuesday in the Octave of Pentecost (Collect)

Lord, may the power of the Holy Spirit assist us: may it come very gently to purify our hearts, and may it protect us from all evil. This we ask of You through our Lord . . . in the unity of the same.

Wednesday in the Octave of Pentecost (Collect)

May the Holy Spirit, the Comforter, who proceeds from You, Lord, come to enlighten our souls and guide us to all truth, according to the promise of Your Son, who lives and reigns with You in the unity of the same.

Friday in the Octave of Pentecost (Collect)

It is the Holy Spirit who gathers together Your Church; God of mercy, grant that Your Church may never be troubled by the attacks of her enemies. This we ask of You through our Lord . . . in the unity of the same.

Saturday within the Octave of Pentecost (Collect)

In Your kindness, Lord, may You see fit to pour into our souls the Holy Spirit whose wisdom has created us and whose providence governs us. This we ask of You through our Lord . . . in the unity of the same.

Hymn for Terce

Come, Holy Ghost, Who ever One,
Reignest with Father and with Son,
It is the hour, our souls possess
With Thy full flood of holiness.

Let flesh, and heart, and lips, and mind,
Sound forth our witness to mankind;
And Love light up our mortal frame
Till others catch the living flame.

Now to the Father, to the Son,
And to the Spirit, Three in One,
Be Praise, and thanks, and glory given,
By men on earth, by Saints in heaven. Amen[10]

LITURGY OF GREEK CHURCH

Hymn from the Greek Church by St. John Damascene from the Pentecostarion

Coming forth from the mysterious cloud that covered him, the tongue-tied Moses promulgated the Law written by God; for, closing his eyes to material things, he learned to see Him WHO IS: and praised, in sacred songs the Spirit he had been taught to know.

The venerable lips, whose words were ever grave, said to his apostles: "Depart not from Jerusalem, my friends! for when I shall be seated on my Father's high throne, I will pour forth, on you who desire light, the infinite grace of the Spirit."

Having consummated his course, the Word, ever faithful to his promise, fills their hearts with sweet peace; for, having accomplished his work, Christ, as he had promised, gladdened his dear disciples, filling the cenacle with a mighty wind, and giving then the Spirit in the form of fiery tongues.

How incomprehensible is the power of our most holy God! Of illiterate men he made orators, whose words silenced philosophers, and, by the bright Spirit that was within them, rescued countless people from the thick night of error.

This almighty Spirit, the illuminating and incorruptible brightness, proceeds from the uncreated Light, from the Father and the Son. To the whole earth, this day, on Mount Sion, is he made known in all his effulgence by a voice of fire.

And thou, O Son of God, one Person in two Natures, hast prepared the divine laver of regeneration; whose water flowed from the wound of thy divine side, O Word of God! The Holy Ghost gives fruitfulness to the font by his own glowing flame.

You who adore the triple lighted Essence, you are the true servants of the sovereign God! This day did Christ, our benefactor, accomplish his divine work: he gave us, for our salvation's sake, the whole grace of the Spirit, and he gave it in the form of fire.

O children of the Church! children of light! receive the dew of the Holy Spirit, the dew that burns away the dross of sin. Now hath a law gone forth from Sion, the grace of the Spirit, in the form of a fiery tongue.

There was a time, when the shrill voice of many instruments bade the multitude adore a lifeless statue of gold: but now, by the life-giving grace of the Paraclete, men are made worthy to sing: "O one, coequal, and unbeginning Trinity! we bless thee!"

The senseless crowd, when they heard the apostles speaking in divers tongues, forgot the prophecy of Joel, and said: "These men are drunk with wine!" But we, instructed by our God, cry out with fervent hearts: "O thou, the Renewer of the world! we bless thee!"

The hour of Tierce was chosen for this effusion of grace, showing us that we should adore three Persons in the oneness of power. Blessed art thou, Father, Son, and Spirit, on this the now first of days, the Sunday.[11]

LITURGY OF ARMENIAN CHURCH

Pentecost Hymn from Armenian Church

The Dove, sent unto men, has descended from heaven, amidst a mighty sound; it came in the form of light, which, with its bright fire, burned not but strengthened the disciples, as they sat in the sacred cenacle.

The dove is the Spirit, the Unsearchable that searcheth the deep things of God. He proceeds from the Father: he announces the second and dread coming. We are taught to believe him consubstantial with the Father.

Praise in the highest heavens to him that proceeds from the Father —the Holy Ghost! The apostles were inebriated with his immortal chalice, and they invited earth to heaven.

O divine and life-giving Spirit! O Lover of mankind! thou didst illumine, with tongues of fire, the apostles who were assembled together in the bond of love. Wherefore, do we also, this day, celebrate thy holy coming.

The holy apostles were gladdened by thy coming, and people of divers tongues were united together, who before were strangers to each other. Wherefore do we also, this day, celebrate thy holy coming.

By them thou didst, by holy and spiritual baptism, beautify the whole earth with a bright and new garment. Wherefore do we also, this day, celebrate thy holy coming.

Thou, O holy Spirit, who sittest on the chariot of the Cherubim, didst this day descend upon the choir of the apostles. Be thou blessed, O immortal King!

Thou, O holy Spirit, that walkest on the wings of the winds, didst this day rest, in divided tongues of fire, on the apostles. Be thou blessed O immortal King!

Thou, O holy Spirit, that carest, in thy providence, for thy creatures, didst this day come to strengthen thy Church. Be thou blessed, O immortal King![12]

Hymn from Armenian Church for Pentecost Monday

O uncreated Spirit! one and the same and coexisting with the Father and the Son; who proceedest inscrutably from the Father, and receivest of the Son ineffably; thou this day descendest into the cenacle, and gavest the disciples to drink of the spirit of grace. Oh! give us also in thy mercy, to drink of the chalice of wisdom.

O Creator of all things, who movest over the waters! thou, in the form of a Dove, lovingly broodest over the water of the font given to us by him who is God together with thee; and thus thou givest birth to a race of God-like men. Oh! give us also, in thy mercy, to drink of the chalice of wisdom.

O Master of the heavenly spirits, and of us men who live on earth; who turnest shepherds into prophets, and fishermen into apostles, and publicans into evangelists and persecutors into preachers of thy word; oh! give us also, in thy mercy, to drink of the chalice of wisdom.

O divine Spirit, who, as a mighty wind, whose rushing sound fills men with fear, appearedst in the cenacle to the choir of the twelve apostles, baptizing them with fire, as gold is cleansed of its dross; oh! drive from us the darkness of sin, and clothe us with the light of glory.

He that is love, out of love for man, sent Thee that art love; by Thee He united his members (that is, his Church), to himself; He, by Thee, built this Church, and set it upon seven pillars, and entrusted her to the stewardship of the apostles, who were adorned with thy seven gifts; oh! drive us from the darkness of sin, and clothe us with the light of glory.[13]

AMBROSIAN LITURGY

Pentecost Preface from Ambrosian Liturgy

It is just and available to salvation, that we rejoice on this great solemnity, whereon the most holy Pasch is veiled with the mystery of the fifty days, and the mystic number is completed, and the division of tongues, caused in times long past by pride, is now remedied by the unity produced by the Holy Ghost. For, on this day, a sound was suddenly heard by the apostles, and receiving the symbol of one faith, they, in divers tongues, taught all nations the glory of thy Gospel. Through Christ our Lord.[14]

MOZARABIC LITURGY

Illation or Preface from Mozarabic Liturgy

It is meet and just, O almighty God, that we acknowledge, to the best of human power, the blessing of thy gifts, and celebrate, by a yearly commemoration, the eternal salvation that was this day granted to mankind. For which of us would dare to be silent concerning the coming of thy holy Spirit, when, through thine apostles, not a tongue of even barbarous nations was silent? But who can narrate the descent of the fire which this day fell, giving to the disciples the divers tongues of all nations, in such wise that, when the Latin spoke to the Hebrew, or Greek to the Egyptian, or the Scythian to the Indian, and used his own language or heard the foreigner's, neither he that listened nor he that spoke failed to understand? Who could describe the power, that by its own free strength, imparted the gift of one and the same heavenly doctrine to them that were to preach the word of truth throughout the whole world? And though the distribution of manifold knowledge was beautiful beyond measure, and the gift of tongues was made admirable by its multiplied variety, yet there was nothing in all this that jarred with the unity of faith. From this we learn that diversity of tongues is no hindrance to men's praising their Lord, and that it matters not that different men profess their faith in different languages provided all believe in the same God.

We therefore, beseech thee, O Lord, to accept this our homage of praise, which comes from the hearts of the children of promise. By the infusion of thy divine Spirit, bless and sanctify our souls, that thus we may hope for and receive the favours thou hast promised to thy faithful people. Among the numberless gifts and operations of the Holy Ghost, which were the generous outpouring of thy glory for our salvation's sake, nothing was grander at the beginning of the Church, than that a few should speak the languages of all nations, and in the same preach the Gospel. Such a prodigy as this could only have been by the inspiring grace of the Holy Ghost, who came to us after the seven weeks of thy Son's glorious Resurrection; hereby showing us, that although he be sevenfold in his gifts, yet that he is the perfection of all the virtues blended into one whole; just as seven is a separate number in itself, yet is it found in each of the other numbers. These, without doubt, are the seven steps of thy temple, whereby man is to mount to the kingdom of heaven. This is the fiftieth year of remission, that celebrated mysterious type of the old Law. This is the harvest of the first-fruits, which we are commanded to offer up on this day: they are fruits which, though eternal and existing before all ages, yet are new because now first made known to us.

Neither was it without a mysterious meaning, that this Gift was poured out upon us on the tenth day after the Ascension of thy Son; it showed us that this was the coin of ten, (the denarius) promised by the Father of the family to the laborers in the vineyard. Great, indeed, and exceedingly necessary was this sign of thy divine Gift, that when the fiery tongues rested on the heads of the disciples, there should be produced nothing in the hearts of believers that was discordant or tepid, but that the preachers of thy Word should be unanimous in the truth, and fervent in charity. O blessed Fire, that burns yet gives fruitfulness! Every intellectual being confesses by the principle of life that is in it, that this Fire is the omnipotent God. The Cherubim and Seraphim—thus called because of their burning more ardently with this Fire—praise the blessed Three, confessing them to be coequal in holiness and almighty power. Together with the hymning choirs of the heavenly hosts, they rest not nor grow tired of their office, but with unceasing jubilation, sing, adore, and praise; saying: Holy! Holy! Holy![15]

An Address Made to the Faithful by the Bishop during the Mass of Whit Sunday in the Mozarabic Liturgy

Let us, dearly beloved brethren, celebrate the gifts of the Holy Ghost, which were promised unto us by the Son of God, and were this day sent; let us celebrate them with all possible faith, intention, virtue, joy, gladness, praise, devotion, homage, and purity. Let us open our hearts, and purify them; let our mind and soul be dilated; for surely narrow hearts are not able to speak the praise and coming of the immense. He is coequal with the Father and Son, of one and the same nature with them; he is the Third in Person, but One in glory. He, whom the heavens cannot contain, for they neither confine nor limit him, is coming down this day to the narrow dwelling of our heart. Who among us, dearly beloved brethren, would dare to think himself worthy of such a guest? Who would think himself able to provide an entertainment worthy of him, who is the life of the very Angels, and Archangels, and all the heavenly Powers? Since, therefore, we acknowledge that we ourselves cannot provide him a suitable dwelling, let us beseech him to prepare one himself within us. Amen.[16]

Sequence from the Ancient Missal of Liège

O Love of the Father and the Son! thou art our true and brightest aid, in whom alone we hope for solace.

O never-failing light of the good! the reward of the just, the resuscitator of sinners!

Giver of all strength, and holiness, and blessing! Lover of all righteousness.

Almighty, and so bounteous! All-governing, and so merciful!

Infinitely just, and dear, and glorious, and holy, and strong and spiritual! No, nothing is so mighty, nothing so good!

Thou enlightener of hearts! by whom we come to the Father of all, and to the Son.

Fount of knowledge; giver of joy; remedy for sin; Spirit of counsel!

Humble, docile, and unchangeable; prudent, noble, and invincible; prompt and endearing!

Choicest of gifts! 'tis thou that givest us understanding and love, and that lovest what is right.

Thou art the Spirit of the Father and the Son; the life-giving Paraclete; the Finger of God's right hand!

He is grandeur and joy, mercy and goodness, benignity and munificence;

Who, as he wills, and when he wills, and where he wills, and as long as he wills, inspires and teaches, fills and exalts, enriches and guides.

He, the Spirit of knowledge, is given to the apostles, on this day, that he may console them. By him is opened to them, in all its fullness, the fount of true wisdom. Amen.[17]

Litany of the Holy Ghost

Lord, have mercy on us.

Christ, have mercy on us.
Lord, have mercy on us.
Father all powerful, have mercy on us.
Jesus, Eternal Son of the Father, Redeemer of the world, save us.
Spirit of the Father and the Son, boundless life of both, sanctify us.
Holy Trinity hear us.
Holy Ghost, Who proceedest from the Father and the Son, enter our hearts.
Holy Ghost, Who art equal to the Father and the Son, enter our hearts.
Promise of God the Father, have mercy on us.
Ray of heavenly light,
Author of all good,
Source of heavenly water,
Consuming fire,
Ardent charity,
Spiritual unction,
Spirit of love and truth,
Spirit of wisdom and understanding,
Spirit of counsel and fortitude,
Spirit of knowledge and piety,
Spirit of fear of the Lord,
Spirit of grace and prayer,
Spirit of peace and meekness
Spirit of modesty and innocence,
Holy Ghost, the Comforter
Holy Ghost, the Sanctifier
Holy Ghost, Who governest the Church,
Gift of God, the Most High
Spirit Who fillest the universe, have mercy on us.
Spirit of the adoption of the children of God,
Holy Ghost, inspire us with horror of sin.
Holy Ghost, come and renew the face of the earth.
Holy Ghost, shed Thy light in our souls.
Holy Ghost, engrave Thy law in our hearts.
Holy Ghost, inflame us with the flame of Thy love.
Holy Ghost, open to us the treasure of Thy graces.
Holy Ghost, teach us to pray well.
Holy Ghost, enlighten us with Thy heavenly inspirations.
Holy Ghost, lead us in the way of salvation.
Holy Ghost, grant us the necessary knowledge.
Holy Ghost, inspire us in the practice of good.

Holy Ghost, grant us the merits of all virtues.
Holy Ghost, make us persevere in justice.
Holy Ghost, be Thou our everlasting reward.
Lamb of God, Who takest away the sins of the world, pour down into our souls the gifts of the Holy Ghost.
Come, Holy Ghost! Fill the hearts of Thy faithful.
And enkindle in them the fire of Thy love.
LET US PRAY.

Grant, O merciful Father, that Thy Divine Spirit enlighten, inflame and purify us, that He may penetrate us with His heavenly dew and make us fruitful in good works; through our Lord Jesus Christ, Thy Son, Who with Thee, in the unity of the same Spirit, liveth and reigneth forever and ever. Amen.[18]

PRAYER FOR THE SEVEN GIFTS OF THE HOLY GHOST

O Lord Jesus Christ Who, before ascending into Heaven didst promise to send the Holy Ghost to finish Thy work in the souls of Thy Apostles and Disciples, deign to grant the same Holy Spirit to me that He may perfect in my soul the work of Thy grace and Thy love. Grant me the Spirit of Wisdom that I may despise the perishable things of this world and aspire only after the things that are eternal; the Spirit of Understanding to enlighten my mind with the light of Thy divine truth; the Spirit of Counsel that I may ever choose the surest way of pleasing God and gaining heaven; the Spirit of Fortitude that I may bear my cross with Thee and that I may overcome with courage all the obstacles that oppose my salvation; the Spirit of Knowledge that I may know God and know myself and grow perfect in the science of the saints; the Spirit of Piety that I may find the service of God sweet and amiable; the Spirit of Fear that I may be filled with a loving reverence towards God and may dread in any way to displease Him. Mark me, dear Lord, with the sign of Thy true disciples and animate me in all things with Thy Spirit. Amen.[19]

NOTES

1. *The Rite of Baptism* (Collegeville, Minn.: The Liturgical Press, 1970). Copyright: International Committee on English in the Liturgy, 1969.

2. *The Sacramentary* (New York: Catholic Book Publishing Co., 1974), pp. 834-837. Copyright: International Committee on English in the Liturgy, 1973.

3. *The Roman Pontifical.* Provisional Text (Washington: National Conference of Catholic Bishops/Bishops' Committee on the Liturgy, 1969). Copyright: International Committee on English in the Liturgy, 1969.

4. Prayers from the Mass, excluding hymns, are taken from *The Sacramentary* (cf. Note 2), pp. 270-273; 429; 940-942, 481, 483.

5. Hymn variously ascribed to Robert II, King of France, Archbishop Stephen Langton, Hermannus Cantactus, and Pope Innocent III. John Julian's *A Dictionary of Hymnology* (New York: Dover Publications, 1957), II, pp. 1213-1214, declares that the sequence is clearly not earlier than about the beginning of the 13th century. The most probable author is Innocent III. This translation is by Edward Caswall, *Lyra Catholica* (London: James Burns, 1849), pp. 234-236.

6. This hymn is sometimes ascribed to Saint Ambrose, Charlemagne, Rhabanus Maurus, and Gregory the Great. Julian declares the evidence is too slight to be conclusive for any of the supposed authors. *Dictionary of Hymnology*, II, 1208. This translation by John, Marquis of Bute, is from the *Garden of the Soul* (London: Keating and Brown, 1834), pp. 178-179.

7. Caswall, *op. cit.*, pp. 104-106.

8. Collects, lessons and antiphon to the Magnificat from the breviary are taken from *The Hours of the Divine Office in English and Latin* (Collegeville, Minn.: The Liturgical Press, 1964), II, 1376-1379; 1390-1393; 1397; 1401; 1404; 1408; 1415-1416; 1419.

9. Caswall, *op. cit.*, pp. 106-108.

10. A hymn of the Ambrosian school translated by Cardinal Newman. *The Roman Breviary* (Edinburg and London: William Blackwood, 1908), p. 52.

11. Abbot Gueranger, *The Liturgical Year.* Translated by Laurence Shepherd. (Westminster: The Newman Press, 1949), III, 320-323.

12. Ibid., pp. 323-324.

13. Ibid., pp. 352-353.

14. Ibid., p. 325.

15. Ibid., pp. 325-328.

16. Ibid., pp. 421-422.

17. Ibid., pp. 375-376.

18. Gabriel Denis, *The Reign of Jesus Through Mary* (New York: Montford Fathers, 1944), pp. 221-224.

19. "Prayers to the Holy Ghost to Implore His Aid in Studies and Examinations" (Washington: The Holy Ghost Fathers).

Miniature—Reichenauer Perikopenbuch, c. 1020, Munich, Staatsbibliothek.

Chapter IV

THE HOLY SPIRIT IN THE WRITINGS OF THE EARLY CHURCH

Introduction

The *earliest* Fathers of the Church had the joy of living in an age that witnessed the immediate results of the new breath of the Spirit sent over the earth after Christ's redemptive death. "I really witness in your community an outpouring upon you of the Spirit," Barnabas wrote delightedly to his followers. Actually, early Christian writers often seemed more interested in the *experience* of the Spirit and the effects of His love in men's lives than in theological discussions about Him. "Test the man who has the Divine Spirit by his life," urged the Shepherd of Hermas. The ultimate gift of self, martyrdom, was offered by saints such as Polycarp and Eulpus with joyful praises for Christ and his Spirit on their lips. In the Christian community created by the Pentecostal Spirit, neither rank nor station was important; what mattered was the very presence of the Spirit in an individual, affirmed the *Didache, The Teaching of the Twelve Apostles*.

Though founded by the Spirit of God, the early Christian community was not exempt from human dissension. Some of the earliest recorded passages concerning the Spirit are admonitions by pastors such as Ignatius and Clement to their flocks to retain the unity of the Spirit in the face of communal strife. Ignatius at one point related how the Spirit of God inspired him to exhort the faithful to submit to the hierarchy even though he had no *human knowledge* that division existed in their ranks.

Severe tension between the institutional and the prophetic Church appeared in the second century with the emergence of the Montanists. Some Christians led by a convert named Montanus believed that they themselves, instead of the established, organized Church, were especially chosen by the Spirit to convey his messages to mankind. One of their most famous converts was Tertullian, a literary genius who was the first to declare that the Spirit proceeded from the Father through the Son.

Tertullian's contemporary, Origen, pointed to the Spirit's role as Sanctifier and likewise taught the procession of the Spirit from the Father through the Son. Origen's prolific writings often begot great controversy, but he bequeathed some sublime passages concerning the Spirit to the Christian theological heritage.

In the mid-fourth century, the Pneumatomachian threat elicited from the Fathers some of the most definite dogmatic affirmations concerning the Spirit. In the struggle against them, Athanasius of Alexandria affirmed in no uncertain terms his belief that God is One in Three. The Eastern Cappadocian Fathers Basil, Gregory of Nazianzus, and Gregory of Nyssa all joined Athanasius in denouncing the Pneumatomachian inanities. In the process, Basil produced a complete treatise on the doctrine of the Holy Spirit, while Gregory of Nazianzus provided the first historical instance of a Christian orator articulating doctrines at length concerning the Spirit. His Pentecostal oration on the Holy Spirit was such a great discourse that over two centuries later another Gregory, this time a great pope, in his own sermon used the same analogies to describe the action of the Spirit in the human soul.

In the West, Bishop Ambrose of Milan, responding to a request from the Emperor Gratian, wrote a clear exposition of the scriptural evidence for maintaining the divinity of the Holy Spirit. The great St. Augustine unified and systematized decades of theological speculation in his treatise on the Trinity. His affirmation that the Spirit is the *soul* of the Church would be echoed centuries later in the doctrine of the Mystical Body. In the Eastern Church, a similar synthesis of the theology of the Trinity was made by St. John Damascene in the eighth century. The writings of Simeon the New Theologian, a Byzantine mystic, are pertinent for the present charismatic movement, for he taught in the eleventh century the need for "an added stage in the Christian life which he called the baptism in the Holy Spirit."[1]

The writings of the Early Fathers are replete with beautifully graphic imagery to describe the operation of the Spirit in the individual and in the Church. Tertullian spoke of Him as the Gift of God; Hilary of Poitiers forcefully developed this idea. To some He was a gentle dove, to others a raging fire. His grace could be a balm, like oil poured on stormy waters. Echoing the Old Testament, some Fathers could best perceive Him as a wind; the Christian's joyous call was merely to open his sails to be sped along the way of salvation by this Divine Wind.

EARLY CHRISTIAN INSCRIPTION IN STONE

In God's Holy Spirit
To Cyriacus, dearest of sons:
Live in the Holy Spirit.[2]

ST. IGNATIUS OF ANTIOCH (*ca.* 50—*ca.* 110)

Epistle to the Ephesians

I have heard of certain persons from elsewhere passing through, whose doctrine was bad. These you did not permit to sow their seed among you; you stopped your ears, so as not to receive the seed sown by them. You consider yourselves stones of the Father's temple, prepared for the edifice of God the Father, to be taken aloft by the hoisting engine of Jesus Christ, that is, the Cross, while the Holy Spirit serves you as a rope; your faith is your spiritual windlass and your love the road which leads up to God.[3]

Epistle to the Magnesians

Be zealous, therefore, to stand squarely on the decrees of the Lord and the Apostles, that in all things whatsoever you may prosper, in body and in soul, in faith and in love, in the Son and the Father and the Spirit, in the beginning and the end, together with your most reverend bishop and with your presbytery—that fittingly woven spiritual crown!—and with your deacons, men of God. Submit to the bishop and to each other's rights, just as did Jesus Christ in the flesh to the Father, and as the Apostles did to Christ and the Father and the Spirit, so that there may be oneness both of flesh and of spirit.[4]

Epistle to the Philadelphians

Even though some were willing enough to lead my human spirit into error, yet the Spirit is not led into error, since he proceeds from God. Indeed, He knows where He comes from and whither He goes, and lays bare what is secret. I cried out, while in your midst, and said in a ringing voice—God's voice: "Give heed to the bishop and to the presbytery and to the deacons." Some, however, suspected I was saying this because I had previous knowledge of the division caused by some; but He for whose sake I am in chains is my witness, that I had not learned it from any human source. No, it was the Spirit who kept preaching in these words: "Apart from the bishop do nothing; preserve your persons as shrines of God; cherish unity, shun divisions; do as Jesus Christ did for He, too, did as the Father did."[5]

SAINT CLEMENT OF ROME (*First Century*)

Epistle to the Corinthians *ca.* 97

Thus all were blessed with a profound and radiant peace of soul, and there was an insatiable longing to do good, as well as a rich outpouring of the Holy Spirit upon the whole community. Filled, moreover, with a desire for holiness, you stretched out your hands, with ready goodwill and devout confidence, to Almighty God, imploring

Him to show mercy in case you had inadvertently failed in any way. . . .[6]

After receiving their instructions and being fully assured through the Resurrection of our Lord Jesus Christ, as well as confirmed in faith by the word of God, they [the apostles] went forth, equipped with the fullness of the Holy Spirit, to preach the good news that the Kingdom of God was close at hand. From land to land, accordingly, and from city to city they preached, and from among their earliest converts appointed men whom they had tested by the Spirit to act as bishops and deacons for the future believers. . . .[7]

Take care, beloved, that His blessings, numerous as they are, do not turn to our condemnation in case we do not—through a life unworthy of Him—do with perfect accord what is good and pleasing in His sight. For somewhere it is said: "The Spirit of the Lord is a lamp that searches the deep recesses of the soul. . . ."

You are given to wrangling, brethren, and are jealous in matters that bear upon salvation. You have looked deep into the sacred writings, which tell the truth and proceed from the Holy Spirit. You know that nothing unjust or fraudulent is written in them . . . Why are quarrels and outbursts of passion and divisions and schisms and war in your midst? Or, do we not have one God and one Christ and one Spirit of grace, a Spirit that was poured out upon us? And is there not one calling in Christ? Why do we tear apart and disjoint the members of Christ and revolt against our own body, and go to such extremes of madness as to forget that we are mutually dependent members?[8]

SOLOMON *(Late 1st Century, A.D.)*

ODES

My heart hath been cleft,
Its flower hath appeared
And grace hath fructified therein,
And hath borne fruits for the Lord.
For the Most High hath opened me by his Holy Spirit.
. . . . He hath filled me with his love
And his wounding hath become salvation for me.
. . . . A water which speaketh has touched my lips,
Generously sprinkled by the fountain of the Lord,
I have drunk, I am inebriated with the living and immortal water.
And my inebriation was wise:
I abandoned my vanity
And I turned to the Most High, my God.[9]

As the hand moves over the zither
    And the strings speak
So doth the Spirit of the Lord speak
    in my members
And I speak in his Love.[10]

THE EPISTLE OF BARNABAS (*ca.* 117 to 130)

Sons and daughters: My best wishes to you for peace in the name of the Lord who has loved us!

Great, indeed, and generous are God's gifts of justification bestowed upon you! And so I am exceedingly, in fact beyond all measure, cheered as I think of your happy and glorious endowments. So deeply implanted is the gift of the Spirit that has been graciously vouchsafed to you! For the same reason I congratulate myself all the more on my own hope of salvation, because I really witness in your community an outpouring upon you of the Spirit from the wealth of the Lord's fountainhead. Such keen delight, on your account, has my longed-for sight of you afforded me![11]

ST. IRENAEUS (135-140—202-203)

The Holy Spirit in the Church

We receive our faith from the Church and keep it safe; and it is as it were a precious deposit stored in a fine vessel, ever renewing its vitality through the Spirit of God, and causing the renewal of the vessel in which it is stored. For this gift of God has been entrusted to the Church, as the breath of life to created man, to the end that all members by receiving it should be made alive. And herein has been bestowed on us our means of communion with Christ, namely the Holy Spirit, the pledge of immortality, the strengthening of our faith, the ladder by which we ascend to God . . . For where the Church is, there is the Spirit of God; and where the Spirit of God is, there is the Church and every kind of grace. The Spirit is truth. Therefore those who have no share in the Spirit are not nourished and given life at their mother's breast; nor do they enjoy the sparkling fountain that issues from the body of Christ.[12]

As a compacted lump of dough cannot be formed of dry wheat without fluid matter, nor can a loaf possess unity, so in like manner, neither can we. . . . be made one in Christ Jesus without the water from heaven. And as dry earth does not *produce* unless it receives moisture, so we also, being originally a dry tree, could never have brought forth fruit unto life without the voluntary rain from above. For our bodies have received unity among themselves by means of that laver which leads to incorruption; but our souls, by means of the Spirit.

Therefore both are necessary, since both contribute toward the life of God. Our Lord compassionated that erring Samaritan woman . . . by promising her living water, so that she would thirst no more, nor *work* to acquire refreshing water, since she had within herself water springing up to eternal life. . . .

Gideon, that Israelite whom God chose . . . prophesied that there would be dryness upon the fleece of wool (a type of the people), on which there had been dew at first. He thus indicated that they should no longer have the Holy Spirit from God . . . [But the Father] did confer this Spirit again upon the Church, sending throughout all the world the Comforter from heaven, from whence also the Lord tells us that the devil, like lightning, was cast down. Therefore we have need of the dew of God, that we be not consumed by fire, nor be rendered unfruitful, and that where we have an accuser there we may have also an Advocate.[13]

HERMAS *(2nd Century)*

The Shepherd of Hermas (*ca.* 140-155)

"Be," said he, "long-suffering and prudent and you shall have power over all evil deeds and shalt do all righteousness. For if you are courageous the Holy Spirit which dwells in you will be pure, not obscured by another evil spirit, but will dwell at large and rejoice and be glad with the body in which it dwells, and will serve God in great cheerfulness, having well-being in itself. But if any ill temper enter, at once the Holy Spirit, which is delicate, is oppressed, finding the place impure, and seeks to depart out of the place, for it is choked by the evil spirit, having no room to serve the Lord as it will, but is contaminated by the bitterness. . . .[14]

Ill temper is first foolish, frivolous, and silly; then from silliness comes bitterness, from bitterness wrath, from wrath rage, and from rage fury; then fury, being compounded of such great evils, becomes great and inexpiable sin. For when these spirits dwell on one vessel, where also the Holy Spirit dwells, there is no room in that vessel, but it is over-crowded. Therefore the delicate spirit which is unaccustomed to dwell with an evil spirit, or with hardness, departs from such a man, and seeks to dwell with gentleness and quietness. . . . .[15]

"Put away," said he, "grief from yourself, for this also is a sister of double-mindedness and bitterness."

"How sir," I said, "is she their sister, for it seems to me that bitterness is one thing and double-mindedness is another, and grief another?"

"You are foolish, O man," he said, "and do not understand that grief is more evil than all the spirits, and is most terrible to the servants of God, and corrupts man beyond all the spirits, and wears out the Holy Spirit—and again saves us." . . .[16]

Test the man who has the Divine Spirit by his life. In the first place, he who has the spirit which is from above, is meek and gentle, and lowly-minded, and refrains from all wickedness and evil desire of this world, and makes himself poorer than all men, and gives no answers to anyone when he is consulted, nor does he speak by himself (for the Holy Spirit does not speak when a man wishes to speak), but he speaks at that time when God wishes him to speak. Therefore, when the man who has the Divine Spirit comes into a meeting of righteous men who have the faith of the Divine Spirit, and intercession is made to God from the assembly of those men, then the angel of the prophetic spirit rests on him and fills the man, and the man, being filled with the Holy Spirit, speaks to the congregation as the Lord wills. Thus, then, the Spirit of the Godhead will be plain. Such, then, is the power of the Lord concerning the Spirit of the Godhead.[17]

ATHENAGORAS *(2nd Century)*

I expect that you who are so learned and so eager for truth are not without some introduction to Moses, Isaias, Jeremias, and the rest of the prophets, who, when the Divine Spirit moved them, spoke out what they were in travail with, their own reasoning falling into abeyance and the Spirit making use of them as a flautist might play upon his flute. . . .

This same Holy Spirit, that works in those who utter prophecy, we call an outflow from God, flowing out and returning like a ray of the sun.[18]

THE BISHOP OF SMYRNA (*ca.* 155-157)

THE MARTYRDOM OF SAINT POLYCARP

There he was, with his hands put behind him, and fastened, like a ram towering above a large flock, ready for sacrifice [by fire], a holocaust prepared and acceptable to God! And he looked up to heaven and said:

"O Lord God, O Almighty, Father of Thy beloved and blessed Son Jesus Christ, through whom we have received the knowledge of you—God of angels and hosts and all creation—and of the whole race of saints who live under your eyes! I bless Thee, because Thou hast seen fit to bestow upon me this day and this hour, that I may share, among the number of the martyrs, the cup of Thy Anointed and rise to eternal life both in soul and in body, in virtue of the immortality of the Holy Spirit. May I be accepted among them in Thy sight today as a rich and pleasing sacrifice, such as Thou, the true God that cannot utter a falsehood, hast prearranged, revealed in advance, and now consummated. And therefore I praise Thee for everything; I bless Thee; I glorify Thee through the eternal and heavenly High Priest Jesus Christ, Thy beloved Son, through whom be glory to Thee together with Him and the Holy Spirit, both now and for the ages yet to come. Amen."[19]

DIDACHE

The Teaching of the Twelve Apostles (*ca.* 170)

Do not, when embittered, give orders to your slave, male or female, for they hope in the same God; otherwise, they might lose the fear of God, who is the Master of both of you. He surely is not coming to call with an eye to rank and station in life; no, he comes to those whom the Spirit has prepared.[20]

TERTULLIAN (*ca.* 160-240 or 250)

After the waters of the deluge, by which the old iniquity was purged—after the baptism, so to say, of the world—a dove was the herald. It announced to the earth the assaugement of celestial wrath after she had been sent out of the ark and had returned with the olive branch—a sign which even among the nations is the fore-token of peace. So by the self-same law of heavenly effect, to earth (that is, to our flesh) as it emerges from the font, after its old sins, flies the dove of the Holy Spirit, bringing us the peace of God, sent out from the heavens, where is the Church, the typified ark.[21]

ORIGEN (*ca.* 185-254)

The grace of the Holy Spirit is added that those creatures which are not holy by virtue of their own being may be made holy by participation in the Spirit. Thus they derive existence from God the Father, rationality from the Word, sanctity from the Holy Spirit. Again when they have once been sanctified through the Holy Spirit they are made capable of receiving Christ, in respect that he is the righteousness of God, and those who have deserved to advance to this stage through the sanctification of the Holy Spirit will go on to attain the gift of wisdom through the power of the Spirit of God and his operation in them . . . Thus the operation of the Father which bestows existence on all, proves more splendid and impressive when each person advances and reaches higher stages of progress through participation in Christ as wisdom, and as knowledge and sanctification; and as a man has become purer and cleaner by participation in the Holy Spirit he is made worthy to receive, and receives, the grace of wisdom and knowledge. Then, when all the stains of pollution and ignorance have been removed and purged away, he receives such advancement in purity and cleanness, that the being which was given by God becomes worthy of God, who bestowed it in order that it might attain its purity and perfection; so that the being is as worthy as is he who gave it existence.[22]

The Spirit Rests on the Pure of Heart

We read that the Spirit rests not on all men whatsoever, but on the holy and blessed. For the Spirit of God rests on the "pure in heart," and on those who purify their souls from sin, just as He does not dwell in a body given over to sins—even if He has dwelt in it in the past; for the Holy Spirit cannot tolerate the partnership and company of an evil spirit. For there is no doubt that when we sin an evil spirit comes and makes play in our heart, whosoever we be . . . Hence our sin grieves the Holy Spirit but our righteous and holy deeds prepare Him a resting place in us.[23]

On Prayer

Origen's Own Prayer for Divine Help in Expounding Prayer

Since . . . to expound prayer is such a difficult task that one needs the Father to shed light upon it and the Word Himself, the first-born, to teach it, and the Spirit to work within us that we may understand and speak worthily of so great a theme, I beseech the Spirit, praying as a man (for I do not lay to my own credit the capacity for prayer), before I begin to speak of prayer. That it may be granted me to speak fully and spiritually . . .[24]

How many things are there which each of us can recount, if he remembers with gratitude benefits done him and wishes to praise God for them? For souls long barren knowing of the sterility of their own minds and the barrenness of their own understanding, have conceived by the Holy Spirit through constant prayer and brought forth words of salvation, filled with true ideas.[25]

ST. CYPRIAN (200?-258)

On the Unity of the Catholic Church

. . . The Church is one and the See of Christ is one. . . . It is this one Church to which the Holy Spirit refers in the Song of Songs, speaking with the voice of the Lord and saying: "My dove, my undefiled, is but one. She is the only one of her mother, elect of her that bore her." . . .

Therefore it was that the Holy Spirit came in the form of a dove, a simple and joyous creature, not bitter with gall, not savage in its bite, not fierce with rending talons. Doves love to find a resting place with men; they cling to association with one house; when they have young they bring them forth together; when they go abroad they keep close in their flight; they spend their lives in mutual and friendly intercourse; they recognize the harmony of peace by the kisses of their beaks; in all things they fulfill the law of unanimity. This is the simplicity that we should know in our Church, this is the charity to which we should attain. The love of our brotherhood should take example from the doves; our gentleness and meekness should be like the lambs and sheep.[26]

ST. ATHANASIUS OF ALEXANDRIA (295-373)

[Heretics say] "If the Spirit is of the Son, then the Father is the Spirit's grandfather." Thus the wretches make mock, like busybodies desiring to "search the deep things of God" which "no one knows but the Spirit of God," against whom they speak evil. We ought therefore to answer them no more, but in accordance with the Apostle's precept, after the warning they have had from what has been said already, to shun them as heretics. . . . .[27]

[After a lengthy refutation of such errors by scriptural quotes, he declares:]

Let us look at the very tradition, teaching and faith of the Catholic Church from the beginning, which the Lord gave, the Apostles preached, and the Fathers kept. . . . There is . . . a Triad, holy and complete, confessed to be God in Father, Son, and Holy Spirit, having nothing foreign or external mixed with it, not composed of one that creates and one that is originated, but all creative; and it is consistent and in nature indivisible, and its activity is one. The Father does all things through the Word in the Holy Spirit. Thus the unity of the holy

Triad is preserved. Thus one God is preached in the Church, "who is over all, and through all, and in all"—over all, as Father, as beginning, as fountain; through all, through the Word; in all, in the Holy Spirit. It is a Triad not only in name and form of speech, but in truth and actuality. For as the Father is he that is, so also his Word is one that is and God over all. And the Holy Spirit is not without actual existence, but exists and as true being. Less than these (Persons) the Catholic Church does not hold.[28]

EULPUS

(Deacon, martyred at Catania, Sicily, ca. *304)*

Prayer

Thank you, Christ, for this. Take care of me, because it is for you that I am suffering. I worship the Father, the Son and the Holy Spirit. I worship the Holy Trinity, apart from whom there is no God. Perish the gods; they had not the power to make heaven and earth and the things that are in them . . .

Thank you, Christ for this. Take care of me, Christ, because it is for you that I am suffering.

BECAUSE HE WAS FULL OF THE HOLY SPIRIT, HE BURST INTO SONG. AND HE SANG:

Great the glory, Lord, that you receive from those of your servants whom in your mercy you have summoned to you. . . .

And when he had finished what he had to say, he knelt down, bared his neck and was beheaded.[29]

ST. CYRIL OF JERUSALEM (315-386)

The Evil Spirit Contrasted to the Holy Spirit

When the unclean devil comes upon a man's soul—may the Lord deliver from him every soul of those who hear me, and of those who are not present—it is like a wolf upon a sheep, greedy for blood, ready to devour. His advent is fierce; there is a sense of oppression; the mind is darkened; his attack is unjust, a seizure of another's possession. He forcibly uses another's body and another's bodily member as his own. He casts down him who stands upright—for he is kin to him who fell from heaven—; he perverts the tongue, he twists the lips; foam comes instead of words; the man is blinded; his eye is open, yet through it the soul sees nothing, and wretched man quivers and trembles at the point of death. The devils are truly enemies of men in abusing them so foully and pitilessly.

Not such is the Holy Spirit; God forbid! His actions on the contrary, effect what is good and salutary. First of all, His coming is gentle, the perception of Him fragrant, His yoke light; rays of light and knowledge shine forth before His coming. He comes with the heart of a true guardian; He comes to save, to cure, to admonish, to strengthen, to console, to enlighten the mind, first of the man who receives Him, then through him the minds of others also. As a man previously in darkness and suddenly seeing the sun gets the faculty of sight and sees clearly what he did not see before, so the man deemed worthy of the Holy Spirit is enlightened in soul, and sees beyond human sight what he did not know. Though his body is upon the earth his soul beholds the heavens as in a mirror.[30]

The Imagery of the Dove

The Holy Spirit descended when Christ was baptized to make sure that the dignity of Him who was baptized was not hidden . . . . It was fitting, as some have explained it, that the firstfruits and the first gifts of the Holy Spirit, who is imparted to the baptized, should be conferred on the manhood of the Savior, who bestows such grace. Perhaps, as some say, it was to reveal an image that He came down in the likeness of a pure innocent, simple dove, working with prayers for the sons He begot and for forgiveness of sins; just as in a veiled manner it was foretold that the beauty of Christ's eyes would be manifested in this way. For in the Canticles she cries out and says of the bridegroom: "Your eyes are like doves beside running waters."

Some have regarded the dove of Noe as prefiguring this dove. In Noe's time salvation and the beginning of a new generation came to men through wood and water; the dove returned at evening carrying a bough of an olive tree; so the Holy Spirit, they say, descended upon the true Noe, the author of the second birth, who unites the aspirations of all nations, of whom the animals in the ark were a figure. After His coming the spiritual wolves feed with lambs, and His Church pastures calf, ox and lion together; just as we see to this day worldly rulers led and taught by churchmen. He descended then, according to some interpreters, as the spiritual dove at Christ's baptism, to show that He is the same who by the wood of the Cross saves them that believe, and who would in the evening, by His death, grant them salvation.[31]

The Saving Fire

[At Pentecost, the Apostles] partook not of burning but of saving fire, which consumes the thorns of sins but renders the soul radiant.

This fire will come to you too, to strip away and destroy your thorn-like sins, and to make the precious possession of your souls shine yet more brightly; and He will give you grace, for He gave it then to the Apostles. He sat upon them in the form of fiery tongues, to crown them with new and spiritual diadems (by the fiery tongues on their heads). A flaming sword of old barred the gates of Paradise; a fiery tongue, bringing salvation, restored the grace.[32]

Why St. John Referred to the Spirit as "Living Water"

Why has He called the grace of the Spirit water? Because all things depend on water; water produces herbs and living things; water of the showers comes down from heaven, and coming down in one form, has manifold effects; one fountain waters the whole of Paradise; one and the same rain comes down on all the world, yet it becomes white in the lily, red in the rose, purple in the violets and hyacinths, different and many-colored in manifold species; thus it is one in the palm tree and other in the vine, and all in all things, though it is uniform, and does not vary in itself. For the rain does not change, coming down now as one thing and now as another, but it adapts itself to the things receiving it and becomes what is suitable to each. Similarly the Holy Spirit, being One and of One Nature and indivisible, imparts to each man His grace "according as he will." The dry tree when watered brings forth shoots; so too the soul in sin, once it is made worthy through penance of the grace of the Holy Spirit, flowers into justice. Though the Spirit is One in nature, yet by the will of God and in the name of the Son, He brings about many virtuous effects. For He employs the tongue of one man for wisdom, He illumines the soul of another by prophecy, to another He grants the power of driving out devils, to another the gift of interpreting the Sacred Scriptures; He strengthens the self-control of one man, teaches another the nature of almsgiving, and still another to fast and mortify himself, another to despise the things of the body; he prepares another man for martyrdom, acting differently in different men, though He Himself is not diverse.[33]

HILARY OF POITIERS (315-367)

Let us make use of those generous gifts and seek to avail ourselves of this most essential boon . . . "We have received the Spirit which comes from God, so that we may know the gifts which have been generously given to us by God." The Spirit, then, is received to give us knowledge. For as the natural human body will be useless if the necessary conditions of its function fail . . . (e.g. eyes without light, ears without sound), so the human mind, unless it has by faith appropriated the gifts of the Spirit, will have the natural faculty of apprehending God, but it will not have the light of knowledge. That gift, which is in Christ, is available to all alike: it is nowhere withheld, but is given to each in proportion to his willingness to be worthy of it. It continues with us to the final consummation of history; it is the solace of our waiting; in the working of its gifts it is the pledge of our hope for the future, the light of our minds, the radiance shed on our hearts.[34]

ST. GREGORY OF NAZIANZUS (*ca.* 329—*ca.* 389)

The Spirit Effects Marvels in Those He Possesses

If this most wise and loving Spirit possesses a shepherd, he makes him a psalmist who charms wicked spirits, as well as designating him king of Israel. If He possesses a goatherd and dresser of sycamores, He makes him a prophet—think of David and Amos. If He possesses an adolescent of admirable disposition, He appoints him a judge of elders even beyond his years. To this Daniel, who overcame the lions in their den, testifies. If he takes possession of fishermen, the whole universe is ensnared for Christ in the nets of their words. Listen to Peter as well as Andrew and the Sons of Thunder thundering about the things of the spirit. If He chooses a publican as his disciple, He makes him a negotiant of souls; witness Matthew, yesterday a publican, today an evangelist. If they are ferocious persecutors, He rechannels their zeal and makes a Paul instead of a Saul, not manifesting less piety than he formerly offended by impiety.[35]

[The Pneumatomachi argued that if the Spirit is begotten of the Father, then there are two sons; if of the Son, then he is a grandson of the Father].

Gregory answers:

We do not admit your dilemma, which allows of no mean between unbegotten and begotten. Therefore your "brothers" and "grandsons" immediately disappear, with the disappearance of your imposing dilemma . . . Now tell me, what place will you assign to that which "proceeds?" For this clearly provides an escape from your dilemma, and it derives from a theologian above your standard, in fact from our Saviour himself. Unless . . . you have removed from your gospels this saying: "The Holy Spirit, who proceeds from the Father."

He is not a creature, in that he proceeds from such a source; he is not a son, in that he is not begotten: he is God, in that his status is a mean between unbegotten and begotten. Thus he escapes the toils of your syllogisms and is revealed as God, being too strong for your dilemmas. What then is "procession?" Well, if you will explain the Father's "ingeneracy," I will give you a scientific account of the "generation" of the Son, and the "procession" of the Spirit; and thus let us both go crazy through peering into the mysteries of God. Who are we to pry into such matters? We cannot understand what is in front of our noses; we cannot count the sands of the seashore, the drops of rain, the days of endless time. Still less can we penetrate the depths of God, and give an account of his nature, which is so ineffable, which surpasses our powers of reason.[36]

ST. BASIL THE GREAT (*ca.* 330-379)

Can anyone fail to have his mind lifted up, when he hears the titles of the Spirit? Can he fail to raise his thoughts to the Supreme Nature? The Spirit is called "God's Spirit," "Spirit of Truth proceeding from the Father," "Right Spirit," "Leading Spirit." But his proper and peculiar appellation is "Holy Spirit," which is a name specially applicable to everything that is incorporeal, purely immaterial, and indivisible. Thus when the Lord was instructing the woman who thought that God was to be worshipped in a particular place, he told her that the incorporeal is not spatially limited and said, "God is Spirit." When we hear the title "Spirit," we cannot picture a nature circumscribed, or subject to change and variation, or in any way resembling created beings. It is inevitable that our imagination should proceed to the highest point, so that we should conceive an intellectual substance, of infinite power, of unlimited magnitude, not measurable by times or ages, unstinting of its good gifts; a being to which all turn when needing sanctification . . . simple in substance, manifold in powers; present entirely in each individual while existing in entirety everywhere; divided without suffering diminution, shared without loss of completeness; after the likeness of the sun's beam, which gracious gift comes to each who enjoys it as if it came to him alone, yet shines on land and sea and mingles with the air. So the Spirit comes to each of these who receive him, as though given to him alone; yet he sends out to all his grace, sufficient and complete, and all who partake in him, receive benefit in proportion to the capacity, not of his power, but of their nature.

When the sun's ray falls on bright and transparent objects, they themselves become radiant and from themselves shed a further shining beam; so the souls inhabited by the Spirit, and illuminated by the

Spirit, themselves are rendered wholly spiritual and send out their grace to others. From this source comes foreknowledge of the future, the understanding of mysteries, the apprehension of things hidden, the partaking of spiritual gifts, the heavenly citizenship, a place in the choir of angels, unending joy, the power to abide in God, to become like God, and highest of all ends to which we can aspire, to become divine.[37]

ST. GREGORY OF NYSSA (*ca.* 335-*ca.* 394)

The Existence of the Spirit

Just as, by a process of ascent from the facts of our own nature, we arrived at a knowledge of the Word in the transcendent nature, in the same way we shall be led to the conception of the Spirit by contemplating in our own nature certain shadows and resemblances of the ineffable Power. But in our case the spirit (or breath) is the drawing in of the air, an element foreign to the constitution of the body, inhaled and breathed out in accordance with a fixed law; and this at the moment when we utter the word becomes a voice, manifesting in itself the meaning (or force) of the word. In the case of the Divine nature it has been held to be consistent with true religion that there is a Spirit (or breath) of God, just as it was granted that there is also a Word of God; for the Word of God must not be deficient as compared with our word, which would be the case if, while the latter was observed to be accompanied with the emission of breath (or spirit), the former was believed to be unaccompanied by Spirit. To suppose, however, that some foreign element, resembling our breath, has an influx from without into God, and in Him becomes the Spirit, is a conception unworthy of God. On the contrary, when we heard that there was a Word of God, we did not conceive of it as something unsubstantial, nor as finding its place in Him as the result of acquired knowledge, nor as being uttered by the voice, and after such utterance as passing away; nor as subject to any of the other accidents which are observed in the case of our word, but as existing after the manner of true being, possessing will and activity and omnipotence. So also, when we have learned that there is a Spirit of God, which accompanies the Word and manifests His activity, we do not conceive of the Spirit which is in Him as like our own. But we conceive of it as a power possessing real existence in its own right and in a subsistence of its own, incapable of being separated from God in Whom it exists, or from the Word of God Whom it accompanies; not dissolving into non-existence, but like the Word of God, possessing an individual existence, able to will, self-moved, active, always choosing what is good, and for the carrying out of every purpose, possessing the power corresponding to its will.[38]

The Wings of the Dove

The soul that is rising upwards must leave all that it has already attained as falling far short of its desire; only then will it begin to grasp something of that magnificence which is beyond the stars.

But how is it possible for us to attain this if our desires are for earthly things? How can we fly to heaven without celestial wings, if we are not already light, and borne on air by a lofty way of life? No one could be so uninitiated in the mysteries of the Gospel as to be unaware that man has but one vehicle that can carry him to heaven; he must assume *the wings of the* descending *Dove*, such as even the prophet David longed for (Ps. 54:7). In this way does the Scripture symbolically express the power of the Spirit. And it takes the dove, perhaps, because as observers report, it has no gall, or else because the bird cannot endure any foul odor.

Thus the man who avoids all bitterness and all the odors of the flesh, will raise himself upon *the wings of the Dove* above all the lowly strivings of the world and, indeed, above the entire universe; he will discover that which alone is worthy of our desire; he will become beautiful because he has drawn near to Beauty; and there he will become as luminous as light because he is in communion with the true light.[39]

ST. AMBROSE (*ca.* 339-397)

The Fire Symbol

. . . Isaias points out that the Holy Spirit is not only light but is also fire, when he says: 'And the light of Israel shall be as fire.' Thus the Prophets called Him a burning fire, because in those three points we notice more readily the majesty of the Godhead, for to sanctify is of the Godhead, and to illuminate is proper to fire and light, and to be expressed and to be seen in the appearance of fire is customary with the Godhead; "for God is a consuming fire," as Moses said.

For he himself saw the fire in the bush, and he had heard God at that time when a voice came from the flame of fire to him saying: "I am the God of Abraham, and the God of Isaac, and the God of Jacob." The voice was from the flame, and the flame was in the bush, and the flame was not harmful. For the bush was burned, and was not burned up, because in that mystery the Lord represented that He would come to illuminate the thorns of our body; not to consume those beset with miseries but to mitigate the miseries; who would baptize with the Holy Spirit and with fire, that He might distribute grace and consume sins. Thus in the appearance of fire God keeps His purpose.

In the Acts of the Apostles also, when the Holy Spirit descended upon the faithful, the likeness of fire was seen, for thus you have it: "And suddenly there came a sound from heaven, as though the Spirit were coming with great might; and it filled the whole house where they were sitting; and there appeared to them cloven tongues as it were of fire."

Therefore, too, did that take place, when Gideon, about to overcome the Midianites, ordered three hundred men to take pitchers, and to hold lighted lamps in the pitchers, and in their right hands trumpets; thus our ancestors preserved what they had received from the Apostles, that the pitchers are our bodies, which, fashioned out of clay, know not how to fear, if they burn with the fervor of spiritual grace, and bear testimony to the passion of the Lord Jesus with a confession of a melodious voice. . . .

What, then, is that fire? Surely not fire made of common twigs, or roaring by the burning of the stubble of the forests, but that fire which, like gold, improves good deeds, and consumes sins like stubble. This surely is the Holy Spirit, who is called both the fire and the light of the Lord's countenance; the light, as we have said above: "The light of thy countenance, O Lord, is signed upon us."[40]

The Water Symbol

. . . The Holy Spirit has been called not only water but also a river, according to what is written: "Out of His belly shall flow rivers of living water. Now this he said of the Spirit which they should receive who believed in Him."

Therefore, the Holy Spirit is a river, and a very large river, which according to the Hebrews flowed from Jesus in the lands, as we have received it in prophecy from the mouth of Isaias. This river is great, which flows always, and never fails. Nor only a river, but also one of profuse stream, and of overflowing greatness, just as David also said: "The stream of the river maketh the city of God joyful."

For that city, the heavenly Jerusalem, is not washed by the course of some earthly river, but the Holy Spirit proceeding from the Fountain of Life, by a short draught of which we are satiated, seems to flow more abundantly among those heavenly Thrones, Dominions and Powers, Angels and Archangels, boiling in the full course of seven spiritual virtues. For if the river spreading over the tops of its banks overflows, how much more does the Spirit, rising above every creature, when He touches the remaining lower field of the mind, as it were, delight that heavenly nature of creatures with a kind of more effusive fertility of His mind![41]

You also have it in the Gospel that the angel at a certain time went down into a pond, and the water was moved. And he that went down first into the pond was made whole. What did the angel announce in this type but the descent of the Holy Spirit, which would take place in our time to consecrate the waters when invoked by sacerdotal prayers? That angel, then, was the herald of the Holy Spirit, because through spiritual grace medicine was to be applied to the infirmities of our soul and mind. The Spirit, too, then has the same ministers as God the Father and Christ. So He fills all things, so He possesses all things, so He operates all things, just as both God the Father and the Son operate.[42]

THE INCARNATION THE WORK OF THE SPIRIT

The birth from the Virgin is the work of the Spirit. The fruit of the womb is the work of the Spirit, according to what is written: "Blessed art thou among women; and blessed is the fruit of thy womb." The flower of the root is the work of the Spirit, that flower, I say, of which it was well prophesied: "There shall come forth a rod out of the root of Jesse, and a flower shall rise up out of his root." The root of the patriarch Jesse is the family of the Jews; Mary is the rod; Christ is the flower of Mary, who sprouted forth from a virginal womb to spread the good odor of faith throughout the whole world, as he himself said: "I am the flower of the field, and the lily of the valley."

The flower, even when cut, keeps its odor, and when bruised increases it, and when torn does not lose it; so, too, the Lord Jesus on that gibbet of the cross neither failed when bruised, nor fainted when torn; and when cut by the pricking of the lance, made more beautiful by the sacred color of the outpoured blood, He grew young again, Himself not knowing how to die and exhaling among the dead the gift of eternal life. On this flower, then, of the royal rod the Holy Spirit rested.[43]

SERAPION OF THMUIS

THE EUCHOLOGIUM OF SERAPION (*ca.* 350)

Prayer after the Homily

God our Saviour, God of the whole universe, Lord and Creator of all that exists, Father of that only Son whom you begot as a true and living Image of yourself and sent out to help the human race, by this means calling men to you and winning them over: we pray you for the people here assembled.

Send them the Holy Spirit, and may the Lord Jesus visit them, speak in the minds of them all and prepare their hearts for faith; may he draw all souls to you, O God of mercies.

Take possession, too, of the people in this town that are yours; make a real flock of them, through your only Son, Jesus Christ, in the Holy Spirit. Through him may glory and power be yours, now and age after age. Amen.[44]

ST. PAULINUS OF NOLA (*ca.* 353-431)

I have written some little verses for your basilicas. . . . The following lines will describe the baptistry . . .

"Here the spring which fathers newborn souls brings forth water living with divine light. The Holy Spirit descends on it from heaven, and mates its sacred liquid with a heavenly stream. The water becomes pregnant with God, and begets from seed eternal a holy offspring in its fostering fount. . . ."[45]

Souls that are now schooled in the faith of the apostles. . . . are ships floating on the waves of the world, armed with the oars of faith in the truth and of works of justice, both on the right hand, as Scripture says, and on the left. The word of God is the rudder that steers them. They open the sails of their senses to the wind of the Holy Spirit, and they lash the sail of their hearts to the sailyard of the cross, using for ropes the bonds of charity. Their mast is the rod out of the root of Jesse, controlling the whole quadrireme of our bodies. If we are fastened to it through the truth of the prophets by voluntary bonds, as in the Homeric story, and if the ears of our hearts, not our bodies, are stopped up with faith, not wax, against the enticements of the world which beguile us variously but harm us equally, then we shall sail safely and harmlessly by the rock of pleasures, the cliffs of the Sirens, so to speak.[46]

THE APOSTOLIC CONSTITUTIONS (*ca.* 380)

Prayer of the Newly Initiated

God the all-powerful, Father of Christ, who is your only Son, give me a clean body, a pure heart, a watchful mind and knowledge free from error. May your Holy Spirit come to me and bring me truth, yes and the fullness of truth, through your Christ.

Through him may glory be yours, in the Holy Spirit, throughout the ages. Amen.[47]

SAINT AUGUSTINE OF HIPPO (354-430)

Breathe in me, O Holy Spirit,
That my thoughts may all be holy;
Act in me, O Holy Spirit,
That my work, too, may be holy;
Draw my heart, O Holy Spirit,
That I may love but what is holy;
Strengthen me, O Holy Spirit,
To defend all that is holy;
Guard me, then, O Holy Spirit,
That I always may be holy.[48]

The Interior Master

Do not suppose that any man learns aught from man. We can admonish by the sound of our voice; if there be not One within that shall teach, vain is the noise we make. Aye, brethren, have you a mind to know it? Have you not all heard this present discourse? And yet how many will go from this place untaught! I, for my part, have spoken to all; but they to whom that Unction within speaks not, they whom the Holy Ghost teaches not, those go back untaught. The teachings of the master from without are a sort of aid and admonition. He that teaches the hearts, has his chair in heaven. . . . Let Him therefore Himself speak to you within, when not one of mankind is there. . . . Let His unction be in the heart, lest it be a heart thirsting in the wilderness, and having no fountains to be watered withal. . . .

The words, brethren, which we speak from without are as the husbandman to the tree: from without he works, applying water and diligently cultivating it. Let him from without apply what he will—does he form the apples? Does he clothe the nakedness of the wood with a shady covering of leaves? Does he do anything like this from within? But whose doing is this? Hear the husbandman, the apostle: "I did the planting, Apollos did the watering, but God made things grow. Neither the planter nor the waterer matter: only God, who makes things grow."[49]

Pentecost

[The] Disciples . . . persevered together in prayer, in one house, awaiting the fulfilment of His promise. Now they began to desire this with faith, with prayer, with eagerness of the spirit. They were the new wineskins, and they looked for the new wine from heaven. For the great Grape Cluster had been trodden out, and glorified. . . .

What great wonder followed, you have already heard. All who were present in that assembly had learned but one tongue. The Holy Spirit came. They were filled with Him, and they began to speak in the tongues of different nations, which they neither knew before, nor had learnt. But He taught them Who had come. He entered into them, and they were all filled with Him. He transformed them. And this then was a sign of whoever had received the Holy Spirit, that of a sudden filled with the Spirit, they began to speak in the tongues of every nation; not these one hundred and twenty alone.

The Sacred Writings teach that after men had believed, were baptized, and received the Holy Ghost, they began to speak in the tongues of all nations. Those present were astonished, some wondering, some mocking, so they said: "These men are full of new wine." They laughed, yet they said a true thing. For these skins were filled with new wine. You heard when the Gospel was being read, how, "no one puts new wine into old wineskins:" the carnal minded cannot grasp spiritual things. The carnal mind is age, grace is newness. To whatever degree a man is changed for the better, so much the more does he grasp the flavour of truth. The new wine bubbled up, and as the must boiled, the tongues of the nations poured forth.[50]

The Holy Spirit Is the Soul of the Church

If you wish to have the Holy Spirit, attend to what I say, my brethren. The spirit within us, by which a man lives, is called a soul; our spirit, by which each single one of us lives is called the soul. Consider what the soul does within the body. It gives life to all the members. It sees through the eyes, hears through the ears, smells through the nostrils, speaks by the tongue, works by means of the hand, walks by means of the feet. It is present at the same time in all the members, that they may live. It gives life to all; to each it allots duties. The eye does not hear, the ear does not see, the tongue does not see, and neither does the eye speak, or the ear; and yet each lives. The duties are diverse, but the life is one.

Such is the Church of God. In some of its saints it works miracles, in others of the saints it utters truth; in some saints it cherishes virginity, in others of the sanctified it upholds conjugal modesty; in others this, in others that. Each one does what belongs to him, but they live in the same manner. What the soul is to the body of man, the Holy Ghost is to the Body of Christ: which the Church is. What the soul does in all the members of one body, this the Holy Spirit does throughout the Church.[51]

ST. JOHN CHRYSOSTOM (354-407)

The Phenomenon of Tongues

The Holy Ghost came in the form of tongues, and He assigned to each one of them [the Apostles] the region of the world where each should teach, making known to them by means of the given tongue, as though by a written tablet, the limits of the realm entrusted to them, and of their teaching.

For this cause the Holy Spirit came in the form of tongues, but not for this cause alone, but to recall the past to our minds. For when of old, men filled with pride, had sought to build a tower to reach the heavens, through the division of their tongues God put an end to the evil purpose of their common speech. Because of this, the Holy Spirit descends upon them now in the form of fiery tongues, that by this means He may join together the divided world. So there then took place something new and wondrous: for as in times past tongues divided the world, and changed an evil accord into division, so now tongues join the world together, and bring together in harmony those that before were divided.

And so He appeared in the form of tongues, and of tongues of fire, because the thorn of sin in us has grown into a forest. For as land, which though rich and fertile is left uncultivated, will bring forth a large crop of thorns, so is our nature which though created good, and suited to the cultivation of the crop of virtue, because it had never felt the plough of reverential love of God, nor received the seed of the knowledge of God, had brought forth impiety as though it were thorns and other useless growth. And as, as often happens, through the dense growth of thorns and unprofitable weeds the face of the earth is not even seen, so the purity and nobility of our soul did not appear until the husbandman of nature of man had come, and, touching it with the fire of the Spirit, cleansed and prepared it, that it might be ready to receive the good seed.[52]

ST. LEO THE GREAT (400-461)

Sermon for Whitsuntide

"While the days of the Pentecost were being completed and the disciples were all together in the same, there came suddenly from heaven a sound as of a vehement wind approaching . . ."

O how rapid is the discourse of wisdom! And where God is the Master, how soon is that learned which is taught! No interpretation was added that they might hear better; they were not familiarised with the words in order to use them, nor had they time given them for study; but by the Spirit of truth blowing where He willed, the peculiar languages of the several nations were made common in the mouth of the Church. It was, then, from this day that the trumpet of the preaching of the Gospel gave forth its sound; it was from this day that showers of spiritual gifts, streams of blessings, watered every desert and all the dry ground, for the Spirit of God was being borne over the waters in order to renew the face of the earth; and new flashes of light were beaming forth to drive away the old darkness, seeing that by the splendour of the radiant tongues was being received that lustrous Word of the Lord, that fiery utterance, wherein were present an illuminating energy and a burning force, to create intelligence and to consume sin.

But, although, dearly beloved, the appearance of the event was indeed wonderful, nor can it be doubted that, in that exultant choir of all human tongues, the majesty of the Holy Spirit was present, yet let no one fancy that in what was seen by bodily eyes His Divine substance showed itself. For His invisible nature, which He shares with the Father and the Son, did exhibit, by such a manifestation as it pleased, the character of its own gift and work. But it retained within its Divinity that which belonged to its own essence; for as the Father and the Son, so also the Holy Spirit is inaccessible to human eyesight.[53]

ST. GREGORY THE GREAT (540-604)

The Spirit Fortifies the Weak

[The Apostles] would not have dared to withstand the rulers of this world, had not the power of the Holy Spirit sustained them. What the Teachers of the holy Church were like before the Coming of the Holy Ghost we know; what their courage became after His Coming we shall now see.

What fear, what weaknesses, the very Pastor of the Church . . . showed before the Coming of the Holy Ghost, the maid who was doorkeeper will tell us, should we ask her. Terrified at the voice of a woman, fearful of death, he denied Life. And Peter denied Him on the ground at the very time when the Thief would confess Him upon the cross. But let us hear what was the courage of this man after the coming of the Holy Ghost. There was an assembly of the Council and of the Ancients, and, after they had been scourged, the Apostles were charged that they must speak no more in the name of Jesus. Peter with firm decision replied: "We ought to obey God, rather than men." And again: "If it be just in the sight of God, to hear you rather than God, judge ye. For we cannot but speak the things which we have seen and heard." And they indeed went from the presence of the Council, rejoicing that they were accounted worthy to suffer reproach for the name of Jesus. Behold Peter, rejoicing at being scourged, who before had trembled at a word. And he who, when she questioned him, was terrified by the voice of a serving maid, after the Coming of the Holy Spirit, though scourged, stands firm against the power of princes.

It is my delight to lift up eyes of faith to the wonders of our Creator; and here and there to dwell upon the Fathers of both the Old and New Testament. I behold with these same eyes, that were opened by faith, David and Amos and Daniel and Peter and Paul and Matthew, and I am moved to consider how great, as Creator, is the Holy Spirit, but in my reflection I fall short. For it is He Who inspires the youthful harpist, and He Who has created the psalmist. He moves the soul of the herdsman dressing Sycamores, and makes him a prophet. He enters into a young boy, disciplined in spirit, and makes him a judge. He enters into a fisherman, and makes of him a preacher of the Gospel. He fills a persecutor of the Church, and makes him the Doctor of the Gentiles. He fills a publican, and makes him an Evangelist. What power of creation has this Spirit! In all that He willed there is not pause to learn. As He touches a soul He teaches it; and simply to have touched is to have taught it. For as His Light illumines it, the human spirit of a sudden changes; it rejects on the instant what it was, and shows itself at once as it was not.[54]

The Spirit Reveals to Us That Which We Cannot Understand Naturally

Take the case of an expectant mother cast into a dungeon where she gives birth to a son. He stays there with her and grows up in the darkness. Suppose this boy's mother described to him the sun, the moon, and the stars, the mountains and fields, birds flying in the air and horses running in the fields. Born and raised in the dungeon, knowing only the perpetual darkness around him, he would doubt whether the things he heard his mother describe actually existed, since he had no experience of them. So it is with men born into the darkness of this earthly exile. They hear about lofty and invisible things, but hesitate to believe in them, because they know only the lowly, visible things of earth into which they were born. It was for this reason that the Creator of the visible and invisible worlds came as the Only-begotten of the Father to redeem the human race and to send the Holy Spirit into our hearts. From Him we were to receive new life in order to believe those truths of which we as yet had no knowledge through experience. All of us, therefore, who have received this Spirit as the pledge of our inheritance are no longer in doubt about the existence of invisible beings. On the other hand, anyone who is not yet solidly grounded in this faith ought to accept what his elders say, putting his trust in them, since they have experimental knowledge of the invisible world through the Holy Spirit. In our story, too, it would have been foolish for the little boy to think his mother was telling him lies about the light, merely because he himself knew nothing but the darkness of the dungeon.[55]

Direction of the Spirit

There are times when the Spirit directs a soul entirely from within. In such cases the guidance of this divine Teacher supplies for the absence of any human instruction. Weaker souls, however, must not try to imitate this freedom in their own lives. For if, on the vain presumption that they, too, are filled with the Holy Spirit, they refuse to be guided by another human being, they will only become teachers of error. The soul that is really filled with the Spirit of God will easily be recognized by its miraculous powers and humility. Where these two signs of holiness are found to perfection they show beyond a doubt that God is truly present. John the Baptist, for example, did not have an instructor, either, as far as we can tell from sacred Scripture. Even the divine Master, who is Truth itself, did not make John one of His disciples as He did the Apostles, whom He taught through His human presence. Instead, Christ left him free of these external ties and continued to instruct him by divine inspiration. Moses, too, after being taught in the desert, received instructions from an angel, not from a human being. But, as I said before, examples like these are rather to be admired by weaker souls than imitated.[56]

ST. JOHN OF DAMASCUS (*ca.* 680-749?)

It is . . . necessary that the Word have a Spirit. Thus, even our own speech is not devoid of breath, although in our case the breath is not of our substance. It is an inhaling and exhaling of the air which is breathed in and out for the sustainment of the body. . . . Having learned that there is a Spirit of God, we conceive of Him as associated with the Word and making the operation of the Word manifest. We do not conceive of Him as an impersonal breath of air, for the majesty of the divine nature would be reduced to low estate if its Spirit were likened to our own breath. Rather, we conceive of him as a substantial power found in its own individualizing personality, proceeding from the Father, coming to rest in the Word and declaring with whom it is associated, having might, not dissipated away into non-existence, but distinctly subsistent like the Word—living, endowed with will, self-moving, active, at all times willing good, exercising His power for the prosecution of every design in accordance with His will, without beginning and without end. For the Word fell short of the Father in nothing, and the Spirit did not fall short of the Word in anything. . . .[57]

We . . . believe in the Holy Ghost, the Lord and Giver of life, who proceeds from the Father and abides in the Son; who is adored and glorified together with the Father and the Son as consubstantial and co-eternal with Them; who is true and authoritative Spirit of God and the source of wisdom and life and sanctification; who is God together with the Father and the Son and is so proclaimed; who is uncreated, complete, creative, almighty, all-working, all-powerful, infinite in power; who dominates all creation but is not dominated; who deifies but is not deified; who fills but is not filled; who is shared in but does not share; who sanctifies but is not sanctified; who, as receiving the intercessions of all, is the intercessor; who is like the Father and the Son in all things; who proceeds from the Father and is communicated through the Son and is participated in by all creation; who through Himself creates and gives substance to all things and sanctifies and preserves them; who is distinctly subsistent and exists in His own Person indivisible and inseparable from the Father and the Son; who has all things whatsoever the Father and the Son have except the being unbegotten and the being begotten. For the Father is uncaused and unbegotten, because He is not from anything, but has His being from Himself and does not have from any other anything whatsoever that He has. Rather, He Himself is the principle and cause by which all things naturally exist as they do. And the Son is begotten of the Father—although not by begetting, but by procession. Now, we have learned that there is a difference between begetting and procession, but what the manner of this difference is we have not learned at all. However, the begetting of the Son and the procession of the Holy Ghost from the Father are simultaneous.[58]

SYMEON THE NEW THEOLOGIAN (949-1022)

Prayer to God, the Holy Spirit

Come, true light,
Come, eternal life,
Come, secret of hiddenness.
Come, delight that has no name.
Come, unutterableness.
Come, O presence, forever fleeing from human nature.
Come, everlasting jubilee.
Come, light without end.
Come, awaited by all who are in want.
Come, resurrection of the dead.
Come, mighty one, forever creating, recreating, and renewing with a mere wave of Thy hand.
Come, Thou who remainest wholly invisible, for none ever to grasp or to caress.
Come, Thou who flowest in the river of hours,
yet immovably stayest above it,
who dwellest above all heavens,
yet bendest to us who are bowed down.
Come, most longed-for and most hallowed name:
to express what Thou art,
to comprehend how Thou art, and how thou existest
is forever denied to us.
Come, perpetual joy.
Come, unwitherable wreath.
Come, O purple raiment of our Lord and God.
Come, girdle, clear as crystal and many-coloured with precious gems.
Come, inaccessible refuge.
Come, Thou whom my poor soul desireth and hath desired.
Come, lonely one, to the lonely one—for lonely I am, as Thou canst see.
Come, Thou who hast made me solitary and forlorn on earth.
Come, Thou who hast become my longing, for that thou has ordained, that I must needs long for Thee whom no human breath has ever reached.
Come, my breath and my life.
Come, joy, glory, and my incessant delight.

I give Thee thanks that without merging or losing Thyself in my nature, Thou art yet one spirit with me, and while Thou remainest God, high above everything. Thou hast become everything to me.

Ineffable nourishment, never to be withdrawn, pouring forth unceasingly into the lips of my spirit and aboundingly filling my inner self!

I give Thee thanks that Thou hast become for me a day without evening and a sun without setting:

Thou, who hast no place to hide, as Thou fillest the universe with Thy power.

Never hast Thou hidden from anyone; we, however, hide from Thee always, if we dare not appear before Thy face.

And where also shouldst Thou hide, Who hast nowhere a place to rest?

O why shouldst Thou hide, Who dost not shrink nor shy away from anything in all the world?

Ah, Holy Lord—make an abode in me, dwell in me, and till my departure leave me not, leave not your servant;

That I too, may find myself after death in Thee, and reign with Thee, O God, who reignest over everything.

Remain with me, Lord, do not forsake me.

Strengthen me interiorly, so that I may be unmoved at all times, and protect me by dwelling in me: that, although dead, I may live in contemplating Thee, and although poor, may be rich in the possession of Thee.

Thus I shall be mightier than all kings:

Eating and drinking Thee, and at chosen hours wrapping myself in Thee, I shall enjoy unspeakable bliss.

For Thou art all Good, all Beauty, all Beatitude,

And Thine is the glory of the universe, Thine, with the Father and the Son, forever and ever. Amen.[59]

NOTES

1. George A. Maloney, *The Mystic of Fire and Light. St. Simeon The New Theologian* (Denville, New Jersey: Dimension Books, 1975), p. 10.

2. *Early Christian Prayers*. Edited by A. Hamman. Translated by Walter Mitchell (Chicago: Henry Regnery Co., 1961), p. 80.

3. *Ancient Christian Writers*. No. 1. *The Epistles of St. Clement of Rome and St. Ignatius of Antioch*. Translated by James E. Kleist (Westminster: Newman Press, 1949), p. 63.

4. *Ibid.*, p. 73.

5. *Ibid.*, p. 88.
6. *Ibid.*, p. 10.
7. *Ibid.*, p. 35.
8. *Ibid.*, pp. 36-38.
9. XI Odes 1-8 in Louis Bouyer, *The Meaning of Monastic Life* (New York: P. J. Kenedy and Sons, 1955), p. 86.
10. *Ibid.* VI Odes I, p. 87.
11. *Ancient Christian Writers* No. 6. *The Didache. The Epistle of Barnabas. The Epistles and the Martyrdom of St. Polycarp. The Fragments of Papias. The Epistle to Diognetus.* Translated by James E. Kleist (Westminster: The Newman Press, 1948), p. 37.
12. *Adversus Haereses* Book III Chapter XXIV in *Early Christian Fathers*. Translated by Henry Bettenson (London: Oxford University Press, 1956), p. 114.
13. *Adversus Haereses* Book III, Ch. XVII in *The Ante-Nicene Fathers*. Translated by Alexander Roberts and James Donaldson (New York: Charles Scribner's Sons, 1925), Vol I., pp. 444-445. Text edited.
14. *The Apostolic Fathers. The Shepherd of Hermas.* Translated by Kirsopp Lake (Cambridge, Mass.: Harvard University Press, 1965), p. 89.
15. *Ibid.*, p. 93.
16. *Ibid.*, p. 113.
17. *Ibid.*, p. 121.
18. *Ancient Christian Writers* No. 23. *Athenagoras. Embassy for the Christians. The Resurrection of the Dead.* Translated by Joseph Hugh Crehan (Westminster: The Newman Press, 1956), pp. 39-40.
19. *Ancient Christian Writers* No. 6 (Cf. Note 11), p. 97.
20. *Ibid.*, p. 18.
21. "On Baptism," Chapter VIII in *The Ante-Nicene Fathers*. Translated by Alexander Roberts and James Donaldson (New York: Charles Scribner's Sons, 1925), Vol III, p. 673.
22. *De Principiis* I, iii, 8. in *Early Christian Fathers* (cf. Note 12), p. 317.
23. *Homilia VI.3 in Numeros* in *Origen and the Doctrine of Grace*. Translated by Benjamin Drewery (London: The Epworth Press, 1960), p. 174.
24. "On Prayer," II.6 in *Ibid.*, p. 183.
25. *Ibid.*, XIII.3, p. 184.
26. "On the Unity of the Catholic Church," Translated by F. A. Wright in *Fathers of the Church* (New York: E. P. Dutton, 1929), pp. 115, 118-119.
27. *The Letters of St. Athanasius Concerning the Holy Spirit.* Translated by C.R.B. Shapland (New York: Philosophical Library, 1951), p. 98.
28. *Ibid.*, pp. 135-136.
29. *Early Christian Prayers* (cf. Note 2), p. 53.

30. Catechesis XVI in *The Fathers of the Church* Vol. 64. *The Works of Saint Cyril of Jerusalem.* Translated by Leo P. McCauley and Anthony A. Stephenson (Washington: The Catholic University of America Press, 1970), Vol II, pp. 85-86.

31. Catechesis XVII in *Ibid.*, pp. 101-102.

32. *Ibid.*, p. 106.

33. Catechesis XVI *Ibid.*, p. 82.

34. "De Trinitate," 2, 35 in *The Later Christian Fathers. A Selection from the Writings of the Fathers from St. Cyril of Jerusalem to St. Leo the Great.* Translated by Henry A. Bettenson (London: Oxford University Press, 1970), p. 56.

35. *Oratio XLI In Pentecosten* in J. P. Migne, *Patrologiae Graecae* (Paris: Garnier Fratres, 1885), Tomus XXXVI, p. 447.

36. Orationes 8-11 in Bettenson, *The Later Christian Fathers* (cf. Note 34), p. 114.

37. *De Spiritu Sancto* in *Later Christian Fathers* (cf. Note 34), pp. 71-72.

38. *The Catechetical Oration of St. Gregory of Nyssa.* Translated by J. H. Srawley (London: Society for Promoting Christian Knowledge, 1917), pp. 30-31.

39. "On Virginity," in *From Glory to Glory. Texts from Gregory of Nyssa's Mystical Writings.* Translated and Edited by Herbert Masurillo (New York: Charles Scribner's Sons, 1961), p. 109.

40. *Theological and Dogmatic Works. Fathers of the Church*, Vol. 44 Translated by Roy J. Deferrari (Washington: Catholic University of America Press, 1963), pp. 87-88.

41. *Ibid.*, pp. 91-92.

42. *Ibid.*, pp. 66-67.

43. *Ibid.*, p. 110.

44. *Early Christian Prayers* (cf. Note 2), p. 118.

45. Letter 32 in *Ancient Christian Writers* No. 36 *Letters of St. Paulinus of Nola.* Translated by P.G. Walsh (Westminster: The Newman Press, 1967), Vol. II., p. 138.

46. Letter 23 in *Ibid.*, p. 33.

47. *Early Christian Prayers* (cf. Note 2), pp. 116-117.

48. Exact source unknown; commonly attributed to St. Augustine.

49. *Homilies on the Gospel According to St. John and His First Epistle* by S. Augustine (London: Walter Smith, 1883), Vol. II, pp. 1136-1137.

50. Sermon 267 (for Pentecost). *The Sunday Sermons of the Great Fathers.* Translated by M.F. Toal (Chicago: Regnery, 1959), Vol III, p. 26.

51. *Ibid.*, p. 27.

52. John Chrysostom, in *Ibid.*, p. 20.

53. *Selected Sermons of St. Leo the Great on the Incarnation.*

Translated by William Bright (London: J. Masters and Co., 1886), pp. 98-99.

54. "Sermon for Pentecost," in *Sunday Sermons of the Great Fathers* (cf. Note 50), pp. 53-54.

55. Dialogue Four. *The Fathers of the Church* Vol. 39. *Saint Gregory the Great. Dialogues*. Translated by Odo John Zimmerman (Washington: The Catholic University of America Press, Inc.), p. 190.

56. Dialogue One, *Ibid.*, pp. 8-9.

57. "An Exact Exposition of the Orthodox Faith," in *Fathers of the Church*. Vol 37 *Saint John of Damascus*. Translated by Frederick H. Chase, Jr. (Washington: The Catholic University of America Press, Inc., 1958), pp. 174-175.

58. *Ibid.*, pp. 183-184.

59. *Come, South Wind: A Collection of Contemplatives* (New York: Pantheon Books, 1957), pp. 134-136.

Albrecht Durer, THE HOLY TRINITY. Woodcut, 1511, Print Room, New York Public Library.

Chapter V

THE HOLY SPIRIT IN THE WRITINGS OF THE MIDDLE AGES AND RENAISSANCE

Introduction

In the earliest days of the Christian era, the organizational network of the Roman Empire had proved a great help in spreading the new faith, even, in the strange dialectic of history, by its persecutions of the early Christians. When the power of Rome waned throughout Europe, early monastic settlements proved to be the only channel of education in areas that had lapsed into political anarchy. In Benedictine monasteries, the motto ruled: "To work and to pray." The work was often the arduous task of clearing virginal forests for human settlement, while the prayer was focused on the chanting of the monastic office and other liturgical celebrations. In both tasks, the emphasis was primarily communal. Yet, out of this tradition emerged great mystics in the Church, such as Bernard of Clairvaux and Hildegarde, to whom the Holy Spirit indeed communicated the mysteries of His love, and who fortunately left notes about their spiritual insights.

When urban and commercial life revived in a grand way in Europe, the Spirit inspired his servants Francis of Assisi and Dominic Guzman to found orders to preach the Word of God in cities—not merely in rural monasteries, as of old. The humble Angela of Foligno found herself in communion with the Spirit while on a pilgrimage to the shrine of Father Francis. The Dominican Thomas Aquinas devoted much of his brilliant intellectual effort to explaining the very inner life of the Father, Son, and Holy Spirit. Like Tertullian and Hilary of Poitiers, Thomas reminded the world that He was a Gift; like Augustine, both Thomas and the German mystic Meister Eckhart forcefully affirmed that God is Love. Following Isaiah the prophet, Thomas bequeathed to Christianity a cogent explanation of the Gifts of the Spirit. Another Dominican, St. Catherine of Siena, reminded the men of her time that when they have arrived at perfect love, like the apostles who received the Holy Spirit, they could fearlessly go forth to announce the Word and His Truth to the mighty of the world. After much "fasting and watching," as she advocated in her writings, Catherine herself boldly proclaimed the truth to popes and high prelates, thus altering Church hisory by persuading the papacy to return once more to the See of Peter in Rome from a long sojourn in Avignon, France.

As the medieval period of history gave way to the Renaissance and the force of the Protestant Reformation, Ignatius Loyola formed his Society of Jesus for the service of the Church. Even while writing the very constitutions of his Society, however, Ignatius affirmed that "the interior law of charity and love which the Holy Spirit writes and engraves upon hearts" must be the guiding force in the lives of his fellow Jesuits. In subsequent decades, a splendid flowering of saintly Spanish mystics appeared whose lives and writings have inspired countless souls. Among them, John of the Cross bespoke in rapturous Spanish poetry his love for the Living Flame who had so cauterized his own ardent soul. In historical perspective, the trials of the Church itself in this era of Reformation may now be viewed as "a sweet cautery," for the Church emerged greatly strengthened in the wake of the Protestant Revolt by its own housecleaning and the action of the Council of Trent. Viewing these disturbed times of the Church, the words of Hans Urs Von Baltasar ring true: "It is the Spirit who makes history into the history of salvation."

ST. BERNARD OF CLAIRVAUX (1090-1153)

THE KISS OF GOD (Sermon on the *Canticle of Canticles*)

It seems to me . . . that a certain ineffable kiss which no creature had ever received was meant by Him who said: "No one knoweth the Son but the Father: neither doth any one know the Father but the Son, and he to whom it shall please the Son to reveal Him." For the Father loves the Son and embraces Him with a singular love. The Most High embraces His Equal; the Eternal, His Co-Eternal; the One, His Only-Begotten . . .

I hold for certain that to so great and so holy an *arcanum* of divine love not even the angelic creation is admitted. . . . See the new Spouse [the Church] receiving the new kiss, not, however, from the *mouth* but from the KISS *of His mouth*. He breathed on them, it is said. There can be no doubt that Jesus breathed upon the Apostles, that is, upon the primitive Church, and said: "Receive ye the Holy Ghost." That was, assuredly, a kiss. What?—the physical breath? No. but the invisible Spirit.

He was communicated by the Lord's breathing so that by this it should be understood that He proceeds from the Son equally as from the Father after the manner of a real kiss which is equally his who gives and his who receives it. And so it is enough for the bride if she is kissed with the *kiss* of the Bridegroom, even if she is not kissed with His *mouth*. Nor does she think it a slight thing or a thing to be despised that she is kissed with a *kiss*, which is nothing else than to be filled with the Holy Ghost. Certainly if the Father is rightly interpreted as giving the kiss and the Son as receiving it, it will not be very far from the fact to understand the kiss itself as the Holy Ghost who is the unalterable peace, the indissoluble bond, the indivisible love, the inviolable unity between the Father and the Son.

It is, therefore, through His inspiration that the bride grows bold and confidently asks under the name of a kiss, that the inpouring of the Holy Ghost be granted her. She holds in memory something which cannot cease to be a motive of confidence. For when the Son said, "no one knoweth the Son but the Father: neither doth any one know the Father but the Son, He added, and he to whom it shall please the Son to reveal HIM." Now, when the Father and the Son are perfectly known to anyone, how can he be ignorant of the Goodness of the Two? And that Goodness is the Holy Spirit.

Therefore, when the bride asks a kiss she begs for the grace to be the recipient of this threefold knowledge, as far as it can be acquired in this mortal flesh. But she asks it of the Son to whom it pertains to reveal things to whomsoever He will. The Son, then, reveals Himself to whomsoever He will and He reveals the Father. But this revelation, beyond a doubt, is made by a kiss, that is, by the Holy Spirit.[1]

ST. HILDEGARDE (1098-1179)

Sequence

O sacred Fire! O Paraclete, Spirit! Thou art the life of every creature's life.

Thou art the Holy One, vivifying all beings!

Thou art the Holy One, healing with thine unction those that are dangerously bruised!

Thou art the Holy One, cleansing our festered wounds!

O breath of holiness! O fire of charity! O thou sweet Saviour of the soul, and the heart's infusion of the pleasing odour of virtues!

O purest fount! wherein is reflected the mercy of God, who adopts aliens for his children, and goes in search of them that are lost.

O breast-plate of life, that givest the members hope of compact strength! O girdle of beautiful energy, save us thy happy people!

Be the protector of them that have been imprisoned by the enemy! Loose the bonds of them whom God's power would save!

O way, which nothing can resist! That penetrates heaven and earth, and every deep abyss, bringing all to order and unity!

'Tis by thee that clouds glide in the firmament, that air wings its flight, that rocks yield springs, that waters flow, and earth gives forth her verdure.

'Tis thou that leadest men to knowledge, gladdening with them the inspiration of wisdom.

Praise, then, be to thee, O thou praise-yielding Spirit, thou joy of life, our hope, our highest honour, the giver of the reward of light! Amen.[2]

WILLIAM OF ST. THIERRY (d. 1148)

Excerpts from the Golden Epistle

Man has not only to be created and formed but also endowed with life. For first God formed man, then he breathed into his face the breath of life, so that man became a living soul. The formation of a man is his moral training, his life is the love of God.

This is conceived by faith, brought forth by hope, formed and endowed with life by charity, that is, the Holy Spirit. For the love of God, or the Love that is God, the Holy Spirit, infusing itself into man's love and spirit, attracts him to itself; then God loves himself in man and makes him, his spirit and his love, one with himself. For as the body has no means of living apart from its spirit, so man's affections, which are called love, have no means of living, that is to say, of loving God, but the Holy Spirit. . . .[3]

When the object of thought is God and the things which relate to God and the will reaches the stage at which it becomes love, the Holy Spirit, the Spirit of life, at once infuses himself by way of love and gives life to everything, lending his assistance in prayer, in meditation or in study to man's weakness. Immediately the memory becomes wisdom and tastes with relish the good things of the Lord, while the thoughts to which they give rise are brought to the intellect to be formed into affections. The understanding of the one thinking becomes the contemplation of one loving and it shapes it into certain experiences of spiritual or divine sweetness which it brings before the gaze of the spirit so that the spirit rejoices in them. . .

But this way of thinking about God does not lie at the disposal of the thinker. It is a gift of grace, bestowed by the Holy Spirit who breathes where he chooses, when he chooses, how he chooses and upon whom he chooses. Man's part is continually to prepare his heart by ridding his will of foreign attachments, his reason or intellect of anxieties, his memory of idle or absorbing, sometimes even of necessary business, so that in the Lord's good time and when he sees fit, at the sound of the Holy Spirit's breathing the elements which constitute thought may be free at once to come together and do their work, each contributing its share to the outcome of joy for the soul. . . .[4]

He is the almighty Artificer who creates man's good will in regard to God, inclines God to be merciful to man, shapes man's desire, gives strength, ensures the prosperity of undertakings, conducts all things powerfully and disposes everything sweetly.

He it is who gives life to man's spirit and holds it together, just as it gives life to its body and holds it together. Men may teach how to seek God and angels how to adore him, but he alone teaches how to find him, possess him and enjoy him. He himself is the anxious quest of the man who truly seeks, he is the devotion of the man who adores in spirit and truth, he is the wisdom of the man who finds, the love of him who possesses, the gladness of him who enjoys.

Yet whatever he bestows here on his faithful of the vision and the knowledge of God is but as in a mirror and a riddle, as far removed from the vision and the knowledge that is to be in the future, as faith is from truth, or time from eternity.[5]

Prayers Asking for the Holy Spirit

O you who are adorable, tremendous, blessed, give him to us! Send forth your Spirit, and we shall be made, and you will renew the face of the earth! For it is not in a flood of many waters, in the disturbance and confusion of our moods, which are as many in number as they are different in kind, that we shall draw near to God. Lord, that disaster, the punishment of Adam's seed, has gone on long enough! Bring in your Spirit on the earth, let the sea draw back, let the wilderness of ancient condemnation draw back, and let the parched earth appear, thirsting for the fount of life! Let the dove come, the Holy Spirit, when the great blackbird has been driven out, and is hunching over his kill! Let the dove, I say, come with the olive branch, proclaiming peace with the branch that speaks of renewal and light! May your holiness and hallowing make us holy, may your unity unite us and, through what is indeed a sort of blood relationship, may we be united to God who is love through the name of love. We shall be made one with him through the power of this name.[6]

Lead me away . . . my refuge and my strength, into the heart of the desert as once you led your servant Moses; lead me where the bush burns, yet is not burnt up, where the holy soul that has earned admission to a like experience is all aflame with the fullness of the fire of your Holy Spirit, and burning like the seraphim, is not consumed but cleansed. And then there comes to pass for the first time a better thing, the miracle of all your miracles, the sight of sights. The soul attains to the holy place where none may stand or take another step, except he be bare-footed—having loosed the shoe-strings of all fleshly hindrances—the place that is, that the soul may enter with her affections clean and pure. This is the place where He Who Is, who cannot be seen as he is, is notwithstanding heard to say, "I Am Who Am," the place where, for the time, the soul must cover her face so that she does not see the face of God, and yet in humble obedience must use her ears to hear what the Lord God will say concerning her.[7]

In the soul of your poor servant . . . Lord, your love is always present; but it is hidden like the fire in the ashes till the Holy Spirit who blows where he wills, is pleased to manifest it profitably the way and to the extent he wishes. Come, therefore, come O holy Love; come, O sacred Fire! Burn up the concupiscences of our reins and our hearts. Hide your thoughts as you will, to furnish more abundantly the rule of humility for your revealing flame. Manifest them when you will, to manifest the glory of a good conscience and the riches it has in its house. Manifest those riches, Lord, to make me zealous to keep them; hide them from me, lest I be led rashly to squander them, until such time as he who has begun the good work shall also perfect it, he who lives and reigns through all the ages.[8]

ADAM OF ST. VICTOR (d. 1177?)

Sequences

The glad and glorious light—wherewith the heaven-sent Fire filled the hearts of Jesus' disciples and gave them to speak tongues—invites us now to sing our hymns with hearts in concord with the voice.

On the fiftieth day, Christ revisited his bride, by sending her the pledge he had promised. After tasting the honeyed sweetness, Peter, now the firmest of rocks, pours forth the unction of his preaching.

The Law, of old, was given on the mount to the people, but it was written on tablets of stone, and not on fiery tongues; but in the cenacle, there was given to a chosen few newness of heart and knowledge of all tongues.

O Happy, O festive day, whereon was founded the primitive Church! Three thousand souls! Oh! how vigorous the first fruits of the new born Church!. . . .

O dear Comforter, come! govern our tongues, soften our hearts:

where thou art, must be no gall or poison. Nothing is joyous, nothing pleasant, nothing wholesome, nothing peaceful, nothing sweet, nothing full, save by thy grace. . . .

O thou the Giver and the Gift. O thou, the only good of our hearts eager to praise thee, and teach our tongues to sound forth thy glory. Do thou, O Author of purity, purify us from sin! Renew us in Christ; and then, give us the full joy of perfect newness! Amen.[9]

Come, O best of Comforters, hope of our salvation, giver of life! aid us with thy grace. O sweet fire, O divine dew! Thou art, with Father and Son, the germ of infinite goodness.

Thou proceedest from both; from neither ever separate, but united to both with an everlasting link. O thou their dew and Spirit! May the Father and Son grant thee to flow in copious gift, even to us.

Christian! He is the dew and Spirit: believe, too, that he is the fragrance that tells thee he is God. The more we drink of this heaven-sent dew, the more we thirst to drink, and pant the more to have.

That we may be regenerated as children of God, he gives water its mystic power, he that moved over the waters when this world began. He is the fount of holiness, the fount that cleanses us from sin, the fount that springs from the fountain Godhead, the fount that consecrates the font.

O living fire, O life-giving stream! Cleanse and fructify our hearts. Inflame us with the fire of charity, and then, in mercy, make us a holy offering to thyself.

Dear Spirit of the Father and the Son! Thou remedy of sin! Be to the wearied, help, and to the sorrowing, consolation! O chaste and beautiful love! O burning, yet purest love! May thine unction heal the wound of seething lust.

O soundless voice! Voice mysterious and still! Voice whispered in the faithful ear! O voice most sweet and dear! Speak to our souls! O lie-dispelling light! O truth-bearing light! Grant to each and all of us thy servants life, and health, and brightness everlasting. Amen.[10]

ST. THOMAS AQUINAS (1226-1274)

Summa Theologica

Whether "Love" Is the Proper Name of the Holy Ghost

The name Love in God can be taken essentially and personally. If taken personally it is the proper name of the Holy Ghost; as Word is the proper name of the Son. . . .

The Holy Ghost is said to be the bond of the Father and the Son, inasmuch as He is Love; because, since the Father loves Himself and the Son with one love, and conversely, there is expressed in the Holy Ghost, as Love, the relation of the Father to the Son, and conversely, as that of the lover to the beloved. But from the fact that the Father and the Son mutually love one another, it necessarily follows that this mutual Love, the Holy Ghost proceeds from both.

The Father loves not only the Son, but also Himself and us, by the Holy Ghost; because. . . . . to love, taken in a notional sense, not only imports the production of a divine person, but also the person produced, by way of love, which has relation to the object loved. Hence, as the Father speaks Himself and every creature by His begotten Word, inasmuch as the Word *begotten* adequately represents the Father and every creature; so He loves Himself and every creature by the Holy Ghost, inasmuch as the Holy Ghost proceeds as the love of the primal goodness whereby the Father loves Himself and every creature.[11]

Whether "Gift" Is the Proper Name of the Holy Ghost

Gift, taken personally in God, is the proper name of the Holy Ghost.

In proof of this we must know that a gift is properly an unreturnable giving, as Aristotle says (Top. iv. 2)—i.e., a thing which is not given with the intention of a return—and it thus contains the idea of a gratuitous donation. Now, the reason of donation being gratuitous is love; since therefore do we give something to anyone gratuitously forasmuch as we wish him well. So what we first give him is the love whereby we wish him well. Hence it is manifest that love has the nature of a first gift, through which all free gifts are given. So since the Holy Ghost proceeds as love, as stated above, He proceeds as the first gift.[12]

On the Truth of the Catholic Faith
That Christ Was Born of the Holy Spirit

Although, of course, every divine operation by which something is accomplished in creatures is common to the entire Trinity . . . the formation of Christ's body, which was perfected by the divine power, is suitably ascribed to the Holy Spirit although it is common to the entire Trinity.

Now, this seems to be in harmony with the Incarnation of the Word. For, just as our word mentally conceived is invisible, but is made sensible in an external vocal expression, so the Word of God in the eternal generation exists invisibly in the heart of the Father, but by the Incarnation is made sensible to us. Thus, the Incarnation of God's Word is like the vocal expression of our word. But the vocal expression of our word is made by our spirit, through which the vocal formation of our word takes place. Suitably, then it is through the Spirit of the Son of God that the formation of His flesh is said to have taken place.[13]

BLESSED ANGELA OF FOLIGNO (1248-1309)

Her Dialogue with the Holy Spirit

As I went unto St. Francis [at Assisi] . . . I prayed . . . that he would implore God for me that I might serve well his Order . . . that I might feel somewhat of Christ, but above all, that he would make me become poor and end my days in poverty.

. . . It was said unto me:

"Thou hast prayed unto my servant Francis, and I have not willed to send thee another messenger. I am the Holy Spirit, who am come unto thee to bring thee such consolation as thou hast never before tasted. . . . I will bear thee company and will speak with thee all the way; I will make no end to my speaking and thou wilt not be able to attend to any save unto me, for I have bound thee. . . .

"My beloved and my bride, love thou me! All thy life, thy eating and drinking and sleeping and all that thou dost is pleasing unto me, if only thou lovest me." And He said, "I will do great things through thee in the sight of all people; thou shalt be known and glorified, so that many shall praise my name in thee."

[Angela replied] "If Thou who has spoken with me from the beginning were truly the Holy Spirit, Thou wouldst not have told me such great things; and if Thou wert verily within me, then my joy would be so great that I could not bear it and live."

Then did He make answer: "Nothing can exist, nothing can be done save according unto my will . . ."

. . . . I had no desire to reach the city or that the road should ever come to an end. I can never describe the joy and sweetness which I felt, especially when He said, "I am the Holy Spirit who am entering into thee;" but briefly, great was the sweetness which I received at each one of his sayings.[14]

ST. GERTRUDE (1256-1303)

Prayer

. . . O Holy Spirit, Love who art God, Thou loving bond of union of the Holy Trinity, Thou dost rest among the children of men, taking Thy delight in holy purity which, in the strength of Thy love and Thy holy joys, gloweth like a rose shut in among thorns.

O Spirit of love, what road shall I follow to reach such happiness? What approach will bring me unto these spiritual joys? Where is the way of life leading unto these meadows whereon God Himself descendeth like dew for the refreshment of thirsting hearts? O Love! Thou alone knowest these paths of life and truth. In Thee the precious nuptial alliance with the Holy Trinity is accorded unto chosen souls. Through Thee the lofty charisms of the Spirit are bestowed. From Thee proceed in all abundance the richest seeds of the fruits of life. Out of Thee floweth forth the indescribable sweetness of God's delights. Down from Thee distilleth the marvellous dewfall of the blessings of the Lord of hosts, those precious pledges of the Spirit, which on our poor earth, alas! are so seldom found. . . .

Come then, O Love, keep me during this wretched life under the shadow of Thy charity; and after this exile bring me, spotlessly pure, amid that virginal band, into Thy sanctuary. There may the fountain of Thy Divine love be my sole refreshment and the enjoyment of Thyself my sole satisfaction. Amen! And let all things that have being say: Amen![15]

MEISTER ECKHART (1260-1329)

Now, you must know that God loves the soul so strenuously that to take this privilege of loving from God would be to take his life and being. It would be to kill God, if one may use such an expression. For out of God's love for the soul, the Holy Spirit blooms and the Holy Spirit is that love. Since, then, the soul is so strenuously loved by God, it must be of great importance. . . .

God is love and love is God, so that to live in love is to live in God and to be lived in by God. Without a doubt, to live in God is to be well housed, and to be God's heir, and to have God live in you is to have a good and worthy lodger. One of the authorities says that God gives the soul a gift that moves it to spiritual things, while another says that the soul is moved immediately by the Holy Spirit, for God loves me with the same love he has for himself! This is also true of the soul. It loves God with the same love it has for itself. If it were not for the love God has for himself, there would be no Holy Spirit. It is an ardor, and a blossoming of the Holy Spirit in which the soul loves God.[16]

JULIANA OF NORWICH (1343-1443)

The Grace of Prayer

Prayer oneth the soul to God. For though the soul be ever like to God in kind and substance, restored by grace, it is often unlike in condition, by sin on man's part . . . When the soul is tempested, troubled, and left to itself by unrest, then it is time to pray, for to make itself supple and buxom to God. . . . And then shall we, with his sweet grace, in our own meek and continuant prayer come to him now in this life by many privy touchings of sweet ghostly sights and feeling, measured to us as our simpleness may bear it. And this is wrought, and shall be, by the grace of the Holy Ghost.[17]

Juliana's Advice to Margery Kempe

The Holy Spirit never inspires anything contrary to the love of God, and if he were to do so He would be contrary to His own self, for He is all love. Also, he inspires a soul to perfect chastity, for those who live chastely are called the Temples of the Holy Spirit: and the Holy Spirit makes a soul firm and steadfast in the true Faith and the right belief. And a man who is divided in his soul is always unfirm and unsteadfast in all his ways. A man always in doubt is like to the sea, which is moved and carried about by the wind; and such a man is not likely to receive the gifts of God. Every created being who receives such tokens of God's love must steadfastly believe that the Holy Spirit dwells in his soul. And even more, when God visits one of his creatures with tears of contrition, devotion, or compassion, he may and he should believe that the Holy Spirit is in his soul.[18]

THE EPISTLE OF PRIVY COUNSEL *(Fourteenth Century)*

The Spirit's Call Innermore

. . . Our Lord is not only porter himself, but also the door: the porter by his Godhead, and the door by his manhood . . .

If this be the door, shall a man when he hath found the door stand ever thereat or therein and come never innermore?

I answer for thee and say: that it is good that he do so ever, until the great rust of his boisterous bodilyness be in great part rubbed away . . . And especially, ever till he be called innermore by the privy teaching of the Spirit of God, the which teaching is the readiest and the surest witness that may be had in this life of the calling and the drawing of a soul innermore to more special working of grace.

Evidence of this touching a man may have thus: if he feel in his continual exercise as it were a soft growing desire to come near God in this life, as it may be by a special ghostly feeling, as he heareth men speak of, or else findeth written in books. For he that feeleth him not stirred in hearing or reading of ghostly working, and especially in his each day's exercise by a growing desire to come near God, let him stand yet still at the door, as a man called to salvation, but not yet to perfection.[19]

ST. CATHERINE OF SIENA (1347-1380)

The Dialogue of the Seraphic Virgin Catherine of Siena

. . . "The Soul who wishes to rise above imperfection should await My Providence in the House of Self-Knowledge, with the light of faith, as did the disciples, who remained in the house in perseverance and in watching, and in humble and continual prayer, awaiting the coming of the Holy Spirit. She should remain fasting and watching, the eye of her intellect fastened on the doctrine of My Truth, and she will become humble because she will know herself in humble and continual prayer and holy and true desire."

"It now remains to be told thee how it can be seen that souls have arrived at perfect love. This is seen by the same sign that was given to the holy disciples after they had received the Holy Spirit, when they came forth from the house, and fearlessly announced the doctrine of My Word, My only-begotten Son, not fearing pain, but rather glorying therein. They did not mind going before the tyrants of the world, to announce to them the truth, for the glory and praise of My Name. So, the soul, who has awaited Me in self-knowledge as I have told thee, receives Me, on my return to her, with the fire of charity. . . .[20]

THOMAS À KEMPIS (1380-1471)

A Prayer for the Cleansing of the Heart, and for Heavenly Wisdom

Confirm me, O God, by the grace of Thy Holy Spirit. Grant me power to be strengthened in the inner man, and to cast out of my heart all unprofitable care and trouble; not to be drawn away with various desires of anything whatsoever, be it vile or precious, but to view all things as passing away, and myself also as passing with them.

For nothing is lasting under the sun, where all is vanity and affliction of spirit. Oh, how wise is he who thus judgeth!

Grant me, O Lord, celestial wisdom, that I may learn above all things to seek Thee and to find Thee; above all things to relish Thee and to love Thee, and to understand all other things as they are, according to the order of Thy wisdom.[21]

IGNATIUS LOYOLA (1491-1556)

Preamble to the Constitutions of the Society of Jesus

Although it must be the Supreme Wisdom and Goodness of God our Creator and Lord which will preserve, direct, and carry forward in His divine service this least Society of Jesus . . . and although what helps most on our own part toward this and must be, more than any exterior constitution, the interior law of charity and love which the Holy Spirit writes and engraves upon hearts; nevertheless,. . . . we think it necessary that constitutions should be written to aid us to proceed better, in conformity with our Institute, along the path of divine service on which we have entered.[22]

Like many other founders of religious orders, Ignatius faced hard opposition in his task. That he practised the love of the Holy Spirit that he preached is evident in the following letter, written in answer to one who had threatened to burn every Jesuit that he found between Perpignan and Seville, Spain.

Rome
August 10, 1546
J.H.S.

Master Doimo,

Tell Father Barbaran that, as he says he will have burned all of Ours to be found between Perpignan and Seville, it is also my desire that both he and all his friends and acquaintances, not only between Perpignan and Seville but throughout the whole world, should be enkindled and inflamed by the Holy Spirit, and that by thus reaching a high degree of perfection they will be distinguished in the glory of His Divine Majesty.[23]

BLESSED JOHN OF AVILA (1500-1569)

Christians acknowledge one God, whose Son is equal to the Father: but if you mention the Spirit to some of them, they will have a heart attack.[24]

The Comforter Cures Us

As Christ during His life on earth performed marvellous cures among the sick who needed Him and asked for His help, so this Teacher and Paraclete performs spiritual cures among those souls in whom He dwells and with whom He is in union through grace. He makes the lame walk, the deaf hear, the blind see, puts the erring on the right path. He teaches the ignorant, consoles the afflicted, strengthens the weak. Christ, as man, went among men performing these holy deeds, which He could not have done if He were not God, so we say that they were the work of God and man. And we call the wonders accomplished by the Holy Ghost in the heart where He dwells, the work of the Holy Ghost and man, though man here plays a lesser part.

If a man does not enjoy this union, has not this Guest in his house, has not this counsellor, this guide, this protector, this tutor, comforter and guardian, do we not consider him unfortunate and unhappy? And since you have not got Him within you, you are as you are—distressed, sad, listless, full of bitterness, lacking in piety, miserable. Tell me, have you received Him? Have you called Him? Have you besought Him to come? Have you sighed and wept for Him? Have you fasted? What prayers have you recited? May God come to you! I do not know how you can bear to live without His great goodness. Remember, all the benefits, all the graces and mercies which Christ came to bring to man, are given to our souls by this Comforter; He preaches to you, cures you, teaches you and gives you innumerable blessings.[25]

The Breath of Christ

. . . . The law of the spirit of life is in Christ Jesus. God planted that law in Adam's heart; it remained living for it contained the spirit; in the same way Jesus Christ placed within you His quickening spirit; it will bring you life. Thus it is fitting that the great Eliseus should place himself over the little dead child, should bow upon him and lie on him and that he should want to breathe upon him. He who does not receive *the breath of Christ*, no matter how rich or powerful he may be, no matter how much he may possess of this world's goods, is poor, weak and wretched, for he has not Christ. Vine and Branches are nourished with the same sap; Head and body are sustained by the same holiness: the spirit of Christ and spirit of those who are incorporated in Him, is all one. He is the vine, and His members are the branches.[26]

FAITH THE FIRST REQUIREMENT FOR THE SPIRIT'S COMING

The *first* requirement for the coming of the Holy Ghost to our souls is that we should believe that He can accomplish marvels. However sad a soul may be, He is sufficient to console; however worthless, He can make it valuable; however lukewarm, He can fire it; however weak, He can strengthen it; however lacking in piety, He can inflame it with ardent devotion. What is the way to bring the Holy Ghost to us? It is to be aware of His might.[27]

THE SPIRIT REVIVES US IN OUR DRYNESS

Has it never happened that your soul has felt dry, lacking in fervour, discontented, full of fear, sorrowful, disillusioned, so that nothing can satisfy you; and while you are in distress, and perhaps distraught in mind, a breath of holiness comes to you, a feeling of relief revives you, strengthens, encourages you, and makes you yourself again; gives you fresh aspirations, ardent love, great and holy peace, and makes you speak words and accomplish deeds that astonish you yourself. That is the Holy Ghost. That is the Comforter who has breathed upon you, has come to you, without warning of any kind. You will be as if touched by a loadstone; you will have renewed vigour, will act and speak differently, and have new desires. Whereas formerly nothing seemed of importance, everything worried and annoyed you, now you have a zest for living, you are content, everything exhilarates you, you learn from everything. A blade of grass, looked at attentively, will make you praise Our Lord God, and will teach you to know the Maker and wonderful Creator of all things, and will so inspire your heart with feelings of piety and gratitude towards the all-powerful Lord, that if you could speak you would tell of the marvels and wonders performed by the Lord of Creation.

O happy Paraclete. O blessed breath of God that wafts vessels to heaven! The sea which we have to navigate is full of perils; but with Thy help and with Thee as pilot we shall arrive safely. Many boats will be destroyed! Contrary winds will blow! Dreadful dangers await us! But when this holy Paraclete breathes upon these vessels, they will arrive safely in port. Who could possibly estimate the favours He has bestowed on us, and the dangers from which He has safeguarded us? The breath of the Holy Ghost comes from heaven and returns there to the Father and the Son; it blows from thence and the Holy Ghost, breathing upon His friends, guides them and brings them to heaven, for it is His wish that they should go there. . . .

Before this Comforter arrives, before the breath of the Holy Ghost comes upon us, we do not exert ourselves, we are sluggish, we feel despondent, everything appears difficult, impossible. There seems to be no way for us to get to heaven. There are obstacles everywhere and we feel as if we are carrying a stone of lead. A stone did I say?—a hundredweight of lead. How can dead bones come to life? How, being dry, can they be covered with flesh and rise again? It is clear that, of themselves, they are powerless, but God, who can do all things, can cover them with flesh, and infuse into them the spirit of life, and make them rise again, and give them the power of movement and energy.

God called the prophet Ezechiel and said to him: "Son of man, dost thou think these bones shall live?" Can they have life and be covered with flesh and sinew? Ezechiel answered, "Lord, what Thou askest me, Thou knowest." And God said, "Behold, dry bones, I will send spirit into you and you shall live. And I will lay sinews upon you and will cause flesh to grow over you and will cover you with skin; and I will give you spirit and you shall live. And you shall know that I am Lord."

Every man who has not the Holy Ghost is dry bone, hard and without marrow or virtue, dead bone. But after the prophet had called upon the divine breath to blow upon those dead bones, they regained life; they were transformed; what was heavy became light and the dead became alive. You were evil, cast down, without the fire of charity, inanimate, and you showed neither kindness nor tenderness to any one; you were overcome with weakness, incapable of doing good of any kind, inert as the dead. In this state, God says to you: "Man, do not be frightened! Do you imagine that you will not be able to rise again? Take courage, because I have more power to save you, to revive you, to give you life and make you happy than all your wickedness has to overthrow you, to destroy you, to kill and dispirit you. If my power for good were not stronger than yours for evil, your sins would finally damn you and make you thoroughly wicked."

May the skies and the earth bless Thee, Almighty God! In a little time many will bear witness that their vessels were on the verge of being lost, were about to be broken in pieces, and would have foundered, when Thy breath blew upon them and rescued them and they arrived safely in port. Many who have lost all hope of life, have been revived by the Spirit, have been given life and new desires, have been cheered and strengthened by fresh hope! By whom is this accomplished? By the Holy Ghost, who breathed upon them and brought them unresisting to God.[28]

ST. JOHN OF THE CROSS (1542-1591)

Stanzas Which the Soul Recites In the Intimate Union With God, Its Beloved Bridegroom

O living flame of love
That tenderly wounds my soul
In its deepest center! Since
Now You are not oppressive,
Now Consummate! If it be Your will:
Tear through the veil of this sweet encounter!

This flame of love is the Spirit of its Bridegroom, which is the Holy Spirit. The soul feels Him within itself not only as a fire which has consumed and transformed it, but as a fire that burns and flares within it, as I mentioned. And that flame, every time it flares up, bathes the soul in glory and refreshes it with the quality of divine life. Such is the activity of the Holy Spirit in the soul transformed in love: the interior acts He produces shoot up flames for they are acts of inflamed love, in which the will of the soul united with that flame, made one with it, loves most sublimely.

Thus these acts of love are most precious; one of them is more meritorious and valuable than all the deeds a person may have performed in his whole life without this transformation, however great they may have been.

The same difference that lies between a habit and an act lies between the transformation in love and the flame of love; it is like the difference between the wood that is on fire and the flame that leaps up from it, for the flame is the effect of the fire that is present there.

Hence we can compare the soul in its ordinary condition in this state of transformation of love to the log of wood that is ever immersed in fire, and the acts of this soul to the flame that blazes up from the fire of love. The more intense the fire of union, the more vehemently does this fire burst into flames. The acts of the will are united to this flame and ascend, carried away and absorbed in the flame of the Holy Spirit, just as the angel mounted to God in the flame of Manue's sacrifice.

Thus in this state the soul cannot make acts because the Holy Spirit makes them all and moves it toward them. As a result all the acts of the soul are divine, since the movement toward these acts and their execution stems from God. Hence it seems to a person that every time this flame shoots up, making him love with delight and divine quality, it is giving him eternal life, since it raises him up to the activity of God in God. . . . .[29]

To sum up the entire stanza now, it is like saying: O flame of the Holy Spirit that so intimately and tenderly pierces the substance of my soul and cauterizes it with your glorious ardor! Previously, my requests did not reach Your ears, when, in the anxieties and weariness of love in which my sense and my spirit suffered because of considerable weakness, impurity, and lack of strong love, I was praying that You loose me and bring me to Yourself, because my soul longed for You, and impatient love did not allow me to be so conformed to the condition of this life in which you desired me still to live. The previous impulses of love were not enough, because they did not have sufficient quality for the attainment of my desire; now I am so fortified in love that not only do my sense and spirit no longer faint in You, but my heart and my flesh, reinforced in You, rejoice in the living God, with great conformity between the sensory and spiritual parts. What you desire me to ask for, I ask for; and what you do not desire, I do not desire, nor can I, nor does it even enter my mind to desire it. My petitions are now more valuable and estimable in Your sight, since they come from You, and You move me to make them, and I make them in the delight and joy of the Holy Spirit, my judgment now issuing from Your countenance, that is, when You esteem and hear my prayer. Tear then the thin veil of this life and do not let old age cut it naturally, that from now on I may love You with plentitude and fullness my soul desires forever and ever.

O sweet cautery,
O delightful wound!
O gentle hand! O delicate touch
That tastes of eternal life
And pays every debt!
In killing You changed death to life.

This cautery, as we mentioned, is the Holy Spirit. For as Moses declares in Deuteronomy, "Our Lord God is a consuming fire," that is, a fire of love, which being of infinite power, can inestimably transform into itself the soul it touches. Yet He burns each soul according to its preparation: He will burn one more, another less, and this He does insofar as He desires, and how and when He desires. When He wills to touch somewhat vehemently, the soul's burning reaches such a high degree of love that it seems to surpass that of all the fires of the world; for He is an infinite fire of love. As a result, in this union, the soul calls the Holy Spirit a cautery.[30]

NOTES

1. *St. Bernard on the Love of God.* Translated by Terence L. Connolly (New York: Spiritual Book Associates, 1937), pp. 79-80.
2. Abbot Guéranger, *The Liturgical Year.* Translated by Laurence Shepherd. Book III (Westminster: The Newman Press, 1949), pp. 406-407.
3. *The Works of William of St. Thierry. Book IV. The Golden Epistle.* Translated by Theodore Berkeley (Spencer, Mass.: Cistercian Publications, 1971), p. 67.
4. *Ibid.*, pp. 92-93.
5. *Ibid.*, pp. 96-97.
6. *The Works of William of St. Thierry.* Book I (Spencer, Mass.: Cistercian Publications, 1971), pp. 58-59.
7. *Ibid.*, p. 116.
8. *Ibid.*, p. 178.
9. Guéranger, *op. cit.*, pp. 387-389.
10. *Ibid.*, pp. 438-439.
11. *Summa Theologica*, Vol. I, Question 37, First and Second Articles (New York: Benziger Brothers, 1947), pp. 189-191.
12. *Ibid.* Question 38, Second Article, pp. 192-193.
13. *On the Truth of the Catholic Faith.* Translated by Charles O'Neill (Garden City, N.Y.: Hanover House, 1957), pp. 205-206.
14. *The Book of Divine Consolation of the Blessed Angela of Foligno.* Translated by Mary G. Steegman (London: Chatto and Windus, 1909), pp. 159-165.
15. *The Exercises of Saint Gertrude.* Translated by a Benedictine Nun of Regina Laudis (Westminster: The Newman Press, 1956), pp. 48-49.
16. *Meister Eckhart.* A Modern Translation by Raymond Blakney (New York: Harper and Brothers, 1941), p. 213.
17. *Revelations of Divine Love Shewed to a Devout Ankress by Name Julian of Norwich.* Ed. by Dom Roger Hudleston (Westminster: Newman Press, 1952), Ch. 41.
18. *The Book of Margery Kempe* in Eric Colledge, *The Mediaeval Mystics of England* (New York: Charles Scribner's Sons, 1961), p. 286.
19. *The Cloud of Unknowing and Other Treatises* by an English Mystic of the Fourteenth Century. Edited by Justin McCann (Westminster: The Newman Press, 1952), p. 126.

20. *The Dialogue of the Seraphic Virgin Catherine of Siena.* Translated by Algar Thorold (Westminster: The Newman Press, 1959), pp. 168-169.

21. *The Following of Christ in Four Books* (St. Louis: B. Herder, 1919), p. 298.

22. *The Constitution of the Society of Jesus.* Translated by George E. Ganss, S.J. (St. Louis: Institute of Jesuit Sources, 1970), pp. 119-120.

23. *Letters of St. Ignatius of Loyola*, Translated by William J. Young (Chicago: Loyola University Press, 1959), p. 100.

24. *The Holy Ghost* (Dublin: Scepter, 1959), p. 44.

25. *Ibid.*, p. 92.

26. *Ibid.*, p. 67.

27. *Ibid.*, p. 11.

28. *Ibid.*, pp. 93-95.

29. *The Collected Works of St. John of the Cross.* Translated by Kieran Kavanaugh and Otilio Rodrigues. (Washington, D.C.: Institute of Carmelite Studies, 1973), pp. 578-581.

30. *Ibid.*, pp. 594-596.

El Greco, THE ANNUNCIATION, c. 1596, Spain. The Toledo Museum of Art, Toledo, Ohio. Gift of Edward Drummond Libbey.

Chapter VI

THE HOLY SPIRIT IN EARLY MODERN WRITINGS

Introduction

How often it happens through the ages that when the faith of a generation seems weakest, the Holy Spirit inspires men and women to live a new type of dedicated life that can witness meaningfully to their age of the love of Christ. The "Age of the Enlightenment" in seventeenth and eighteenth century France was a time when deism or rationalism prevailed among men of fashion. But Voltaire, the intellectual leader of the new thinkers of the "Enlightenment," had for a contemporary the saintly Alphonsus Liguori who prayed so ardently to the Spirit of God, "YOU are a light; ENLIGHTEN me that I may know eternal things." The gentle Francis de Sales, fluent himself with pen and oratory, pointed out that Christians could penetrate to the mysteries of their faith not by curiosity and study "as the theologians do," but through meditation and prayer.

Throughout these centuries when the *savants* were so engrossed with discovering the order and laws governing the universe, the saints repeatedly and clearly spoke of the joy, the harmony, the order of a life lived in tune with the Spirit. If you open yourself to the action of the Spirit of God, you go by giant steps, you fly, declared Lallement. Indeed you do fly, repeated Mother Barat. But if you remain mediocre, you are swimming between two currents. So, she urged her daughters, "Hurry up and plunge into midstream. The Holy Spirit will then carry you."

With the opening up of the New World to colonization, the Spirit inspired countless men and women such as Marie of the Incarnation to leave family and homeland to labor for Christ beyond the seas. Important as was the actual *work* of their hands among the savages, these Spirit-filled missionaries accomplished much more by their saintly *presence* and dedicated self-surrender.

When faith had grown dim among his rural flock and the gentle Curé of Ars sadly observed the peasants trundling off with their carts toward field work on Sunday instead of praising God, he reminded them that without the Spirit of God, they were no better than stones in the road. His words were often even more blunt: "If the damned are asked: 'Why are you in Hell?' they answer: 'For having resisted the Holy Spirit.' " His flock listened and repented. Like many another minister of the Gospel who surrendered himself completely to the action of the Spirit, the Curé found that there were not enough hours in the day to minister to the souls who came to him seeking forgiveness of sins and knowledge of the ways of advancing in holiness.

SAINT FRANCIS DE SALES (1567-1622)

Sermon for Pentecost: The Gifts of the Spirit

Let us begin with that of fear. . . . This gift not only makes us dread divine judgment, heaven and hell, but it makes us fear God as our Lord and our judge and consequently inclines us to flee evil and all that we know to be disagreeable to him. . . .

Piety is nothing more than filial fear, which makes us not look upon God so much as our judge as our father whom we dread to displease and desire to please.

But it would hardly serve for us to desire to please God and fear to displease him if the Holy Spirit did not concede to us the third gift—knowledge, by which we learn what is virtue and what is vice. . . .

It is also necessary that the Holy Spirit give us the fourth gift—that of strength, because otherwise the preceding ones serve for nothing, since it does not suffice to have the will to shun evil and do good, less still to know the one and the other, if we fail to put our hand to the task. For that, we have great need of fortitude. . . . This is not to act like Alexander the Great, who conquered the whole world by arms. He did not have the gift of fortitude . . . His strength consisted in the balls of lead which crashed the walls of towns and battered chateaux. He had even less of the courage of which he is so much praised; the test is that he lacked the power to overcome himself and not drink a glass of wine; he was a drunkard.

Let us make a small comparison between the valiance and courage of Saint Paul the Hermit, or rather the great Apostle Saint Paul with this Alexander. The latter ruins villages, batters chateaux, subjugates the world by force of arms, and in the end is conquered by himself. On the contrary, our great Apostle seems to want to subjugate and travel through the whole world—not to overthrow walls but the hearts of men . . . Not content with that, look, I beg you, at the power he had over himself, subjecting his affections and passions to the rule of reason, and everything to the very holy will of the divine majesty.

But being thus resolved and fortified to embrace the true practice of virtue, we need the gift of counsel to choose the most necessary means according to our vocation. . . .

After the gift of counsel comes that of understanding, which makes us penetrate the mysteries of our faith by means of meditation and choose the maxims of interior perfection in the depth of these mysteries. But mark, I pray you, that I say by meditation and prayer, and not by curiosity, speculation, and study, as the theologians do. A simple and poor weak woman will be more capable of doing it than the most excellent doctors with less piety. . . .

[The gift of wisdom gives] a taste, a savor, an esteem, a contentment in the practice of Christian perfection. . . . Thus, acting completely contrary to the men of the world who esteem riches, who are honored and live delightfully, the soul thinks the poor in spirit are blessed, since it has found that virtue in the heart of God himself.[1]

Letter to a Lady

[The Holy Spirit is] that uncreated love, which without regard to his own advantage is everywhere occupied in seeking our good, often sending forth his fairest flames when we were least thinking of this holy splendour, to engage us to love him with all our power; and because this love is a gratuitous gift of his love, therefore ought we to love it with all our strength. We must not disturb ourself about our offences, for this Divine Spirit is often more liberal of his gifts to those who have been more ungenerous with their heart and affections towards him.

But, my dear daughter, we must testify to Jesus Christ all our confidence, with the holy Apostles and disciples, on whom he did not will to send his Holy Spirit till after he had ascended into heaven. If you ask me why this was, you must first know that the Holy Spirit is the wine of heaven, according to St. Bernard, who said that in heaven there was an overflowing abundance of this wine, I mean the joy of the Holy Ghost and beatific jubilee—but they had not that sacred bread of Christ's humanity. The earth, on the other hand, had this sacred bread, which it made its delight and its joy; it had not that sweet and sparkling wine of the Holy Ghost, which was to inebriate our souls and crown them with joy.

And hence that admirable inference of Jesus Christ, when he showed his Apostles that it was not right to keep the humanity of Jesus Christ, and at the same time to have this admirable wine of heaven. There must be then, said Jesus Christ, a holy bargain between you and the Angels: you shall infallibly have from heaven that mighty wine of the Holy Ghost, if you share with it your sacred bread which is still on the earth and as it were in your hands—that is, the humanity of Jesus Christ. I think, my dear daughter, that this is enough to open your heart wide for the reception of the Holy Ghost, and of those tongues of fire and adorable flames. Adieu.[2]

JOHN DONNE (1573-1631)

The Litany

O Holy Ghost, whose temple I
Am, but of mud walls, and condensèd dust,
And being sacrilegiously
Half wasted with youth's fires, of pride and lust,
Must with new storms be weather-beat;
Double in my heart Thy flame,
Which let devout sad tears intend; and let
(Though this glass lanthorn, flesh, do suffer main)
Fire, Sacrifice, Priest, Altar be the same.[3]

LOUIS LALLEMENT S.J. (1587-1635)

The Nature of Docility to the Guidance of the Holy Spirit

In What This Docility Consists

When a soul has given itself up to the leading of the Holy Spirit, he raises it little by little, and directs it. At the first it knows not whither it is going; but gradually the interior light illuminates it, and enables it to behold all its actions, and the governance of God therein, so that it has scarcely ought else to do than to let God work in it and by it whatever He pleases; thus it makes wonderful progress.

We have a figure of the guidance of the Holy Spirit in that which God adopted in regard to the Israelites in their exodus from Egypt during their journeying in the wilderness towards the land of promise. He gave them as their guide a pillar of cloud by day, and a pillar of fire by night. They followed the movements of this pillar, and halted; they did not go before it, they only followed it, and never wandered from it. It is thus we ought to act with respect to the Holy Spirit.

The Means of Attaining This Docility

The principal means by which we obtain this direction of the Holy Spirit are the following:

1. To obey faithfully God's will so far as we know it; much of it is hidden from us, for we are full of ignorance; but God will demand an account at our hands only of the knowledge He has given us; let us make good use of it, and he will give us more. Let us fulfill his designs so far as He has made them known to us, and He will manifest them to us more fully.

2. To renew often the good resolution of following in all things the will of God, and strengthen ourselves in this determination as much as possible.

3. To ask continually of the Holy Spirit this light and this strength to do the will of God, to bind ourselves to him, and remain his prisoners. . . . In every important change of circumstances, to pray God grant us the illumination of the Holy Spirit, and sincerely protest that we desire nothing else, but only to do his will. After which if he impart to us no fresh light, we may act as heretofore we have been accustomed to act, and as shall appear best for the time being.

This is why at the commencement of important affairs, as the opening of the law courts, the assemblies of the clergy and councils, the assistance of the Holy Spirit is invoked by votive masses said in his honour.

4. Let us watch with care the different movements of our soul. By such attention we shall come gradually to perceive what is of God and what is not. That which proceeds from God in a soul which is subjected to grace, is generally peaceable and calm. That which comes from the devil is violent, and brings with it trouble and anxiety. . . .[4]

That Perfection and Even Salvation Depend on Docility to Grace

The two elements of the spiritual life are the cleansing of the heart and the direction of the Holy Spirit. These are the two poles of all spirituality. By these two ways we arrive at perfection according to the degree of purity we have attained, and in proportion to the fidelity with which we have cooperated with the movements of the Holy Spirit and followed his guidance.

Our perfection depends wholly on this fidelity, and we may say that the sum of the spiritual life consists in observing the ways and the movements of the Spirit of God in our soul, and in fortifying our will in the resolution of following them, employing for this purpose all the exercises of prayer, spiritual reading, the sacraments, the practice of virtues and good works.

Some exercise themselves in many commendable practices and perform a number of exterior acts of virtue; thus their attention is wholly given to material action. This is well enough for beginners, but it belongs to a far higher perfection to follow the interior attraction of the Holy Spirit and be guided by his direction. It is true that this latter mode of acting yields less sensible satisfaction, but there is more of the interior spirit and of virtue in it.

The end to which we ought to aspire, after having for a long time exercised ourselves in purity of heart, is to be so possessed and governed by the Holy Spirit that he alone shall direct all our powers and all our senses, and regulate all our movements, interior and exterior, while we, on our part, make a complete surrender of ourselves, by a spiritual renunciation of our own will and our own satisfaction. We shall thus no longer live in ourselves, but in Jesus Christ, by a faithful correspondence with the operations of his divine Spirit, and by a perfect subjection of all our rebellious inclinations to the power of his grace. . . .

The lights of grace come to use by degrees according to our interior disposition, and depart also in the same manner, leaving us in darkness. So that we have an alternation of day and night, and resemble in some wise the inhabitants of the polar regions, who have more or less of day in proportion as they are nearer to or farther removed from the pole. Now we ought to aspire after the enjoyment of a perpetual day; nor will it fail to shine into our soul, when, having thoroughly purified it, we shall continually follow the guidance of the Holy Spirit.

There are but few perfect souls, because there are but few who follow the guidance of the Holy Spirit. . . .

We may say with truth that there are but very few who persevere constantly in the ways of God. Many wander from them perpetually; the Holy Spirit calls them back by his inspirations, but as they are intractable, full of themselves, attached to their own opinions, puffed up with their own wisdom, they do not readily let themselves be guided. They enter but seldom into the way of God's designs, and make no stay therein, returning to their own inventions and ideas, which deceive and delude them. Thus they make but little progress, and are surprised by death, having taken but twenty steps where they might have taken ten thousand, had they abandoned themselves to the guidance of the Holy Spirit.

On the other hand, truly interior persons who are guided by the light of the Spirit of God, for which they have disposed themselves by purity of heart, and which they follow with perfect submission, proceed at a giant's pace, and fly, so to say, in the ways of grace. . . .

We do great wrong to God in two ways. First, in that we confess, with truth, that we have need of the Holy Spirit and of his assistance, and yet take from him the direction of our soul, and wish to manage his graces our own way, without depending on his holy guidance both in the use of them and in the conduct of our interior life. This is to usurp the rights of the Holy Spirit, and to arrogate to ourselves his office; for him alone it belongs to guide souls. Secondly, in that our inmost soul being destined for God only, we fill it with creatures to his prejudice; and instead of dilating and enlarging it indefinitely by the presence of God, we straighten it exceedingly by occupying it with a few wretched nonentities. This is what prevents our attaining to perfection.[5]

MÈRE MARIE OF THE INCARNATION (MARIE GUYARD) (1599-1672)

Her Experience of the Trinity

On the morning of Pentecost Monday (1625), while assisting at Mass in the chapel of the Feuillant Fathers . . . I was looking in the direction of the altar when all of a sudden my eyes were closed and my mind elevated and absorbed in a view of the most holy and august Trinity in a way I cannot explain. At once all the powers of my soul were suspended and felt the impression made upon them by this sacred mystery, an impression without form or figure, yet more clear and intelligible than any light. This impression begot in me the conviction that what my soul was experiencing was the truth, and this truth caused me to see in a flash the inner life which exists between the three Divine Persons: the love of the Father, who in contemplating Himself generates the Son, and this from all eternity unto all eternity. . . . Then it understood that the mutual love of the Father and the Son originates the Holy Spirit, which takes place by an immersion in each other's love without any prejudice to the distinction of the Persons. I received the impression that this origination is a spiration, but a spiration so elevated and so sublime that I have no terms for expressing it. . . . . My soul was quite lost in these splendors, and it seemed that the Divine Majesty was pleased to illuminate it more and more regarding those things which creatures are impotent to express . . . And when my soul received this illumination it understood and experienced at the same time how it was created to the image of God; that the memory relates it to the eternal Father, the understanding to the Son, and the will to the Holy Spirit. . . . This vision continued during the time of many Masses. Upon returning to myself I found myself on my knees just as I was when the vision began. . . .

I really didn't have in mind to write the above, but the interior Spirit moved me to do it. May He be eternally blessed![6]

The Holy Spirit as Guide of Her Soul

I should remark that, in keeping with our Lord's invariable plan for my spiritual life, the Holy Spirit has throughout the entire course of my interior life always furnished me with the maxims of the Gospel for my guiding principles. And this He did without my having reflected on them for the purpose of choosing one of them as a subject, for they came to my mind in a flash, without my having previously read about them . . . And even if I had first read about them, my memory was unretentive on this point to such a degree that the maxim made operative in me through the activity of the Holy Spirit who guided me obliterated in me all other memories, however holy. For that which the Holy Spirit presented to my spirit contained within itself whatever was useful for my spiritual progress at that time, and every sort of good and significant grace was granted me through my union with the sacred Lord Incarnate. But with the passing of time and the changes of spiritual states, the effects of the operations of the Spirit of God change in a degree depending on the state upon which the soul enters. Thus a passage of Holy Scripture will at different times be operative in the soul of quite different effects, but always with a greater perfection, not indeed with regard to God, who is immutable, but in regard to the soul, which will increase in sanctity until the end of life.[7]

Description of the Seventh State of Her Prayer Life

The soul no longer lives in itself but in Him who holds it completely absorbed in His love. While continually experiencing this ecstasy of love, it sometimes finds itself moved by the Holy Spirit who possesses it, at other times it is languishing, and at yet other times it is in suspension. He leads it whither He wills; it is unable to resist Him. For the will is so much His captive that, if any object seeks to detain it, at that very moment this Divine Spirit who wills to possess it for Himself alone attracts it to Himself by stirring up its love for Him. Since that time I've read the Canticle of Canticles in Holy Scripture, and I know of nothing which better expresses what the soul feels (in this state of prayer) but the actual experience of it begets an impression quite different from that begotten by merely listening to the words of that canticle. It affords a divine nourishment which human language is unable to express, an intimacy and boldness, an inexplicable reciprocity of love between the Word and the soul.[8]

JEAN JACQUES OLIER (1608-1657)

Since my great desolations, I can not doubt that the Spirit of my Master dwells in me . . . I experience his guidance in the use of my natural faculties, and even to the disposition of my body, which formerly was so out of order. I now sense that Spirit who regulates and directs me in my bearing, my proceedings, and even my words . . .

At the moment I want to write, I feel that this Divine Spirit wishes to lead and direct all the movements of my hand. I lend and give myself to him as an instrument which no more acts of itself.

He is diffused throughout my being, as if He took the place of my soul. I perceive Him as a second soul who animates me and supports me and avails himself of all my being, as the soul disposes the movements of the body, but with more gentleness and dominion.

Finally, I experience him as a person who takes great care of us, speaking to me of something that he has to do there, and I respond to him naively: "I have an infirmity which prevents me from doing what I want; I can only do what he allows me, and I can't in any way free myself from that dependence."

I experience the same change in respect to the faculties of my soul and to supernatural gifts. Instead of darkness so heavy, I have now so many lights; instead of confusion of spirit, so much clearness in my thoughts; instead of my former stammerings, so much liberty of speech; instead of the desolating dryness that I would experience and that I would cause to others, so many good effects from words; instead of that cursed occupation with self, so many uplifting sentiments of love toward God. I am constrained to confess: it is the Divine Spirit who thus fills me and possesses me.[9]

JOHN MILTON (1608-1674)

. . . . Darkness profound
Covered the abyss: but on the watery calm
His brooding wings the spirit of God outspread,
And vital virtue infused, and vital warmth,
Throughout the fluid mass. . . .

And chiefly thou, O Spirit, that dost prefer
Before all temples the upright heart and pure,
Instruct me, for thou knowest; thou from the first
Wast present, and with mighty wings outspread
Dove-like satest brooding on the vast abyss,
And madest it pregnant: what in me is dark
Illumine, what is low raise and support;
That to the height of this great argument
I may assert eternal Providence,
And justify the ways of God to men.[10]

JACQUES-BÉNIGNE BOSSUET (1627-1704)

THE SPIRIT LEADS THROUGH DARKNESS

We must not forget that one of the great secrets of the spiritual life is that the Holy Spirit leads us—not only by light, sweetness, consolation, tenderness, and easy things; but even more through obscurity, blindness, insensibility, chagrin, anguish, sadness, revolts of our passions and humors.

I say even further that this crucifying way is necessary, that it is good, that it is the best, the most assured way, and that we arrive sooner at perfection this way.

The enlightened soul esteems dearly the guidance of God who allows it to be exercised by creatures and overwhelmed with temptations and diversions. It understands well that these are favors rather than disgraces, loving more to die on the cross on Calvary, than to live amidst the delights of Thabor. . . .

After purgation of the soul in the purgatory of sufferings through which it must pass, will come illumination, repose, joy, which will render this world, complete exile that it is, as a little paradise. The best prayer is that in which one abandons oneself the most to the sentiments and dispositions that God himself puts in the soul, and where one studies with the most simplicity, humility and fidelity to conform himself to His will and to the example of Jesus Christ.[11]

LOUIS BOURDALOUE (1632-1704)

"The charity of God is poured abroad in our hearts, by the Holy Ghost, who is given to us" (Romans 5:5).

What then was the most excellent means that God made use of to inspire men with his love? It was to send us the Holy Ghost, who is himself, personally and substantially the love of God. How did this divine spirit descend? In the form of fire; to give us to understand that he was all love by his ardour, and that he came to inflame every soul with that ardour. . . .[12]

O divine spirit, essential and always subsisting Charity; inexhaustible source of that sacred fire which consumes the blessed angels and all the elect of God! Descend, I beseech thee; open my soul, and come thyself to inflame it. If it be still shut up, make use of a salutary violence. Thou dost penetrate through every thing; and thou needest but one glance, to set my whole heart on fire and consume it . . . O Spirit of Love! I now deliver myself entirely to thee, being resolved to attach myself to my God by an indissoluble tie and an eternal love. What part of my life would I still deprive him of? and on whom would I bestow the part of which I would deprive him? Alas, O Lord! I have but too often divided my heart between thee and other objects: but as it was not solely attached to thee, it was not thine at all; for thou art a jealous God, and thou wilt have a love without reserve. Thou dost well deserve it, O my God! and I am most unworthy of thy graces, if the manifold graces which I have received from thy liberal and paternal hands are not sufficient to teach me to love thee. Alas, O Lord, have I known it to this very day! But what other science ought I to know? With this alone, I would have known all the rest; that is to say, I would have known how to fulfill all the duties of my state, and to practise all the virtues thereof. This, thy Spirit will teach me. Heaven grant that it may always inspire me; and above all, Heaven grant that I may always follow its divine inspirations, and never extinguish its holy ardours in my soul![13]

FRANCOIS DE SALIGNAC DE LA MOTHE-FÉNELON (1651-1715)

The Spirit of God Dwells Within

It is certain from scripture that the Spirit of God dwells within us; that He works there and prays without ceasing, that He groans and desires and begs those things that we do not know to ask for ourselves. He moves us, animates us, speaks to us in silence, suggests all truth to us, and unites us in such a way to Himself that we are one and the same spirit with God. . . .

He is the soul of our soul; we would know how to form neither a thought nor a desire without Him. How blind we are then. We reckon as if we were alone in the interior sanctuary, and completely to the contrary, God is there more intimately than we are there ourselves.

You say to me perhaps, "Are we always inspired?" Yes, without doubt, but not like the prophets and the apostles. Without the actual inspiration of the Spirit of grace, we could neither do, nor wish, nor believe any good. We are, then, always inspired, but we continually stifle this inspiration. God does not cease to speak, but the noise of creatures from outside and our passions from within deafen us and prevent us from hearing Him. One must hush creatures and silence oneself in order to hear in that profound silence of the whole soul the quiet, ineffable voice of the Spouse. One must listen attentively because

His voice is soft and delicate and is not heard except by those who can no longer hear anything else. Oh, it is rare that the soul quiets itself enough to let God speak. The least murmur of our vain desires and self-love muffles all the words of the Divine Spirit. We realize that He is speaking and asking something, but we do not know what He is saying, and sometimes it is easier on one not to find out. The least resistance, the least turning in upon self, the least fear of hearing too clearly that God demands more than we wish to give Him obscures the interior word. Should one then be astonished if so many people, even pious ones, but still occupied with amusements, vain desires, false wisdom and confidence in their virtues, can not hear it, and look upon that interior word as a chimera of fanatics? . . .

Oh my God, I give you thanks with Jesus Christ that you hide your ineffable secrets from the great and wise while you take pleasure in revealing them to souls feeble and small.[14]

THE SPIRIT COMPLEMENTS OUR PRIVATION AND POVERTY

Lord, Thou didst begin to perfect Thine apostles by taking away what seemed essential to them—the actual presence of Thy Son, Jesus Christ. Thou dost destroy all to establish all. Everything is taken away that all may be returned a hundredfold. This is Thy method. Thou art pleased to overturn human logic.

Then, having withdrawn the presence of Christ, Thou didst send Thy Holy Ghost. It is possible for privation to operate more powerfully than possession; yet cowardly souls cannot see this. Blessed are they who lack everything, even the conscious perception and experience of God Himself. Blessed are they from whom Jesus is hidden and withdrawn. The Holy Ghost, the Comforter, will come to them. He will soothe their sorrows and dry their tears. Woe to them who have their joy on earth; whose affection and protection are separate from God. The right spirit, promised to all those who ask it, is not sent to them. The Comforter comes to souls who belong neither to the world nor to themselves.

Ah, Lord, where is this spirit that ought to be my life? It should be the soul of my soul, but where is it? I do not feel it. I cannot discover it. I am conscious only of physical inertia and spiritual dullness. My weak will is divided between Thee and a thousand pointless pleasures. Where is Thy Spirit? Will it come to create in me a new heart like unto Thine? O God, at last I understand—it is in an impoverished soul that Thy Holy Spirit deigns to dwell, provided the soul is opened to It without measure. Awareness of the absence of the Saviour and all His gifts attracts the Holy Ghost.

Come, Holy Ghost, Thou canst find nothing more barren and stricken than my heart. Come and bring it peace.

Eternal Truth teaches us the unity of the Father, Son, and Holy Ghost: the Father, Creator, who creates in us all that He wills, making us children like unto Him; the Son, the Word of God, who becomes the voice and secret language of the soul silent to all else save God; and lastly, the Holy Ghost, who abides with us, loving the Father and the Son in us.

The Holy Spirit fills the soul with light. Those truths taught by Christ while He was on earth are implanted in the depths of our being. We are strengthened and inspired. We are made one with Truth; no longer is it something outside ourselves: we become the truth and are inwardly aware of it as the soul is aware of itself.

The Spirit of Love teaches the soul without words; without sound or sign everything is illumined. Nothing is demanded, and yet the soul is trained in silence for any sacrifice. After experiencing Holy Love we are dissatisfied with any other and we learn to distrust and forget ourselves. What utter joy is ours then without our having sought it! Love becomes the fountain of life flowing through our hearts.

O my Love who art my God, love and glorify Thyself within me! My joy and my life are all in Thee. Thou art my All![15]

ST. JOHN-BAPTIST DE LA SALLE (1651-1719)

Come, then, Holy Spirit, possess my heart, and enliven all my actions so that it can be said that you produce them more than I do, and that I would have no more life, nor movement, nor action than you yourself give me.[1]

ST. ALPHONSUS LIGUORI (1696-1787)

Prayer To Ask the Grace of the Holy Spirit

O Holy Spirit, divine Paraclete, Father of the poor, Consoler of the afflicted, Sanctifier of souls! Here, prostrate in your presence, I adore you with the most profound submission, and I repeat a thousand times with the seraphim who remain before your throne: Holy! Holy! Holy!

I firmly believe that you are eternal, consubstantial with the Father and the Son. I hope that, by your bounty, you will sanctify and save my soul. I love you, O God of love! I love you more than all the things of this world; I love you with all my affection, because you are infinite goodness who alone merits all our love. And, since, insensible to all your holy inspirations, I have had the ingratitude to offend you by so many sins, I beg of you a thousand pardons and I supremely regret having displeased you, O Supreme Good. I offer you my heart, completely cold though it is, and I beg you to make a ray of your light and a spark of your fire enter into it to melt the icy hardness of my iniquities.

You who have filled with immense graces the soul of Mary, and inflamed with a holy zeal the hearts of the apostles, deign also to embrace my heart with your love. You are a Divine Spirit, fortify me against evil spirits; you are a fire, illumine in me the fire of your love; you are a light, enlighten me that I may know eternal things; You are a dove, give me pure ways; You are a breath full of sweetness, dissipate the storms which excite passions in me; You are a tongue, teach me the manner of praising you without cease; You are a cloud, cover me with the shadow of your protection; and finally, You are the author of all celestial gifts: Ah! I implore you, vivify me by grace, sanctify me by your charity, govern me by your wisdom, adopt me for your child through your goodness, and save me by your infinite mercy, in order that I never cease to bless you, to praise you, to love you, first on earth during my life, and then in heaven during all eternity.[17]

PÈRE GROU (1731-1803)

MARY RECEIVES THE HOLY GHOST

The Holy Ghost, on the day of Pentecost, diffused among the disciples limited portions of the sacred fire of charity, but he concentrated all its intensity in the heart of Mary; in her he particularly delighted to dwell, penetrating and inflaming her with his divine ardors; uniting himself to her once more, and establishing with her a more perfect and intimate communication than ever. Without limiting the power of God, it may be safely asserted that the Holy Ghost never did or will dispense his gifts so liberally to any creatures as to Mary. On this day the apostles were miraculously transformed from gross and earthly-minded men into beings altogether spiritual and divine; but a still greater alteration was effected in Mary—not by the substitution, as in them, of holiness for imperfection, but by the exchange of one degree of perfection for another yet more sublime. This we shall believe to be literally true if we reflect that the sanctity of God, being infinite in itself, nothing can restrict its external communication, which with respect to Mary was limited only by her finite capacity as a mere creature. And as the capacity of man may perpetually expand without ceasing to be finite, we can have no difficulty in believing that in Mary it attained an extent surpassing the comprehension of men and angels.[18]

ST. MADELEINE SOPHIE BARAT (1779-1865)

A SOUL SURRENDERED TO THE SPIRIT

A soul that is given over to the Holy Spirit no longer walks; she flies. The greatest sacrifices no longer cost, the roughest crosses no longer weigh her down. What am I saying, my daughters? The cross is her joy; she loves it, she desires it, for God allows that a soul that is thus given over, yielded up to Him, feels only the consolations instead of the pains of the cross. It is very different for weak souls who do not know the sweetness of the cross and who find only afflictions and thorns that tear them; the Holy Spirit makes a soul that has surrendered find flowers under the thorns. It is thus that St. Catherine of Siena chose the crown of thorns, and when she pressed it upon her head she found delight in the pain that she suffered.

Who can say, dear daughters, what goes on in souls who are thus given over to the operations of the Holy Spirit? You see it in the lives of the saints that you read every day, in an Aloysius Gonzaga and many others who are, indeed, more admirable than imitable, since the duties of your vocation and the obedience by which you have the joy of being bound do not allow you to follow in their steps on certain points. Look first at those who went to seek souls in that other world where there are so many needs. If you read their letters you will see how, in the midst of their difficulties, of the hardest kind of work and of incredible sufferings, they were filled with consolations, and said to themselves that they would not exchange their poverty and suffering, their crosses, for a more secure lot. And why? Because they had given themselves over entirely to God; they had kept back nothing of themselves, and the Holy Spirit filled them with His gifts.[19]

Oh if it were given to me, if I were not unworthy to speak to you of the happiness of a soul who surrenders to the Holy Spirit, fully and with no reserves! If I could tell you what goes on in her, if I could picture for you her joy! It is not she who acts, it is God; she only moves, only walks by His inspiration. Everything becomes easy to her. She knows no more difficulties, she meets no more obstacles. The Holy Spirit enchains such a soul. She is His; He binds her to Himself . . . The soul of whom I have been speaking finds the secret of penetrating hearts; as it is no longer she who acts, there is no turning back upon herself. She does not know that she is doing good; in one sense she does not even want to, or rather, she has only one desire; to follow the impulse of the Spirit and obey Him in all.

Few give themselves over to the Holy Spirit, and what a mistake we make in not being among the privileged few! Believe me, it costs much more to stay in a miserable mediocrity in which one belongs neither to God nor to oneself. It is swimming between two currents; it is difficult and dangerous. Hurry up and plunge into mid-stream. The Holy Spirit will then carry you and you will get to port much more quickly.[20]

ST. JEAN-MARIE VIANNEY, CURÉ OF ARS (1786-1859)

CATECHISM ON THE HOLY SPIRIT

O my children, how beautiful it is! The Father is our Creator, the Son is our Redeemer, and the Holy Ghost is our Guide. . . . Man by himself is nothing, but with the Holy Spirit he is very great. Man is all earthly and all animal; nothing but the Holy Spirit can elevate his mind, and raise it on high. Why were the saints so detached from the earth? Because they let themselves be led by the Holy Spirit. Those who are led by the Holy Spirit have true ideas; that is the reason why so many ignorant people are wiser than the learned. When we are led by a God of strength and light, we cannot go astray.

The Holy Spirit is light and strength. He teaches us to distinguish between truth and falsehood, and between good and evil. Like glasses that magnify objects, the Holy Spirit shows us good and evil on a large scale. With the Holy Spirit we see everything in its true proportions; we see the greatness of the least actions done for God, and the greatness of the least faults. As a watchmaker with his glasses distinguishes the most minute wheels of a watch, so we, with the light of the Holy Ghost distinguish all the details of our poor life. Then the smallest imperfections appear very great, the least sins inspire us with horror. That is the reason why the most Holy Virgin never sinned. The Holy Ghost made her understand the hideousness of sin; she shuddered with terror at the least fault.

Those who are led by the Holy Spirit experience all sorts of happiness in themselves, while bad Christians roll themselves on thorns and flints. A soul in which the Holy Spirit dwells is never weary in the presence of God; his heart gives forth a breath of love. Without the Holy Ghost we are like the stones on the road. . . . Take in one hand a sponge full of water, and in the other a little pebble; press them equally. Nothing will come out of the pebble, but out of the sponge will come abundance of water. The sponge is the soul filled with the Holy Spirit, and the stone is the cold and hard heart which is not inhabited by the Holy Spirit.

A soul that possesses the Holy Spirit tastes such sweetness in prayer, that it finds the time always too short; it never loses the holy presence of God. Such a heart, before our good Saviour in the Holy Sacrament of the Altar, is a bunch of grapes under the wine press. . . . You who are not great saints, you still have many moments when you taste the sweetness of prayer and of the presence of God: these are visits of the Holy Spirit. When we have the Holy Spirit, the heart expands—bathes itself in divine love. A fish never complains of having too much water, neither does a good Christian ever complain of being too long with the good God. There are some people who find religion wearisome, and it is because they have not the Holy Spirit.

If the damned were asked, Why are you in hell? they would answer, For having resisted the Holy Spirit. And if the saints were asked, Why are you in heaven? they would answer, For having listened to the Holy Spirit. . . . The Holy Spirit is a power. The Holy Spirit supported St. Simeon on his column; He sustained the martyrs. Without the Holy Spirit, the martyrs would have fallen like the leaves from the trees. When the fires were lighted under them, the Holy Spirit extinguished the heat of the fire by the heat of divine love. The good God, in sending us the Holy Spirit, has treated us like a great king who should send his minister to guide one of his subjects, saying, "You will accompany this man everywhere, and you will bring him back to me safe and sound." How beautiful it is, my children, to be accompanied by the Holy Spirit! He is indeed a good Guide; and to think that there are some who will not follow Him. The Holy Spirit is like a man with a carriage and horse, who should want to take us to Paris. We should only have to say "yes," and to get into it. It is indeed an easy matter to say "yes"! . . . Well, the Holy Spirit wants to take us to heaven; we have only to say "yes," and to let Him take us there.

The Holy Spirit is like a gardener cultivating our souls. . . . The Holy Spirit is our servant. . . . There is a gun; well you load it, but someone must fire it and make it go off. . . . In the same way, we have in ourselves the power of doing good . . . when the Holy Spirit gives the impulse, good works are produced. The Holy Spirit reposes in just souls like the dove in her nest. He brings out good desires in a pure soul, as the dove hatches her young ones. The Holy Spirit leads us as a mother leads by the hand her child of two years old, as a person who can see leads one who is blind.

The Sacraments which our Lord instituted would not have saved us without the Holy Spirit. Even the death of our Lord would have been useless to us without Him. Therefore our Lord said to His Apostles, "It is good for you that I should go away; for if I did not go, the Consoler would not come." The descent of the Holy Ghost was required, to render fruitful that harvest of graces. It is like a grain of wheat—you cast it into the ground; yes, but it must have sun and rain to make it grow and come into ear. We should say every morning, "O God, send me Thy Spirit to teach me what I am and what Thou art."[21]

NOTES

1. *Oeuvres de Saint Francois de Sales. Edition Complète* (Annecy: J. Niérat, 1897), Vol III, pp. 318-322.

2. *Letters to Persons in Religion.* Translated by Henry Benedict Mackey (Westminster: Newman Bookshop, 1943), pp. 424-425.

3. *Poems*. Edited by Hugh l'Anson Fausset (New York: E.P. Dutton, 1943), p. 262.

4. *The Spiritual Doctrine of Father Louis Lallement* (Westminster: The Newman Book Shop, 1946), pp. 108-119.

5. *Ibid.*, pp. 112-117.

6. *The Autobiography of Venerable Marie of the Incarnation.* Translated by John J. Sullivan (Chicago: Loyola University Press, 1964), pp. 45, 50.

7. *Ibid.*, p. 158.

8. *Ibid.*, p. 63.

9. Etienne Michel Faillon, *Vie de M. Olier* (Paris: Poussielgue, 1873), I, 343-345.

10. "Paradise Lost," in *The Complete Poetical Works of John Milton*. Edited by Harris Francis Fletcher (New York: Houghton Mifflin, 1941), p. 155.

11. *Oeuvres Complètes de Bossuet* Par Une Société D' Ecclesiastiques (Par-le-duc: Louis Guerin, 1870), VIII, p. 619.

12. *A Spiritual Retreat for Eight Successive Days* (Baltimore: F. Lucas, 1833), pp. 309-310.

13. *Ibid.*, pp. 316-317.

14. "Instructions et Avis sur divers points de la morale et de la perfection chrétienne," in *Oeuvres Complètes de Fénelon* (Paris: Lerous et Jouby, 1850), Book VI, pp. 118-119.

15. *Meditations and Devotions from the Writings of Francois de Salignac de la Mothe Fénelon.* Translated by Elizabeth C. Fenn (New York: Morehouse-Gorham, 1952), pp. 107-109.

16. St. Jean-Baptiste de la Salle *Methode d'Oraison* (Paris: 1739).

17. *Oeuvres Complètes de S. Alphonse de Liguori.* Translated from Italian by Leop. J. Dujardin. (Tournai Vve H. Casterman, 1882), Book VI, pp. 542-543.

18. *The Interior of Jesus and Mary.* Edited by S.H. Frisbie (New York: Benziger, 1893), pp. 331-332.

19. Margaret Williams, *St. Madeleine Sophie. Her Life and Letters* (New York: Herder and Herder, 1965), p. 247.

20. *Ibid.*, pp. 513-514.

21. *The Curé of Ars to His People. Instruction on the Catechism* (St. Meinrad, Indiana: Grail Publications, 1951), pp. 35-39.

Domenico Zappi, BLESSED MOTHER AS TEMPLE OF THE HOLY SPIRIT, Benedictine Convent of Perpetual Adoration, Kansas City, Missouri.

Chapter VII

THE SPIRIT IN THE WRITINGS OF 19TH AND EARLIER 20TH CENTURY AUTHORS

Introduction

The nineteenth and early twentieth centuries are not noted in Roman Catholic tradition for emphasis upon devotion to the Spirit of God. In this era, humble Thérèse of Lisieux inspired countless souls to follow her "Little Way" of love; Bernadette Soubirous rekindled a devotion ancient in the Eastern and Western churches to the Mother of God; St. Margaret Mary Alacoque's devotion to the Sacred Heart was spreading in an age undergoing the throes of the dehumanizing forces of industrialization.

But, even though devotion to the Holy Spirit was not in great vogue, the Spirit of God still had his devotées. As literacy spread throughout the Western world to the bourgeois class, people of various classes began to keep spiritual journals. The devoted wife and mother, Lucie-Christine found the Comforter present at the bedside of her dying husband. The brilliant Cardinal Newman could avow to the Sanctifier, "If I differ at all from the world, it is because Thou hast chosen me out of the world, and hast lit up the love of God in my heart."

A line in Martin Vonier's excerpt points to a characteristic which is manifestly apparent—since the time of St. Paul—among souls consciously surrendered to the Spirit: "He makes us love with tenderness of heart." When Love Himself possesses the soul, then love for *all* humanity becomes easier. Lucie Christine sought in prayer the way to make souls love God more and obey the Holy Spirit more faithfully. Her answer: "I have found no more powerful means than kindness."

Through the ages, the saints have never ceased to affirm that when the soul is completely possessed by the Spirit of God, a love of the Cross, as well as love of fellow men, becomes a reality. In prayer, Teilhard de Chardin realized: "That the Spirit may always shine forth in me . . . you, Lord, will send me . . . disappointments, sorrow." In the mysterious plan of Providence, Chardin lived through the agony of seeing his own writings suppressed, only to be resurrected in a later age when both his words and his humbly submissive life could doubly inspire others along the road to sanctity.

In this century of the Virgin and the Sacred Heart, along with the humble diarists, there emerged noteworthy poets who praised the Spirit of God in sublime verses, reminding us that, through all the vicissitudes of history, in fashion or out of fashion,

> "the Spirit of God hovers . . .
> with ah,
> bright wings."

JOHN HENRY NEWMAN (1801-1890)

THE PARACLETE, THE LIFE OF ALL THINGS

I adore Thee, my God and God, the Eternal Paraclete, co-equal with the Father and the Son. I adore Thee as the Life of all that live. Through Thee the whole material Universe hangs together and consists, remains in its place, and moves internally in the order and reciprocity of its several parts. . . . Through Thee our own dead souls are quickened to serve Thee. From Thee is every good thought and desire, every good purpose, every good effort, every good success. . . .

I adore Thee, O dread Lord, for what thou has done for my soul. I acknowledge and feel, not only as a matter of faith but of experience, that I cannot have one good thought or do one good act without Thee. I know, that if I attempt anything good in my own strength, I shall to a certainty fail. I have bitter experience of this. My God, I am only safe when Thou dost breathe upon me. If Thou withdraw Thy breath, forthwith my three mortal enemies rush on me and overcome me. I am as weak as water, I am utterly impotent without thee. The minute Thou dost cease to act in me, I begin to languish, to grasp, and to faint away. Of my good desires, whatever they may be, of my good aims, aspirations, attempts, successes, habits, practices, Thou art the sole cause and present continual source. I have nothing but what I have received, and I protest now in Thy presence, O Sovereign Paraclete, that I have nothing to glory in, and everything to be humbled at.

O my dear Lord, how merciful Thou hast been to me. When I was young, Thou didst put into my heart a special devotion to Thee. Thou hast taken me up in my youth, and in my age. Thou wilt not forsake me.[1]

THE PARACLETE, THE FOUNT OF LOVE

My God, the paraclete, I acknowledge thee as the Giver of that great gift, by which alone we are saved, supernatural love. Man is by nature blind and hard-hearted in all spiritual matters; how is he to reach heaven? It is by the flame of Thy grace, which consumes him in order to new-make him, and so to fit him to enjoy what without Thee he would have no taste for. It is Thou, O Almighty Paraclete, who hast been and art the strength, the vigour and endurance, of the martyr in the midst of his torments. Thou art the stay of the confessor in his long, tedious, and humiliating toils. Thou art the fire, by which the preacher wins souls, without thought of himself, in his missionary labours. By Thee we wake up from the death of sin, to exchange the idolatry of the creature for the pure love of the Creator. By Thee we make acts of faith, hope, charity, and contrition. By thee we live in the atmosphere of earth, proof against its infection. By Thee we are able to consecrate ourselves to the sacred ministry, and fulfill our awful engagements to it. By the fire which Thou didst kindle within us, we pray, and meditate, and do penance. As well could our bodies live, if the sun were extinguished, as our souls, if Thou art away.

My most Holy Lord and Sanctifier, whatever there is of good in me is Thine. Without Thee, I should but get worse and worse as years went on, and should tend to be a devil. If I differ at all from the world, it is because Thou hast chosen me out of the world, and hast lit up the love of God in my heart. If I differ from Thy Saints, it is because I do not ask earnestly enough for thy grace, and for enough of it, and because I do not diligently improve what Thou hast given me. Increase in me this grace of love, in spite of all my unworthiness. It is more precious than anything else in the world. I accept it in place of all the world can give me. O give it to me! It is my life.[2]

HENRI-DOMINIQUE LACORDAIRE (1802-1861)

The Intimate Life of God

[The Father] can say, in contemplating his thought, in regarding his image, in hearing his Word, He can say in the ecstasy of the first and most real paternity, that word heard by David: "You are my Son. This day have I begotten Thee." Today! On this day which is eternity, that is to say, the indivisible duration of being without change. . . . .

But is that the whole life of God? The generation of his Son, is it his only act, and does it complete with its fecundity all its beatitude? No, Messieurs; because in us, the generation of thought is not the terminus in which our life stops. When we have thought, a second act is produced: we love. Thought is a regard which leads its object into ourselves; love is a movement which draws us outside toward that object, mutually to unite it to us and to accomplish in its plentitude the mystery of relations, that is the mystery of unity in plurality. . . .

Love is both distinct from spirit and distinct from thought; distinct from spirit where it is born and where it dies; distinct from thought even by its definition, since it is an embracing movement, while thought is a simple view. . . .

In God it is the same. From the coeternal glance between Father and Son comes forth a third term in the relation, proceeding from the one and the other, really distinct from both, elevated by the power of the infinity to a personality, who is the Holy Spirit. He is the holy movement of Divine Love without measure and without blemish. Just as the Son is the consummation of *knowledge* in God, the Holy Spirit is the consummation of Love. By Him the cycle of the fecundity of divine life is terminated.[3]

VENERABLE FRANCOIS-MARIE LIBERMANN (1804-1852)

Letter to a Seminarian

My very dear brother,

May the Holy Spirit fill your soul and be your consolation, your joy, your strength, your light and your love.

Our good Savior has sent us his divine Spirit in order to be our complete life, to effect in us all the perfections and sanctity that he effected in our Savior Himself. See, what bounty on the part of our God, what a miracle of grace and of love it was to send us such a grand Master to instruct us in all the marvels the Father has sent in his well-beloved Son, and to accomplish them in our souls.

What must be our sanctity, if we are faithful in listening interiorly to the Divine Spirit, if we are docile in following his movements, if we yield ourselves and give Him full liberty to establish in our souls his own life, at the expense and to the detriment of our life of the flesh. It is an incomprehensible thing that God has deigned to look favorably on men as corrupt as ourselves and that He has desired to come to establish his dwelling in our souls. . . .

[What a wonder it is] that such a pure and holy spirit can dwell in the midst of continual imperfection and ceaselessly suffer revolt against Him. . . . That is where, in an admirable manner, the divine goodness and mercy are shown. It is inconceivable—but that must confuse us and force us to humble ourselves before God, at the same time that it must make us enter into transports of love toward the Holy Trinity; because *there* is the great mystery of the love of our God . . .

Be faithful to that which the Divine Spirit wishes to do in you—follow it very meekly and in great interior humiliation before Him. Hold yourself always in repose; aim to weaken, to soften all your harshness, all your movements of inquietude, all the discouragements and troubles which tend to rise up in your soul. Try to live in a certain liberty of spirit, without constraint, or effort. While you feel yourself assailed by the desire to dissipate yourself in creatures, don't trouble yourself about it. Don't you know what you are? What do you fear? The Spirit of Jesus is in you—doesn't He hold you between his hands? Oh, surely yes, because if it were not so, you would be far from Him—a long time ago . . .

Don't be astonished that I insist so much on that, because I think —I am persuaded well—that to be perfect it is necessary to be absolutely empty of all that is not God. The Holy Spirit knocks every instant at the gate of our heart; we desire ardently that He enter, and *by* that desire we open the gate to Him. But how can He enter there if he finds no place there, if He finds that heart which would so belong to him full of alien affections? He is then obliged to remain outside, and He has the inconceivable goodness to wait until He finds a small place, measured by how much we disencumber ourselves of these miserable affections.

The more the Holy Spirit has entered our heart, the more fortified we become to chase out little by little the enemies of God who have seized power there. It is for this that it is essential that we aid the Divine Spirit to put them outside, because without our firm will He will not force them alone.

We must then pray ardently and use all the strength He gives us to help Him accomplish that work.

Prayer to the Holy Spirit

O very holy and adorable Spirit, make me hear your sweet, loving voice. I wish to be as a light feather before you, so that your breath can carry me away where it wishes, and never oppose it with the least resistance.[4]

Act of Consecration to the Holy Ghost

On my knees, before the great multitude of heavenly witnesses I offer myself, soul and body to Thee, Eternal Spirit of God. I adore the brightness of Thy Purity, the unerring keenness of Thy justice and the might of Thy love. Thou art the Strength and the Light of my soul. In Thee I live and move and am. I desire never to grieve Thee by unfaithfulness to grace and I pray with all my heart to be kept from the smallest sin against Thee. Mercifully guard my every thought and grant that I may always watch for Thy light and listen to Thy voice and follow Thy gracious inspirations. I cling to Thee and give myself to

Thee and ask Thee by Thy compassion to watch over me in my weakness. Holding the pierced feet of Jesus and looking at His Five Wounds and trusting in His Precious Blood and adoring His opened side and stricken Heart, I implore Thee, adorable Spirit, helper of my infirmity, so to keep me in Thy grace that I may never sin against Thee. Give me Grace, O Holy Ghost, Spirit of the Father and the Son, to say to Thee always and everywhere, "Speak, Lord, for Thy servant heareth." Amen.[5]

CARDINAL MANNING (1807-1892)

The Spirit Impels Us to Goodness

All the day long the Spirit of God is in your hearts; all hours of the day He is calling on you to correspond with the will of God, that by it you may be sanctified. But do you correspond with it? You know that if you strike a note of music, all the octave notes will vibrate. Does your heart vibrate in correspondence and harmony with the voice of the Holy Ghost, prompting you to holy thoughts, good works, charitable actions, peace with all men, prayer and piety towards God? No grace that God gives ever fails of its effects except through our fault. The seeds that fall upon the barren sand can bear no fruit; that which is cast upon the sea cannot strike a root; that which falls upon a mind which is like the troubled sea, or a heart which is like the barren sand, will bear no spiritual fruit. Nevertheless, the grace of God in itself is always fruitful; it never fails of its effect, unless we mar it. Are you, then, corresponding with the exuberant graces, which God is always bestowing upon you? Think of what you have received from your childhood. The lights that have come down on you from heaven all your life long are not more abundant than the graces of the Holy Spirit, which have been bestowed upon you to impart the knowledge of self and the knowledge of God. The showers that water the earth are not more exuberant than the graces of sanctity which God has poured out into your hearts. How have you corresponded with them? How have you wasted them? Let us all learn, for we all alike have need—and what I say to you I say first to myself—let us learn to have a delicate conscience, to understand promptly, and to correspond, if we can, proportionately; not to receive great graces languidly, and squander one half of them, and correspond faintly with the rest. Try with your whole soul and strength to rise up and to obey, when the grace of God calls you to any higher state or to any better action.

You have seen a lock in a river; and you have watched how, when the lock is shut, the water rises against the gate. It presses with its full weight against the gate until a hand—it may be the hand of a child, with such facility it is accomplished—opens the gate of the lock; at once the flood pours in, the level of the water rises, the stream runs strong, and carries forward those that float upon it, almost without effort of their own. The grace of God is always pressing against our will, always in contact with our heart, moving us onward towards God, impelling us to good. And this pressure of the Holy Ghost against our will waits only for our will to open.[6]

The Spirit Illumines Our Soul

The Holy Spirit of God illuminates us, and if we receive that illumination, we receive from Him larger measures of light; but the condition on which we are illuminated is, that we co-operate with the light we already have. The way in which we learn the science of God, in all its greatest principles, and all its least details, is by following the working of the Spirit of God in our hearts. The whole, then, of our sanctification is a personal action of God dwelling in our soul, and unfolding the intelligence and the will to a conformity with His own.[7]

Just as we keep a lamp alight by careful watching, and by pouring in fresh oil when the wick begins to burn dim, so the Holy Ghost lovingly and tenderly watches over the state of our hearts. When He sees there is spiritual decay, and that the light is declining, that our charity is less, or that our piety is faint, He pours in larger measures of His grace, whereby the spiritual life within us is kept vigorous and strong, and its decays are continually repaired.[8]

Neglect of the Holy Spirit

If there be one thing that is to our shame, one thing which ought to cast us down with our faces in the dust, it is this: that we live all the day long as if there were no Holy Ghost, as if we were like the Ephesians who, when the Apostle asked them if they had received the Holy Ghost since they believed, said: "We have not so much as heard whether there be a Holy Ghost." We live in the world and are worldly; we live on the earth and are earthly; we live for pleasure, we live for trade, for money, for levities, for frivolities, for the indulgence of our own will. Many live for worse, for they live in pride, in covetousness, in jealousies, in envies, in animosities, in malice, one with another. Many live in worse still, if it were possible so to say. They spend their years in revelling, wallowing in gross sins of sensuality; and yet they have been made temples of the Holy Ghost. They have been born again, they are regenerate, they have been made sons of God, heirs of His Kingdom: and to all eternity they will bear the mark of their regeneration, the indelible character stamped upon them at the font, and they will bear also the mark of their confirmation—two terrible and divine witnesses against them: the evidence of their disobedience, because they have grieved the Holy Ghost until they quenched His light, and died in their sin. Is it not true if you look round the world you see men on every side living as if they had never been born again? . . .[9]

Let us then resolve, from this time, all we can, to love the Spirit of God, to conform ourselves to His will, to worship him day by day, to pray to him personally, to place ourselves under His guidance, to beware of disobedience—of those three degrees of disobedience of which He Himself has warned Us; "Grieve not the Spirit of God, whereby ye are sealed unto the day of redemption; Resist not the Spirit; Quench not the Spirit." These are the three degrees by which we may fall from His love and from His presence. Beware also not of actual disobedience only, but of that tardy slothful negligence by which you may provoke Him to a just impatience. . . . Nothing provokes the Holy Spirit of God, Who is the fire of the love of God, more than the lukewarmness with which we allow His graces and mercies to pass by us, and to pass by us unperceived. Ask, then of the Holy Spirit of God to give you light to know Him, to know his presence, to be conscious of His indwelling in your hearts. Say to Him: "O my God, I give myself to Thee with all my liberty, all my intellect and heart and will. I desire to be bound to Thee; for 'where the Spirit of the Lord is, there is liberty.' No other liberty is true; I desire to be free from the servitude of my own false freedom, which is the worst bondage of the human soul. To be Thy servant is to be in the liberty of the sons of God. They that are led by the Spirit of God are the sons of God. O holy Spirit of God, take me as Thy disciple, guide me, illuminate me, sanctify me, bind my hands that I may not do evil, cover my eyes that I may see it no more, sanctify my heart that evil may not rest within me. Be Thou my God, be Thou my Guide: wheresoever Thou leadest me I will go; whatsoever Thou forbidest I will renounce; and whatsoever Thou commandest, in Thy strength I will do."[10]

SØREN KIERKEGAARD (1813-1855)

O Holy Spirit

O Holy Spirit—we pray for ourselves and for all—O Holy Spirit, Thou who dost make alive; here it is not talents we stand in need of, nor culture, nor shrewdness, rather there is here too much of all that; but what we need is that Thou take away the power of mastery and give us life. True it is that a man experiences a shudder like that of death when Thou, to become a power in him, dost take the power from him—oh, but if even animal creatures understand at a subsequent moment how well it is for them that the royal coachman took the reins which in the first instance prompted them to shudder, and against which their mind rebelled—should not then a man be able promptly to understand what a benefaction it is towards us that Thou takest away the power and givest life?[11]

Send Therefore Thy Spirit; Be Ye Therefore Sober (1 Pet. 4:7)

Father in Heaven, Thou art a spirit, and they that worship Thee must worship Thee in spirit and in truth—but how in spirit and in truth if we are not sober, even if we are striving to be? Send therefore Thy Spirit into our hearts; ah, it is so often invoked that it may come to bring courage, and life, and power, and strength, oh, that it first (this is indeed the condition for all the rest, and that the rest may be to our profit), oh, that first it might make us sober![12]

Bless This Our Gathering
Thou Holy Ghost, Thou makest alive, bless also this our gathering, the speaker and the hearer; fresh from the heart it shall come, by Thine aid, do Thou let it also go to the heart.[13]

Thou Spirit of Holiness
We have our treasure in earthen vessels, but Thou, O Holy Spirit, when Thou livest in a man, Thou livest in what is infinitely lower. Thou Spirit of Holiness, Thou livest in the midst of impurity and corruption; Thou Spirit of Wisdom, Thou livest in the midst of folly; Thou Spirit of Truth, Thou livest in one who is himself deluded. Oh, continue to dwell there, Thou who dost not seek a desirable dwelling place, for Thou wouldst seek there in vain, Thou Creator and Redeemer, make a dwelling for Thyself; oh, continue to dwell there, that one day Thou mightest finally be pleased by the dwelling which Thou didst Thyself prepare in my heart, foolish, deceiving, and impure as it is.[14]

Enlighten Our Minds
Lord Jesus Christ, let Thy Holy Spirit enlighten our minds and convince us thoroughly of our sin, so that, humbled and with downcast eyes, we may recognize that we stand far, far off and with a sigh, "God be merciful to me a sinner;" but then let it befall us by Thy grace as it

befell that publican who went up to the Temple to pray and went down to his house justified.[15]

MATTHIAS JOSEPH SCHEEBAN (1835-1888)

THE SPIRIT: THE KISS OF GOD

Just as the soul as child of God is sealed and is united to God the Father through the Holy Spirit, and as the Holy Spirit is the *osculum*, or kiss, of the Father whereby the Father takes the soul to Himself as His child and unites it to Himself, so He is likewise the *osculum* of the Son, by which the soul becomes the latter's bride. As bride of the Son the soul in grace prays to Him in the Canticle: "Let Him kiss me with the kisses of His mouth," so that by His spiritual kiss it may become one with Him in one Spirit. The soul becomes one with the Son as one Spirit in the Holy Spirit, whom He breathes forth into the soul and with whom the soul merges through the breath of love aroused by Him: like a flame which, after it has been enkindled from another flame, meets and fuses with the latter and unites with it to form a single flame. The real indwelling of the Spirit of the bridegroom in His bride is to the spiritual marriage of the Son of God with the soul what corporal union is in corporal marriage, a union to which bride and bridegroom aspire in their reciprocal love. Hence it can be regarded as the consummation and sealing of the affectional union between the Son of God and the soul.

Thus, the soul. joined by the Holy Spirit to the Son as sister and bride, and to the Father as child, is taken up by the same Holy Spirit into the intimate communion, into the fellowship and company of both, into the wonderful fellowship of the Father and the Son, which St. John depicts as the purpose of the Incarnation. The Holy Spirit is the bond uniting the Father with the Son in His procession from both, and is likewise the bond uniting the Father and the Son with the creature by His coming to lodge in the latter. This is in the highest sense the communication or society (koinonia) of the Holy Spirit of which the Apostle speaks, that is, it is not only a fellowship with the Holy Spirit Himself, but a fellowship of the creature with the divine persons through Him and based on His procession from them and His entrance into the creature, a fellowship in which the Holy Spirit unites every individual, and also all sanctified creatures as a body, to the divine persons, and therefore also among themselves, threading and joining all together into a great, golden chain. The spiritual unity which the Apostle exhorts us to preserve consists not only in the union of affection, not only in the concord of the love poured into our hearts by the Holy Spirit. We are to guard the unity of love among us because a spiritual "bond of peace," the Holy Spirit Himself, embraces us all, because there is one Spirit for all who come together in one body, and because the union perfected in the Holy Spirit demands on our part a unity of disposition of all of us with the divine persons, similar to that which the Father and the Son exemplify in the spiration of the Holy Spirit.[16]

BARTHÉLEMY FROGET (1843-1905)

The Indwelling God

God is everywhere, in every being and in every place as the immediate cause of everything outside of Himself. But He unites Himself and is present to the souls of the just in a very particular way, that is to say—as the object of their knowledge and love. It is not only by His image imprinted on the mind and by His memory, or by His favours bestowed that He is present to the justified. He comes to them veritably in Person, inaugurating here below that life of union and beatitude which is to be consummated in heaven. It is simply a matter of fact, that as soon as the sinner returns to the friendship of God, He Who is Subsistent personalized Love in God, i.e., the Holy Ghost, is sent to seal, as it were, by His presence the covenant of reconciliation, to co-operate in the great work of sanctification, and to become in the just soul the active principle of a new life, a life comparably superior to the life of man's nature. Nor does the Holy Spirit make merely a passing visit, precious as that might be; but He comes to establish Himself in the soul with the Father and the Son, fixes His abode there, there to remain whilst the soul's love for God remains.

Entering into the soul, the Spirit of God gives Himself to it, and this is His great favour. Then begins the work of beautifying and adorning the living temple in which He is pleased to dwell. To this end He pours into it that grace of infinite value called sanctifying, the effect of which is to purify from every stain, to efface sin, to justify, to transform, yea, to deify the recipient, to make him a child of God and the object of his complacency, with a right to the celestial and eternal inheritance. Nor is this all; for grace never comes alone. Rather it is always accompanied by a whole throng of virtues and supereminent qualities, which are at once an adornment of our faculties and a source of their supernatural activity. These are the theological virtues of Faith, Hope, and Charity; furthermore, the infused moral virtues; and also the Gifts of the Holy Ghost; all of these being living germs of the fruits God wishes to harvest in us; divine energies, the sources of those admirable acts called Beatitudes, because they are the meritorious cause and, as it were, a foretaste of the felicity we await in eternity.

Thus endowed, we are able to go forward, having need of naught else to steer our barque directly and surely towards the eternal shores, unless it be these impulses of the Holy Spirit, which are the constantly renewed portion of the children of God. Nor have we long to wait for these. From the depths of the soul where He dwells, that Divine Spirit enlightens our intelligence, inflames our heart, quickens us and incites us to good. Who will count all the holy thoughts He arouses in us, the good impulses He imparts, the salutary inspirations of which He is the source? Why is it that obstacles too frequently come to more or less paralyze His beneficent activity and to hinder His purposes? This is why so many Christians in the possession of habitual grace and of the Divine energies which accompany it, remain, nevertheless, so feeble and so sluggish in God's service, so little zealous for their perfection, so inclined to earth, so forgetful of the things of heaven, so easily fascinated by evil? . . .

There is another reason which finally explains why a seed so prolific of holiness produces oftentimes so sorry a harvest. It is this: that knowing but very imperfectly the treasure of which they are guardians, a number of Christians form only a faint estimate of it, and put themselves to little pains to make it yield fruit. Yet what power, what generosity, what respect for self, what watchfulness, and what consolation and joy, would not this thought, if constantly held before the mind and piously meditated upon, inspire: The Holy Ghost dwells in my heart! He is there, a Powerful Protector, always ready to defend me against my enemies, to sustain me in my combats, to assure me the victory. A Faithful Friend, He is always disposed to give me a hearing, and, far from being a source of sadness and weariness, his conversation brings gladness and joy. . . .

THE HOLY SPIRIT DWELLS IN MY HEART! I am His temple, essentially the temple of holiness; I must, therefore, sanctify myself, since the first characteristic of God's house is holiness. . . . Let us love, honor, and often invoke the Holy Ghost; let us be docile to His inspirations; and determined finally to occupy the throne of glory which is prepared for us in heaven, let us commence by glorifying here below in our body and in our soul that Holy Trinity Whose abiding place and temple we are.[17]

GERARD MANLEY HOPKINS (1844-1889)

God's Grandeur

The world is charged with the grandeur of God.
It will flame out, like shining from shook foil;
It gathers to a greatness, like the ooze of oil
Crushed. Why do men then now not reck his rod?
Generations have trod, have trod, have trod;
And all is seared with trade; bleared, smeared with toil;
And wears man's smudge and shares man's smell; the soil
Is bare now, nor can foot feel, being shod.

And for all this, nature is never spent;
There lives the dearest freshness deep down things;
And though the last flights off the black West went
Oh, morning, at the brown brink eastward, springs—
Because the Holy Ghost over the bent
World broods with warm breast and with ah! bright wings.[18]

LUCIE-CHRISTINE (1844-1908)

Spiritual Journal of the Action of the Holy Spirit in a Wife and Mother

May or June, 1877. It was on Whit Sunday that I heard that call —my soul being profoundly recollected in the Holy Ghost and united to that adorable Person. I felt drawn to a life of prayer and, according as grace might move me, to kneel down and recollect myself from time to time during my ordinary daily life. This proved a most efficacious help to the interior life.[19]

June 24, 1879. On that day my eldest child was confirmed. Whilst I was praying fervently for her and for all those who were being confirmed with her, I received the grace of union with the Holy Ghost, a union which imparts a powerful love to the soul and raises her above all perishable affections. Since then this grace has been repeatedly renewed.

O my God! O Eternal Love! How many in my place would have become saints![20]

1880. About that time the Confirmation of my second child took place (May 16), and on that occasion the grace of union with the Holy

Ghost was again granted me, and with much greater force than in the preceding year.[21]

April, 1882. I was ill and deprived of Holy Communion for 16 days. During this painful privation my good Master sustained me by His intimate presence in the depths of my soul; it was there that I adored Him, as fever impeded me from visiting the church even in thought. . . . But the characteristic grace of this time of sickness and privation was the union of my soul with the Holy Ghost. This is a very great and precious grace; it carries the soul straight to God, if I dare so express it. Since then my soul has conserved a very special gratitude and attraction for the Divine Spirit Who is so little known and so little invoked, although He is more intimate with our souls than we ourselves.[22]

October 14. This morning—O Holy Ghost, today after the absolution it was Thy presence which took possession of my soul in a sweet union of complacency. Thou givest a peace and a security all Thine own, for Thou art Light Itself and the Divine Director of the soul, and it seems to her when Thou art there in a sensible manner that no doubt or sorrow dare assail her.[23]

July 18, 1883. I saw by a divine illumination that just as the Holy Ghost is the term of the Divine processions, so also He must be the term of the Divine manifestations, that is to say, in the Old Testament men have mostly known and adored the Father, the Creator. In the New Testament they have attached themselves to their adorable Savior Jesus Christ.

But in the latter days, the Holy Ghost will make His heat and light more strongly felt in the heart of the faithful; they will find therein a renewal of faith and they will the better know and love the Father and the Son, and particularly Our Lord in the Eucharist, for better knowing and loving Eternal Love; and this in the same way as they have already learned from the Word to know the Father and to be "adorers in spirit and in truth."[24]

December 27. [At the bedside of her husband who has just died] I remained long there on my knees. My grief was completely dominated by the thought of the judgment of God. . . .

Then I invoked the Holy Ghost, imploring Him to take the direction of my new life and to inspire me in the accomplishment of all my duties. . . .[25]

January 1, 1889. O Holy Trinity, I consecrate my soul to Thee at the beginning of this year. I did so at my first waking in the night. Do not refuse this creature which Thou hast made, however poor it may be, but acknowledge and complete Thy work! Of myself I cannot, neither do I know how to, become holy, but I am ready for all that Thou desirest, and mayest desire, of me day by day as Thou shalt reveal it to me. I only will Thy holy Will and Thy love; my God, thou knowest this![26]

January 16, 1896. I have been seeking how to make God better loved by souls . . . how to make them understand that suavity, that sweetness, that unspeakable peace . . . how to obey the Holy Ghost, that fire which I feel in my soul and which longs to impart itself . . . how to communicate to all other souls that which touches my soul. I have found no more powerful means than kindness.[27]

CARDINAL MERCIER (1851-1926)

His Spirit lives within us by sanctifying grace. He gives Him to us for our instruction, for our guidance through life, for our sanctification in His love. The mission of the Holy Spirit is a prolongation of the Word, with the special object of elevating towards the Father all docile souls and realizing in this world the union of souls upon the model of the perfect union of the three persons of the Holy Trinity—until God, one in three, will one day show Himself to us face to face as He is.[28]

Lie still in the hand of God, patiently waiting till, in His own good time, the Holy Spirit breathes upon your soul. . . . You must repress the hurry and agitation to which nature is prone, so as to let your souls repose in calmness under the inspiration of the Holy Spirit of God.[29]

I am going to reveal to you the secret of sanctity and happiness. Every day for five minutes control your imagination and close your eyes to the things of the world, in order to enter into yourself. Then, in the sanctity of your baptized soul (which is the temple of the Holy Spirit, say to Him:

O Holy Spirit, beloved of my soul . . . I adore You. Enlighten me, guide me, strengthen me, console me. Tell me what I should do . . . give your orders. I promise to submit myself to all that you desire of me and to accept all that You permit to happen to me. Let me only know Your will.

If you do this, your life will flow along happily, serenely and full of consolation, even in the midst of trials. Grace will be proportioned to the trial, giving you the strength to carry it and you will arrive at the gate of Paradise, laden with merit. This submission to the Holy Spirit is the secret of sanctity.[30]

MAURICE LANDRIEUX (1857-1926)

THE HOLY SPIRIT: THE BOND OF THE TRINITY

In the bosom of the Trinity, each of the divine Persons is for the other two a subject of inexhaustible delight. And that vital transport which is force, light and heat—that is power, knowledge and love—which proceeds from the Father, passes through the Word, to end in the Holy Spirit, does not cease there; for the Holy Spirit returns into that ocean of love from which he proceeds, and this reflux of love which returns to the Father through the Word completes the circuit of divine activity without interrupting it. And the gift and the ecstasy, unchangeable in this incessant exchange of infinite love, are eternal.

Nothing created can give an idea of that intensity of life, of that ineffable bliss; not the noblest raptures of human genius, nor the purest transports of the human heart, nor the ideal tenderness of mothers; for the love is in proportion to the perfection. And if our hearts suffer because of their impotence, because there is an abyss between what they wish to do and what they can do, in God, and in God alone, the power is equal to the will.

No; God is not solitary, the Trinity is the divine family: the Holy Spirit is the intervening bond.[31]

THE SPIRITUS-BREATH

Love in its extreme degree has no longer words, has no longer song. It is silent; it is exhaled in a sigh, in a breath in which the whole soul vibrates.

It is in this sense that the name of spirit is given to the third person of the blessed Trinity—SPIRITUS, a breath, a sigh . . . of the ardent soul exhaling love; burning breath that seems to come rather from the heart than from the lungs, that bursts forth from the very sources of being, that goes forth but to return, that is recovered, that is inhaled again with as much pleasure as it is exhaled, in that incessant mysterious rhythmic movement of respiration which is the sign and condition of interior life, SPIRACULUM VITAE, a veritable thermometer of love, so great is the effect of the repercussion of the slightest affective motion in accelerating or in lessening it.[32]

THE FOUNT OF LIFE

The Holy Ghost, like grace, is sometimes compared to a fountain of living water, and again to a glowing fire. O FONS VIVUS, IGNIS,

CHARITAS. Water is life. In nature water circulates as the blood circulates in the human body. Whether it gushes forth from the deep arteries of the globe, whether it rushes down in torrents from the highest mountains, or falls from the sky in rain, it is water that fertilises the earth. Without it the richest soil remains sterile. But, as soon as there is water, life awakens from sleep, the seed germinates and springs up, the sap circulates in the plants and trees. At its touch all becomes verdant, everything grows luxuriantly, everything is fructified. For a right estimate of the value of water, of the transcendent importance of a spring, of a fountain, of a well, residence in a country, where there is scarcity or absence of water, would be necessary. Water causes the oasis to arise in the desert. Now, there is nothing that expresses so well the action of grace in souls as this providential part that water plays in nature.

Just as in the beginning of the world the Holy Ghost moved over the waters, brooding over them, if we may say so, as the bird broods over her eggs to produce life in them, so does the divine Spirit again and with greater effect brood over the waters of baptism in which supernatural life has birth. For the moral world, like the physical world, is generated in water. Divine grace, like water, purifies, refreshes, vivifies. Holy souls are compared to gardens that are watered and fertilised by living waters—"like a watered garden and like a fountain of water, whose waters shall not fail."[33]

And Fire of Love

Water fertilises the earth, but it is the sun, the beneficent sun in the heavens, that makes the sap to rise, that gives to the flower its resplendent bloom, to the fruit its delicious taste . . . The sole secret of the wealth of tropical vegetation is water and heat in abundance.

Hence fire also is a condition of life. Like water, it is hidden everywhere, mingled with everything.

Fire not only vivifies, but it purifies as well; it gives light, it kindles; thus, it is a figure of the work of grace in its three stages of the purgative, the illuminative, the unitive life.

Fire refines precious things; in the crucible it separates gold from the dross that tarnishes it. Fire makes the bar of rigid iron flexible. And whilst it renders the hardest metals malleable, it gives to the clay that the artist has modelled the consistency of stone. Similarly, under the influence of the Holy Ghost the most sin-stained souls wash out their stains in the burning waters of sincere repentance, and cast off the bonds of Satan; hearts hardened and warped by vice grow soft and correct themselves; weak souls grow strong and acquire energy and vigour, as did the souls of the Apostles at Pentecost. . . .

And because this interior fire has its centre in the very bosom of the Trinity, the souls that yield to its operations tend as to their normal, natural end towards divine union—union with God—in which is consummated the supernatural life.[34]

DOM COLUMBA MARMION (1858-1923)

MARMION'S JOURNAL, MARCH 3, 1900

When the Word espoused and endowed His Humanity, the Spouse being God, the dowry had to be divine. According to the Fathers and the Doctors of the Church, what the Word truly gave as dowry to His Humanity was the Holy Spirit, Who proceeds from Him as well as from the Father, and is substantially the plenitude of holiness. . . .

For some time I have felt more and more a special attraction towards the Holy Spirit. I have a great desire to be guided, led, moved in all things by the Spirit of Jesus. Our Lord, as Man, did nothing except under the impulsion of the Holy Spirit and under His dependence. Hence it followed that possessing in Himself and Himself alone—as to the hypostatic union—this Holy Humanity, the Word never operated or wrought anything in His Human Nature save through His Holy Spirit.

We too, have received the same Spirit in baptism, and in the Sacrament of confirmation. . . . All that, in our activity, comes from this *Holy* Spirit is holy. . . . He who yields himself up without reserve or resistance to this Spirit who is Father of the Poor, will be infallibly led by the same path as Jesus, and in the manner that Jesus wills for each one. This Spirit led Elizabeth to praise Mary, and Mary is led by the same Spirit of Jesus to magnify the glory of the Lord.

The Holy Spirit leads us to call upon the Father in the same way as Jesus did . . . to pray as is right, in offering the supplications He makes for us in our hearts. It is by Him that we do good to souls (the Apostles did so little before Pentecost). It is He Who fructifies all our activity.

I will strive to live in this Holy Spirit.

THE SPIRIT ENGRAVES THE DIVINE WORD ON THE SOUL

Christ, the Incarnate Word, together with His Father, gave us His Spirit on the day of our baptism, which made us children of the heavenly Father and Christ's own brethren. This Spirit abides in us. And what does He do in us, this Divine Spirit, the Spirit of Truth? He brings to our mind the words of Jesus. Our Lord Himself tells us so. What does this mean? It means that when we contemplate the actions and mysteries of Christ Jesus—either in reading the Gospel or a life of Our Lord—or when, under the Church's guidance, in the course of the liturgical year, one day it happens that some word, such as we have many times read and re-read without it having particularly struck us, suddenly stands out in supernatural relief in a way we have not hitherto known. It is a flash of light that the Holy Spirit makes all at once to rise from the depth of the soul; it is like the sudden revelation of a source of life hitherto unsuspected, like a new and wider horizon that opens out before the eyes of the soul; it is like a new world that the Spirit discovers for us. He Whom the liturgy names "the finger of God," engraves this Divine word on the soul, ever to remain there a light and principle of action; if the soul is humble and attentive, this Divine word works therein, silent but fruitful.

When we are faithful each day to consecrate a time, longer or shorter according to our aptitudes and duties of state, in speaking with our Heavenly Father, in gathering up His inspirations and listening to what the Holy Spirit "brings to mind," then the words of Christ, the *Verba Verbi*, as St. Augustine calls them, go on multiplying, inundating the soul with Divine Light and opening out in it fountains of life so that the soul's thirst may be ever assuaged.

Prayer: The True Voice of the Spirit within Us

Never forget that prayer is a *state*, and that with souls who seek God prayer becomes continuous, often in an unconscious manner, in the spiritual depths of the soul. It is there, in this sanctuary, that the Word espouses the soul in pure faith. . . . These silent longings, these sighings are the true voice of the Holy Spirit within us which touches the heart of God.[35]

LEONCE DE GRANDMAISON (1868-1927)

The Pursuit of God's Will

Doing God's will . . . consists in being content with the portion He has chosen for us; of being satisfied to flow along with the current He sets in motion; of seeing our lives in its true framework. When we seek this and embrace it and ask the proper directions from those ordained to guide us, we become docile and accustom ourselves to interpret the urgings of the Interior Master.

The pursuit of God's will, if it is sincere, will always bring us to its discovery. The Holy Spirit will supply what intelligence we lack to detect divine paths and signposts. But it is not sufficient just to know; we must fulfill and daily carry out this Holy Will unless we want to build an apostolic life on sand.[36]

Come Good Spirit, Holy Spirit! Make us see, make us love, make us cherish and embrace those ways chosen by the Divine Word in His power and wisdom and love. Show me that outside of those paths, so strange, so steep and difficult as they may seem at times, I would be lost. O Guide, Advocate and Consoler! O Spirit of Jesus, make me taste the ways which Christ has prepared for me.[37]

Lord, consume all that blocks your passage. Purify everything whether we see it or not, but which truly exists and prevents us from enjoying your presence and being sanctified in your truth. Jesus, free us from the secret attachments, from these unseen chains, from all that escapes our limited human vision. Let nothing come between us, Lord. Let nothing screen your Light from me. Let not my callousness prevent your anointing. Let not my set ways impede the Holy Spirit. Let me be docile to you; docile to the Holy Spirit; docile to the Father. Amen.[38]

PAUL CLAUDEL (1868-1955)

Pentecostal Hymn

Before He ascends to Heaven at the hour of noon,
The Master to faithful Apostles is promising a boon;
"The Spirit, the Comforter, in ten days you shall receive. . . .

"Expedient it is that My person depart, for I send you My soul,
That you may embrace My heart, My soul with your soul,
And the Spirit Who tells what things He has heard."

Wherefore, ten days past the Ascension, seven weeks since Easter having gone,
Around Mary clustered, the Church, in guide of Peter, James, and John,
Feels the Spirit of God like a torrent and His speech like a resonant word!

O sun of God's light among us! O Splendor of His light, conceived before day!
The body with water is cleansed and water with the spirit's play!
Nay, water could not suffice, He must recreate with swift fire. . . .

Thunder above our heads, great bells of this holy day!
For double-major the feast, feria of Truth's straight way.

The sun at the hour of Sext gleams, brighter than sight can endure.

Ah, heal Thou my mortal eyes! Awaken my sleeping heart!
Devouring Spirit, come! And death unto death impart!
O fullness of power that lives in fullness of sheer excess! . . . .

When evening comes, blotting out capital letters and rubrics,
And down to the last chapter, I have said every verse of my Office,
Without book or beads, I relax as the world has done. . . .

Two planets in slanting line, one low and the other high,
Are traveling after the sun as it fades down the Pentecost sky,
Like a silver falcon that hovers and a pearly dove that goes.

All is still, but the Spirit that contains all things within me cannot be held.
The Spirit that holds all together knows of the voice unquelled
Within me, its ceaseless cry like a water that ebbs and flows![39]

ST. THÉRÈSE OF LISIEUX (1873-1897)

Soon after my First Communion I went into retreat again for Confirmation, and I prepared myself with great care for the coming of the Holy Spirit; I can't understand how anyone could do otherwise before receiving this Sacrament of Love.

As it happened the ceremony was put off, and I was only too glad to have longer in retreat. How happy I was! Like the Apostles I waited for the promised Holy Spirit, and was overjoyed that soon I would be a perfect Christian, and have my forehead sealed eternally with the mystic cross of this great sacrament.

There was no rushing wind as on the first Pentecost, but just the gentle breeze which murmured on Mount Horeb to Elias. On that day I was given the strength to suffer, strength I was to need, for the martyrdom of my soul was going to begin very soon.[40]

MARTIN VONIER (1875-1938)

The Bride as the Sign of the Spirit

Even a superficial reading of the account given by St. Luke of the coming of the Spirit reveals the fact that the group of men on whom the Holy Ghost descended were the principal object of wonder on that day. The transformation that took place in them, the powers which they showed forth, the ecstasy in which they moved, were an overwhelming prodigy. The mighty wind and the parted tongues were transient signs; the eloquence of the disciples was the permanent sign. . . .

That body of Christians was the real and permanent sign of the coming of the Spirit. To the external symbols of wind and parted tongues of fire was added the more astonishing sign of human beings thus taken out of themselves and made an object of amazement to all men. This leads us to a consideration of paramount importance in the doctrine of the Spirit: the Spirit is truly said to have come because He has made use of created signs to show His advent and His presence. Now the principal created sign is that entirely transformed group of human beings, the hundred and twenty persons who had gone to the upper room with Peter and John, James and Andrew, Philip and Thomas, Bartholomew and Matthew, James of Alpheus and Simon Zelotes and Jude the brother of James, with the women and with Mary the Mother of Jesus and His brethren; they were the Church, and they were made by the Spirit the external sign of His having come forever. . . .

It will be necessary for the Church if she is to be a Pentecostal sign—in other words if she is to embody the Spirit, as Christ's humanity holds the divine Word—to keep forever the enthusiasm of the first Pentecost. She must be like one who is intoxicated with an entirely new life; she must speak to all men the wonderful things of God; she must be able to approach every man under the sun with the same message; she must proclaim, with an unfaltering voice, that Christ is risen from the dead and now sits at the right hand of God, for this is the Pentecostal message. She must work wonders, she must have the faith of miracles, she must have ecstasies, she must, in short, realise that all prophecies have been fulfilled: the prophecy of Joel, quoted by Peter on the first outpouring of the Spirit, must be true of the Church of all times. Spiritual life must be the possession of young men and old, great supernatural gifts must be abundant, faith in the coming Judgment and the second advent of Christ must be an uninterrupted hope. Unless these things be present, no body of men, however spiritually minded, would constitute a true sign of the Spirit.[41]

THE SPIRIT: THE GOD OF THE CHRISTIAN EXPERIENCE

By the divine action of the Holy Ghost we are made to feel, we are made to taste, we are made to enjoy the sublime things of God. So the Spirit Himself may be truly called the God of the Christian experience, and whatever metaphor can represent the ineffable joys of life is appropriate to the Holy Ghost. He is the breath of spring, He is the unction of the mind, He is the comforting voice, He is gladness of heart. He makes us believe with vision; He makes us hope with the feeling a child has when its hand is held in the warm palm of a strong man; He makes us love, not only with resolve and detachment, but with unspeakable tenderness of heart. This is the work of the Holy Ghost, and all the glorious marvels of the holiest Christian experience may thus be viewed and explained.[42]

DOM EUGÈNE VANDEUR (1875-1967)

The Fire of God

Lord Jesus, Thou hast said: "I am come to cast fire on the earth: and what will I, but that it be kindled?"

That is the prodigy which is taking place at this moment in the innermost depths of my being. Suddenly a fire has been lighted there—the saints are conscious of it—a fire which devours the soul and its powers. . . .

Who art Thou, O consuming fire, brought by Jesus Christ my Saviour? The Church replies to me that it is His Holy Spirit, the eternal Love of the Father and the Son, the Love inflaming the whole Trinity and the sacred humanity of Jesus. Thence it comes into my soul, my body; and behold me invaded by the same fire so as to burn, with God, in the same love which devours Him.

That is the daily wonder which my faith adores when, recollecting my faculties at the time of Holy Communion, I surrender myself to the love of the Sacred Heart of our Lord Jesus Christ. What a mutual gift! I give myself, opening to Him all the avenues of my soul, nothing remains hidden from Him; He invades my being even unto its remotest recesses. Then He breathes upon it the flames of that divine fire which devours His own humanity, the adorable burning bush which the prophet had recognized and reverenced, of which I am but a miserable representation.

Breathe upon me, Lord Jesus, that fire of the Holy Spirit invading the Host at the moment of consecration so as to change it into Thee, to make of it the august victim well-pleasing to the heavenly Father, which He takes unto Himself, so as to pour forth from it upon us all the fullness of blessings and graces! It is that Host which I have just received, Thyself, O Jesus, the sacred humanity delivering itself over to me, the fire it casts upon this earth which I am.

Sacred Heart of my Saviour, send forth into my own heart some beams from that Flame whom I adore, that Spirit which has just renewed the face of this earth of mine; laying hold upon my love, may

He transform it into Thine, causing me to communicate in the love of the Father, the Son, and the Holy Spirit![43]

GERTRUDE VON LE FORT (1876-1971)

PENTECOST

Your voice speaks:
Jubilation is my name and rejoicing is my countenance,
I am like a young meadow wreathed in dawn,
Like a sweet shepherd's pipe among the hills.
Hear me ye swelling valleys, hear me ye waving meadows,
hear me ye happy songful forests.
For I am no longer lonely among your splendours, I have become your
sister and one of your kin: greet me fair likeness of myself,
glad earth that the Lord has fulfilled.
Nearness is still far, Grace is yet but an upward step; He is in me as
eternally mine.
He has come over me as buds come on a spray, he has
sprung forth in me like roses on the hedgerows.
I bloom in the red-thorn of His love, I bloom on all my branches in the
purple of His gifts.
I bloom with fiery tongues, I bloom with flaming fulfillment, I
bloom out of the Holy Spirit of God.[44]

JOSEPH SCHRYVERS (1876-1945)

UNDER THE GUIDANCE OF THE DIVINE Spirit, ALL THINGS WORK TOGETHER FOR THE ADVANCEMENT OF THE SIMPLE SOUL

O Divine Spirit! Thou takest my hand, to lead me straight to my God. I wish to be docile; I wish to forget myself and to surrender myself to Thy direction. This, for me, is supreme wisdom.

The traveler who does not know the map of the country in which he journeys does not trust his own ideas; he employs a sure guide to accompany him.

And what do I know of the country of sanctity? All is strange to me: the inhabitants, the laws, the customs, the conditions, and even the language. Oh, that I may not go astray!

Moreover, I have enemies who are bent upon deceiving me. . . . Ah, how I need to distrust myself and to cling to my Guide!

This Guide is the Divine Spirit, the Paraclete, the Consoler in sadness and dejection, the Support in the difficulties of the way, the Light in darkness.

He is especially concerned with the sanctification of souls. What does the fate of empires matter to Him, provided that the souls He guides attain to holiness? His Providence governs the world, bestows crowns, confers power or takes it away, all as it pleases Him, all for the good of souls. Why are there revolutions, wars, epidemics, great social evils? Why are there persecutions? Why are feeble nations oppressed? Why does brutality triumph? Why are there public scourges, family sorrows, hecatombs of human life, the tears of mothers? Ah, how short-sighted is human reason! There are chosen souls, perhaps very many, whom these trials purify and sanctify. There are souls that, without these trials, would never work out their salvation. The entire world is not worth one of these souls. To have one single additional act of love from a little soul hidden in the obscurity of some hamlet, God would permit terrible catastrophes.

O wise and powerful ones of this age! You believe that you are the judges of the world, the dictators of peace or war. God sets little store by your power which endures for one day. You are instruments that serve Him for an instant; then you disappear. And the divine work goes on; and souls of good will are sanctified.

Not only is my Guide devoted to my soul and determined to sanctify it; He also sets in order all the means to accomplish the work. To Himself He reserves the choice of these means.

Under His guidance, all ways become good; all lead to the end. He is pleased to leave the soul in ignorance as to His plans. He conducts it over precipices and makes it climb steep mountains. He leads it into vast, uncultivated forests, exposes it to the inclemencies of the weather and to the teeth of wild beasts. Sometimes He conceals Himself from its sight.

But the surrendered soul does not lose courage. It has learned to forget self and to trust its Master. Soon the darkness is dispelled, calm returns, the way becomes straight. The Divine Guide is again at hand. He desires to teach the soul to give itself without reserve, to leave to Him the exclusive care of its sanctification.

Divine Spirit, let us march forth together. I abandon myself to Thee. No more fear, no more hesitation! I cast myself blindly upon the Bosom of Thy Providence. Lead me; sanctify me. My role is to efface myself, to disappear.[45]

KARL ADAM (1876-1966)

THE SPLENDOR OF WHITSUNTIDE

At Whitsuntide nature keeps high festival. Around us we see an overflowing energy of life, in flower and shrub and tree, in bird and in beast. It is an abundant, even an extravagant life. The power that called such luxuriance into being was no niggardly power, no miser dealing out his favours with anxious children. Consider the millions of blossoms, spread lavishly in field and wood, of which but a small fraction will ever come to fruit or seed. What generous luxuriance, splendid extravagance, rich exuberance! And out of this unstinted largesse spring the beauty of the world, its gay abundance, its rich and varied play of form and scent and colour.

There seems a special appropriateness in such splendor at Whitsuntide, when we are celebrating the feast of the Holy Spirit. It seems emblematic of His power, the rich language of abundant natural life announcing the great Giver of spiritual life. For it is the proper and characteristic quality of the Holy Spirit that He is the creative Spirit, the giver of the new life and of the abundant fullness of that life. That is the Church's meaning when she addresses the Holy Spirit, in the vesper hymn, as "Creative Spirit", when she hails Him as "fountain of life" and as "fire;" and when in the liturgy of the Mass she prays: "Send forth Thy Spirit and they shall be created; and Thou shalt renew the face of the earth."[46]

THE SPIRIT, SOURCE OF FAITH

Only the creative Spirit, who made the individual soul, can reach the innermost shrine of personality and fashion there a faith that, growing intimately and organically out of the individual personality, determines the whole mental and moral outlook of the believer. . . .

As a consequence, if it be genuine divine faith, the faith of a Christian is in very truth a "showing of the spirit and of the power" of the Holy Ghost. It is not we who believe, but the Holy Ghost within us. The experience of Pentecost is continually repeated, and our faith is in its essence nothing else than the pentecostal faith of the apostles.

From out of that pentecostal faith grows the pentecostal marvel of the new man. So soon as the loving importunities of the Holy Spirit have opened the soul's eyes to God and to His truth, then that truth bursts into the confused darkness of our natural being and illumines it with its brilliant radiance. Then does a man first realize the great gulf between what he is and what he should be. He is afraid, trembles and draws back. But whithersoever he may go, the loving importunity of the Holy Spirit pursues him, even to the most secret recesses of his soul. The new light may pierce him, yet it is constantly giving a new insight into things. He may kick against the goad, yet he finds himself with ever new yearnings for God and with new impulses towards good. A pitched battle begins between grace and freedom, the new love and the old, spirit and flesh, God and man; and the conflict is so fierce and thrilling, yet at the same time so glorious, that the angels of heaven rejoice to witness it.[47]

The Spirit Re-Creates Personality

The Christian in grace is a temple of the Holy Ghost, a heaven on earth, a being of mystery, a mystery full of deep silence and devout stillness, and yet a mystery which strikes a hidden spring of vigorous life and casts a radiant beauty over the soul. The result is a new man . . . The whole personality is reorganized. Its centre of gravity is now no longer the old, earthbound self, but the new self which is bound to God in the Holy Spirit. There descends upon the soul—as at Pentecost upon the apostles—a new power, a new love, a new and stronger will. Nor does it come from ourselves. It is not already present in our desolation, or in our prayer, or in our sorrow and penance. It comes from above—like the mighty wind of Pentecost—and breaks down what is old and decayed, so that the excellency of the power of God is made manifest in earthen vessels. Then is fulfilled the word of the prophets: "I will give you a new heart and put a new spirit within you. I will take away the stony heart out of your body and give you a heart of flesh."[48]

SISTER ELIZABETH OF THE TRINITY (1880-1906)

Prayer to the Trinity: November 21, 1904

O my God, Trinity whom I adore! Help me to become wholly forgetful of self, that I may be immovably rooted in Thee, as changeless and calm as though my soul were already in eternity. May nothing disturb my peace or draw me forth from Thee, O my unchanging Lord, but may I, at every moment, penetrate more deeply into the depths of Thy mystery!

Establish my soul in peace; make it Thy heaven, Thy cherished abode, and the place of Thy rest. Let me never leave Thee alone, but remain ever there, all absorbed in Thee, in living faith, plunged in adoration, and wholly yielded up to Thy creative action!

O my Christ whom I love! Crucified for love! Would that I might be the bride of Thy Heart! Would that I might cover Thee with glory and love Thee . . . even until I die of love! Yet I realise my weakness and beseech Thee to clothe me with Thyself, to identify my soul with all the movements of Thine own. Immerse me in Thyself; possess me wholly; substitute Thyself for me, that my life may be but a radiance of Thy life. Enter my soul as Adorer, as Restorer, as Saviour!

O eternal Word, Utterance of my God! I long to spend my life in listening to Thee; to become wholly "teachable," that I may learn all from Thee! Through all darkness, all privations, all helplessness, I yearn to keep my eyes ever upon Thee, and to dwell beneath Thy great light. O my beloved Star! so fascinate me that I may be unable to withdraw myself from thy rays!

O consuming Fire, Spirit of Love! Come down into me and reproduce in me, as it were, an incarnation of the Word; that I may be to Him a superadded humanity, wherein He may renew all His mystery! And Thou, O Father, bend down towards Thy poor little creature and overshadow her, beholding in her none other than Thy beloved Son in whom Thou art well pleased.

O my "Three," my all, my beatitude, infinite solitude, immensity wherein I lose myself! I yield myself to Thee as Thy prey. Immerse Thyself in me that I may be immersed in Thee, until I depart to contemplate in Thy light the abyss of Thy greatness![49]

Our God Is a Consuming Fire

St. Paul writes that our God is a consuming fire. That means a fire of love which destroys, transforms into itself everything that it touches. The joys of the divine embrace are renewed in the depths of our soul by an activity that never ceases. It is the embrace of love in a mutual and eternal delight. It is a renewal of the bond of love that takes place every moment. There are souls who have chosen this abode, there to rest forever, and "there is the silence wherein they are, as it were, lost." Delivered from their prison, they sail in the ocean of the divinity, finding no obstacle or difficulty in anything created. For these, the mystic death, of which St. Paul spoke yesterday is so simple and sweet! They think much less of spoliation and destruction which remains to be accomplished than of plunging themselves in the furnace of love that burns within them, and which is none other than the Holy Spirit.[50]

LUIS MARIA MARTINEZ (1881-1956)

Docility to the Spirit

. . . Our love for the Holy Spirit should be marked by loving docility, by full surrender, and by a constant fidelity that permits us to be moved, directed, and transformed by His sanctifying action.

Our love for the Father tends to GLORIFY Him; our love for the Son, to TRANSFORM ourselves into Him; our love for the Holy Spirit, to LET OURSELVES BE POSSESSED AND MOVED BY HIM.

In order to attain this holy docility to the motions of the Spirit, the soul must be so silent and recollected that it can hear His voice; so pure and so filled with light that it can clearly perceive the meaning of the divine inspiration; so surrendered to the will of God that it embraces that will without hesitation; and so selfless that it performs that will without stopping at any sacrifice. Love accomplishes all this alone, or through the virtues and gifts which it co-ordinates and directs; for love, as St. Paul teaches, "believes all things, hopes all things, endures all things."

Love brings recollection and silence to the soul. Whosoever loves, distinguishes among thousands of voices the voice of the beloved. Does not a mother know the voice of her child among all other sounds, does she not hear it even when she is asleep? Love causes silence because it brings solitude and recollection; because it concentrates all its activity and desire on the beloved. The Holy Spirit frequently speaks to souls, breathes upon them, and inspires them. But they do not hear Him except in the measure of their love for Him, in the proportion in which love has anointed them with silence. Closely united with the Holy Spirit through love, souls feel the secret palpitation of the heart of God.

One of the characteristics, then, that love for the Holy Spirit should have is this solicitous attention to the sound of His voice, to His inspirations, to His most delicate touches. We should struggle against all disturbances, all distracting noises; we must bravely detach ourselves from all creatures, from every affection. Little by little love will have power over our heart and spread its deep influence through all our faculties.

The voice of the Spirit is gentle; His movement is very delicate. To perceive it, the soul needs silence and peace. But it is not enough to hear: the divine language must be understood. . . . The things of the Spirit have a spiritual and secret sense that not everyone perceives. To know divine things, the soul has to be pure, and in proportion to its purity it judges spiritual things and penetrates inspirations. Such purity is produced by love and wondrously brought to perfection by it, for purity considered negatively is withdrawal from earthly things, while under its positive aspect it is deification; and love deifies by uniting the soul to God.

Human love, by the union it produces between those who love

each other, makes one penetrate the mind of the other, and in a certain manner guess his hidden thoughts. Who has not admired the amazing intuitions of the mother discovering what her little one suffers from its all but intelligible cry? Even so, divine love, leading the soul into the intimacies of God and bringing God to the soul, produces that marvelous understanding of spiritual things which we see in the lives of the saints. . . .

The loving soul perceives through silence the divine inspirations, and by its own purity discovers their deep meaning, allowing itself to be taken along, docile and gentle, by the breath of the Spirit. Love offers no resistance to that divine breath, because to give and to let itself be possessed, to surrender to the exigencies of infinite Love, are of its very essence. By its nature, love is the union of wills, the fusion of affections, of identical inclinations. . . .

One of the most intense and delicate joys of love is precisely this abandonment to the dispositions and action of the beloved, this sweet slavery that makes the soul lose its own sovereignty in order to surrender itself to love; this ineffable happiness of having a Master—sweeter perhaps than knowing oneself to be master of the Beloved. . . .

This sweet abandonment to all the movements of love is the characteristic mark of devotion to the Spirit. To love this divine Spirit is to let ourselves be taken along by Him, as the feather is carried along by the wind; to let ourselves be possessed by Him, as the dry branch is possessed by the fire that burns it; to let ourselves be animated by Him, as the sensitive strings of a lyre take life from the artist's touch. . . .

Undoubtedly this docility requires abnegation, for it will always be true that love and pain are proportionate, and that the perfection of the one cannot be attained without the perfection of the other. The soul abandoned to the Holy Spirit exposes itself to every sacrifice, every immolation. The soul of Jesus was possessed by the Holy Spirit in a singular manner. We shall never comprehend to what depths of pain He was led thereby.

The path of the divine Dove is ever the same. His flight is always toward Calvary. The shining white wings can always be described above the blessed Cross, for that is where love is to be found on earth, as in heaven it is found in the bosom of the Father.[51]

The Consuming Fire of the Spirit of Love

When charity pours itself out, it increases. Fire is like that: the more it burns, the more intense is the flame. In a conflagration stirred by a strong wind, the dry stalks tremble, cross over each other, and the victorious flames throw themselves on this fuel, spreading rapidly in their eagerness to soar upward. So with the soul touched by the flame of merciful love; when the wind of the Spirit of God blows over it, it is on fire within, bursting forth with uncontrollable strength, enfolding the miseries of others; and the more it goes out of itself, the more it burns; the more it does for its neighbor, the nearer to heaven rise the flames of its love.[52]

PIERRE TEILHARD DE CHARDIN (1881-1955)

Fire over the Earth

In the beginning was *Power*, intelligent, loving, energizing. In the beginning was the *Word*, supremely capable of mastering and moulding whatever might come into being in the world of matter. In the beginning there were not coldness and darkness: there was the *Fire*. . . .

Blazing Spirit, Fire, personal, super-substantial, the consummation of a union so immeasurably more lovely and more desirable than that destructive fusion of which all the pantheists dream: be pleased yet once again to come down and breathe a soul into the newly formed, fragile film of matter with which this day the world is to be freshly clothed.

I know we cannot forestall, still less dictate to you, even the smallest of your actions; from you alone comes all initiative—and this applies in the first place to my prayer.

Radiant Word, blazing Power, you who mould the manifold so as to breathe your life into it; I pray you, lay on us those your hands—powerful, considerate, omnipresent, those hands which do not (like our human hands) touch now here, now there, but which plunge into the depths and the totality, present and past, of things so as to reach us simultaneously through all that is most immense and most inward within us and around us.[53]

Lord Jesus, when it was given time to see where the dazzling trial of particular beauties and partial harmonies was leading, I recognized that it was all coming to centre on a single point, a single person: yourself. Every presence makes me feel that you are near me; every touch is the touch of your hand; every necessity transmits to me a pulsation of your will.

That the Spirit may always shine forth in me, that I may not succumb to the temptation that lies in wait for every act of boldness, nor ever forget that *you alone* must be sought in and through everything, you, Lord, will send me—at what moments only you know—deprivations, disappointments, sorrow.

What is to be brought about is more than a simple union: it is a *transformation*, in the course of which the only thing our human activity can do is, humbly, to make ourselves ready, and to accept.[54]

RAOUL PLUS (1882-1958)

God Is Perpetually with the Soul in Grace

St. John, resting on the heart of Jesus! . . . We envy his familiarity! There is another: the Holy Spirit is in my own heart . . . This familiarity is mine!

The Holy Spirit is the *highest* reality—*donum Dei altissimi*—the most intimately *ours*—*dulcis hospes animae*! It is a reality which I may attain either by ascending to the ineffable splendours of the heart of God, or by descending into the great silent depths of my divinized being.

When we say: The Holy Ghost dwells in the souls of the just, we do not mean that the Third Person alone abides there. Where the Holy Ghost is, there also are the Father and the Son. This dwelling-place is *attributed* to the Spirit of Love because it is essentially a work of love. . . .

Those who communicate receive the body of Christ—a wondrous fact. But His body lasts only the short time as the sacred species.

He who lives in a state of grace possesses the divinity of the Father, of the Word, and of the Holy Ghost, not only for a quarter of an hour, but for as long as he will, and, if it is his wish, forever.

Is it a lesser thing to receive lastingly the divinity of the Father, the Son, and the Holy Ghost, than to receive, when it must inevitably pass, the Sacred Humanity of the Incarnate Word?

This detracts in no way from the happiness of communion—rather it adds, in a singular manner, to the happiness of living in a state of grace.[55]

God present in us, abiding within us, living within us . . . Let us invest these phrases with their full wealth of meaning. What words can explain the mystery of the constant companionship of the Three Persons *in the centre of our souls*, and their wish to share it with us?

Within me . . .

At this very moment, God the Father begets His Son. The Father and the Son together send for the Holy Ghost. This invisible and mysterious travail of the Holy Trinity, which constitutes its peculiar being, takes place in me now, invisibly but in very truth.

Within me . . .

I close my eyes. At this very moment, far down in the depth of my soul, in a dark basement strangely lighted up at times, my inmost being gushes forth in a continuous stream . . . *And right down there*, beside my meagre thread of life, the great fountain of eternal Life silently bubbles forth.

Let my faith be ever watchful, listening for the springing waters of eternal life *deep down within me . . .*

Let me admire above all how God unites me in a wonderful consortium with the inmost secret of His being.

I participate through grace in the divine generation of the Word by the Father which takes place in me. I am involved by means of grace in the continuous sending of the Holy Ghost which takes place within me.[56]

EDWARD LEEN C.S.SP. (1885-1944)

THE DIVINE EMISSARY OF PEACE

The Son of man . . . established terms of peace [between an offended God and sinful man], and in that His work as mortal man was ended. It devolved on the Holy Ghost to strengthen, consolidate and perfect that peace so dearly purchased. Jesus had swept away misunderstanding: it remained for the Holy Ghost to create a perfect understanding. It is for that He is sent. When a treaty has been struck between two powers, a representative from each is sent to reside close to the seat of government of the other. Christ our Chief has ascended to the court of our heavenly Father, where He lives, "always living to make intercession for us." Keeping the Sacred Wounds of His flesh ever before the eyes of God, He constantly pleads the cause of humanity at the throne of God. The Creator on His side, at the request of Jesus, sends His ambassador to represent His interests in the world of souls. That divine envoy is none other than the Holy Ghost. . . . .

The Holy Spirit is always in the soul, but when this latter has been justified in the blood of Christ He begins to exist there in a manner entirely different from the former manner. He is now there as "Divine Envoy." Having been already in the kingdom of the soul, He now takes up new functions there. He is invested by God the Father with the role of ambassador to the court of man's soul.[57]

The Spirit Illumines the Truths of Faith

The Spirit of Jesus not only consoles hearts: He enlightens minds as well. Mutual communication of secrets is a characteristic of friendship. Most men find it difficult to carry alone the burden of some important piece of knowledge. It is a profound relief to share the burden with one who is loyal, devoted, and trustworthy. . . . The Holy Ghost is laden with all the secrets of God—secrets not only of surpassing interest in themselves but of great import for the creature. . . . These deep things of God, the Holy Ghost is all eagerness to communicate to the soul, as is the tendency of friendship. Unfortunately the creature, too often, is a listless and inattentive listener and the accents of the Spirit fall on deaf ears. But, nevertheless, even the most heedless catch, at times, something of the divine whisper. Those who are better disposed and are most exact in satisfying the obligation of the divine friendship are favoured with many an insight into the mysteries of the supernatural life. To none other than the Holy Ghost are to be attributed those sudden illuminations which, at times, cast a flood of light on the mysteries of faith, and on the words of Sacred Scripture. When the meaning of the sacred text is laid bare in this manner, there is a deepening of faith in, and a strengthening of attachment to, the doctrine and Person of Jesus. The soul becomes, as it were, more malleable to His teachings when, through the radiance shed on them by the Spirit of God, the mysteries of religion are lighted up, their inner harmonies are disclosed and their correspondence with all the needs and aspirations of the human heart are revealed. A great love for them follows.[58]

The Radiant Presence of the Spirit

. . . The airman, when beating his way upwards through the atmosphere vitiated by earth's exhalations, and then through the heavy clouds hanging like a canopy over that atmosphere . . . emerges suddenly into a world flooded with unstained splendour, a world of pure sunshine, a world where the radiant beams that stream directly from the great source of all material light suffer no dimness. This experience bears an analogy to that which thrills the mind of the theologian, when having mounted through all the different degrees of God's presence in nature, he emerges into the contemplation of this radiant presence of the Holy Ghost in the soul through divine habitual grace. In the lower regions the light that streams from the Divinity falls on the soul in broken and refracted rays. Here the Everlasting Fount of light and glory pours out its beams on the soul through the intervening veil of faith. That veil does not refract, distort or divert those beams; it merely arrests the radiance which otherwise would scorch and shrivel the soul as yet inapt to bear their full splendour.[59]

ROMANO GUARDINI (1885-1968)

Christ, after Receiving the Spirit at Baptism

What a privilege it must have been to see the Lord in that early period of abundance when he carried holiness into the crowds. How straightly he spoke to the souls of men! Pressed forward by the *élan* of the Spirit, he reached out to people with both hands. The rush of the Holy Spirit swept the kingdom of God forward, and the human spirit, shaken by the force that demands entry, felt it beat against the door. The accounts of these first events are vibrant with spiritual power. Thus Mark: "And they were astonished at his teaching; for he was teaching them as one having authority, and not as the Scribes." They were "astonished," literally shaken out of themselves. Such was the divine power that poured from his words. Jesus' sentences were not merely correct and pointed as were those of the Scribes, they were the words of one "having authority!" His speech stirred; it tore the spirit from its security, the heart from its rest; it commanded and created. It was impossible to hear and ignore. . . .

Then, buoyed by the stream of the Spirit, came the first healings: "Now Simon's mother-in-law was keeping her sick bed with a fever, and they immediately told him about her. And drawing near, he took her by the hand and raised her up; and the fever left her at once, and she began to wait on them." First the single old woman in her house, then the many; stirring accounts of innumerable sick being carried through the cool evening to the Master's door. In the loving, healing strength of the Spirit, Jesus looms like a rescuing cliff above the tides of human suffering.[60]

The Spirit Gives Hope

The Holy Ghost teaches us to understand Christ, and in Christ, God; Christ, and in Him, ourselves. It is the kind of understanding which comes from the heart, not from the intellect. It is true comprehension; more than that, it is illumination.

The Holy Ghost gives the answers to those questions which the mind cannot answer because the mind invariably couples the word "why" with the word "I." "Why must I endure this suffering? Why am

I denied what others have? Why must I be the way I am, live the way I do?" These are some of the most essential and decisive questions in the life of the individual, and to those questions men and books remain silent. The true answer comes only when our heart is free from revolt and bitterness; when our will has come to terms with life *as it is for us*, recognizing in it the working of the will of God. The intellect may acquiesce readily enough, but this is not sufficient: instruction must go deeper; acceptance must come from our inmost heart. Only then will we find the answer to the WHY, and with it, peace, for truth alone brings peace: This is the work of the Holy Ghost. . . .

The hope of the Christian is linked to the Holy Ghost. Our life is shrouded in insufficiency and darkness. Faith teaches us that there is a mysterious process of *becoming* in us; the becoming of the new man, fashioned in the image of Christ; the becoming of the new heaven and the new earth of which the secret Revelation speaks. But this becoming is hidden and everything we perceive within ourselves and around us seems to belie it. Therefore we stand in need of hope—it springs from the Holy Ghost, for it is He who effects this becoming. He is the recreator of creation; He fashions the future which is to become eternity. He alone can assure us of this future.

Our own being is hidden from us. The Scriptures tell man what he is and he must believe it. He must not only believe in God, but must accept God's message and promise about his own Christian destiny. This is not always easy and we must pray to the Holy Ghost for that inmost assurance which we call faith and hope, and which is sustained by Love.[61]

KARL BARTH (1886-1968)

The word "spirit," in Greek *pneuma* means: breath, wind, spirit. Wind is a movement of air from one place to another. It was here, and now is there. This is both the image and the reality of man's regeneration by the Holy Spirit: God's Spirit was with God and now is with man. The Holy Spirit is then God going from one place to another, from his place to our place, from the height of his majesty to the baseness of our sin, from the holiness of his glory to the misery of our weakness. The Holy Spirit is God giving us the freedom we were seeking in vain within ourselves: freedom for him. . . .

The Holy Spirit brings about the new creation. Being God, his contact with us means a complete change. Where the Holy Spirit is, there we cannot remain as we are. The Holy Spirit attacks us, even kills us that we may live again. And this must be a continuous death because the "old man within us is a fool who ever again allows himself to come up to the surface and who ever again needs to be put back under the surface of the water of baptism, in order to be drowned. Our new birth is not a fact accomplished once for all. . . .

If we wanted to give a material description of the Holy Spirit, we must say he is the Spirit of love. And we might also step into the theology of the Trinity and show that the Holy Spirit is, already in God himself, the bond between the Father and the Son, at the same time the means and expression of their love. Let us confine ourselves to stressing that the Holy Spirit, being God "for us," is the very reality of the divine love. . . . . It is not in vain that the two definitions of God in the New Testament are: *God is Spirit* (John 4:24) and *God is Love* (I John 4:8).[62]

NOTES

1. *Meditations and Devotions of the Late Cardinal Newman* (New York: Longmans Green, 1893), pp. 397-398.
2. *Ibid.*, pp. 403-404.
3. *Conférences de Notre Dame de Paris par Le R.P. Henri-Dominique Lacordaire* (Paris: Sagnier et Bray, 1848), Book III, pp. 58-59.
4. *Lettres du Vénerable Père Libermann présentées par P. L. Vogel* (Paris: Desclee de Brouwer, 1965), pp. 190-191.
5. *Living with God* (New York: Catholic Book Publishing Co., 1949), pp. 254-255.
6. *The Internal Mission of the Holy Ghost* (London: Burns and Oates, 1895), pp. 25-26.
7. *Ibid.*, p. 45.
8. *Ibid.*, p. 49.
9. *Ibid.*, pp. 20-21.
10. *Ibid.*, pp. 28-29.
11. *The Prayers of Kierkegaard.* Edited by Perry D. Le Fevre (Chicago: University of Chicago Press, 1969), p. 109.
12. *Ibid.*, p. 108.
13. *Ibid.*, p. 107.
14. *Ibid.*, p. 106.
15. *Ibid.*, p. 105.
16. From *The Mysteries of Christianity* (St. Louis: B. Herder, 1947), pp. 172-173.
17. *The Indwelling of the Holy Spirit in the Souls of the Just.* Translated by Sidney A. Raemers (Westminster: The Newman Press, 1955), pp. 237-239.

18. *Poems of Gerard Manley Hopkins*. Edited by Robert Bridges. 2nd Edition (Oxford University Press, 1938), p. 26.

19. *Spiritual Journal of Lucie-Christine* (1870-1908). Translated by A. Poulain (St. Louis: Herder, 1915), p. 16.

20. *Ibid*., p. 20.

21. *Ibid*., p. 26.

22. *Ibid*., p. 62.

23. *Ibid*., p. 87.

24. *Ibid*., p. 144.

25. *Ibid*., p. 242.

26. *Ibid*., p. 261.

27. *Ibid*., p. 330.

28. *Cardinal Mercier's Conferences. Delivered to His Seminarists at Mechlin in 1907*. Translated by J.M. O'Kavanagh (New York: Benziger, 1910), p. 121.

29. *Ibid*., p. 84.

30. *Exact source unknown*.

31. *The Forgotten Paraclete*. Translated by E. Leahy (New York: Benziger, 1924).

32. *Ibid*., p. 7.

33. *Ibid*., pp. 36-37.

34. *Ibid*., pp. 40-43.

35. *The Trinity in Our Spiritual Life. An Anthology of the Writings of Dom Columba Marmion*, compiled by Dom Raymond Thibaut (Westminster: Newman Press, 1954), pp. 249-250, 236-237, 247.

36. *Come, Holy Spirit. Meditations for Apostles*. Translated by Joseph O'Connell (Chicago: Fides, 1956), p. 64.

37. *Ibid*., p. 29.

38. *Ibid*., p. 86.

39. "Pentecostal Hymn," in *Paul Claudel*. Translated by Sister M. David (New York: Pantheon Books, 1943), pp. 51-67.

40. *The Story of a Soul. The Autobiography of Saint Thérèse of Lisieux*. Translated by Michael Day (Westminster: Newman Press, 1952), p. 55.

41. *The Collected Works of Abbot Vonier* Volume II. *The Church and the Sacraments* (Westminster: The Newman Press), pp. 14-16.

42. *Ibid*., p. 91.

43. *Pledge of Glory. Meditations on the Eucharist and the Trinity*. Translated by Dominican Nuns (Westminster: Newman, 1958), pp. 167-169.

44. "Pentecost" in *Hymns to the Church*. Translated by Margaret Chanler (New York: Sheed and Ward, 1942), p. 49.

45. *The Gift of Oneself*. Translated by a Religious of Carmel (Bettendorf, Iowa: Carmel, 1943), pp. 48-51. Copyright: Newman Press.

46. *Christ Our Brother* Translated by Justin McCann (New York: Macmillan, 1961), p. 146.

47. *Ibid.*, pp. 164-166.

48. *Ibid.*, p. 171.

49. *Reminiscences of Sister Elizabeth of the Trinity. Servant of God.* Trans. by a Benedictine of Stanbrook Abbey. (Westminster: Newman, 1952), p. 233.

50. *Ibid.*, p. 199.

51. *The Sanctifier.* Translated by Sister M. Aquinas (Paterson, N.J.: St. Anthony Guild, 1961), pp. 68-72.

52. *Ibid.*, p. 293.

53. *Hymn of the Universe* (New York: Harper and Row, 1965), pp. 21-22.

54. *Ibid.*, pp. 153-154.

55. *Living with God* (New York: Benziger, 1923), pp. 18-20.

56. *Ibid.*, pp. 70-72.

57. *The Holy Ghost and His Work in Souls* (New York: Sheed and Ward, 1939), pp. 172-173.

58. *Ibid.*, pp. 228-229.

59. *Ibid.*, pp. 159-160.

60. *The Lord.* Translated by Elinor Castendyk (Chicago: Henry Regnery, 1954), pp. 40-41.

61. *Prayer in Practice.* Translated by Prince Leopold of Lowenstein-Wertheim (New York: Pantheon, 1957), pp. 117-119.

62. *The Faith of the Church. A Commentary on the Apostle's Creed According to Calvin's Catechism.* Edited by Jean-Louis Leuba. Translated by Gabriel Vananian (New York: Meridian Books, 1948), pp. 130-131.

French (Limoges) thirteenth century Champleve enamel, copper-gilt, EUCHARISTIC DOVE, Metropolitan Museum of Art, The Cloisters Collection.

Chapter VIII

THE HOLY SPIRIT IN THE CONTEMPORARY AGE

Introduction

The relationship of men of the twentieth century to the Spirit of God bears some common features with the early days of Christianity. The ordeals of Dietrich Bonhoeffer and Alfred Delp hark back to the age of martyrs, while Delp's beautiful prison commentary recalls the heart-rending cries of Eulpus and Polycarp. This century has no dearth of voices, like Merton's, who have reminded us that as St. Paul earlier pointed out, the Spirit will indeed pray within us if we let Him.

Much more than the immediately preceding century, the twentieth can indeed be called the Age of the Spirit. "The Spirit has a way of defeating human calculations," declared Carmelite Father Cyril Papali in 1957. "Often it is just when your archeologists are preparing to shelve the Church as an interesting fossil that she erupts into unprecedented activity." To anyone who has witnessed over twenty thousand Catholics gathered together in praise of God at recent annual charismatic conferences, these words seem quite prophetic.

The writings of twentieth century theologians are full of warnings that the Spirit cannot be limited, that the charismatic is not dead in the Church, that the Spirit breathes where he will. In the first half of the century, Protestant churches saw the growth of a "pentecostal" movement in their ranks. Much to their surprise, the Holy Spirit became a forceful living reality in the lives of a small group of Catholics gathered for a retreat in 1966 at Duquesne University, Pittsburgh—a story ably described in Kevin and Dorothy Ranaghan's *Pentecostal Catholics*.

No one can deny that this new charismatic movement, which has grown in the Catholic Church from the Duquesne retreat, is changing the Church. In America, groups of laymen have formed covenants to live and praise God in truly Christian communities, united by the love of the Spirit. Throughout parishes and religious orders, those whose lives have been touched by the Spirit gather in groups for spontaneous prayer and sharing of the experience of God in their lives. Countless members of the clergy have gained new life in their apostolates; laity and religious have experienced a reawakening of their prayer life, a deeper commitment to Christ, and greater realization of the beauty of Scripture and power of the Word of God to enlighten and heal. Touched by the manifest love existing in such groups of committed Christians, even souls enmeshed by the sins and temptations abounding on every side in twentieth century urban life have found the liberating force of the Spirit freeing them from their subservience to dope and other trappings of the Spirit of Evil.

Nevertheless, some Christians, seeing their Roman brethren engaging in "tongues" and praying for the Spirit's healing power to descend upon their fellow men, have been genuinely scandalized. For them, perhaps the Protestant Frederick Bruner's analysis may prove enlightening: "Perhaps indeed, the phenomenon of tongues is a voice calling the people to hear what the Spirit is capable of saying and doing in a Church that listens."

Since the beginning of Christianity, members of the Church have been urged to listen to the voice of the Spirit in their individual lives and in their Christian communities. At the same time, from the earliest days, Christian leaders have had to remind their flock that they must also listen to the voice of the established Church's hierarchy. Finding the proper means between the two has posed a problem throughout the history of the Church from the very days of Ignatius and Clement.

Echoing the idea of many twentieth century theologians, Rahner, in urging openness to the Spirit, pointed out that "God has not resigned in favor of the Church's administrative apparatus." He warned, however, that "all charismatic and pentecostal gifts must ever remain IN the Church." (This sentence was published in 1966 and was possibly written before the emergence of the American charismatic movement. The term "charismatic" in Europe at the time had a different connotation.) Cardinal Suenens reminded us that in striking a delicate balance between older and newer attitudes, a delicate discernment is needed. To those who find the new movements and forms of prayer disquieting, it may be some comfort to read Suenens' reassuring words that the Spirit of God is still indeed in the Church to guide in this discernment. Often what seems revolutionary is but a return to sources, and the Spirit will Himself enlighten Christians concerning which innovations to accept—if only they listen. While prayerfully listening, however, it seems wise to remember, as Rahner has noted, that when the Christian assumes the attitude of prayerful listening, he indeed "reckons with the incalculable."

SISTER M. MADELEVA WOLFF (1887-1964)

INVITATION TO THE PARACLETE

In wonder
Of thunder.
In love

And the Dove,
In the Father's Word
Heard:
In these you came.

Let me mind
The wind,
And desire
The fire.
Let me claim
The flame:
Let my tongue be stirred
With your diverse Word.

To me frightened, dumb,
Wise, bitter sweet
Paraclete,
Come![1]

JOHN T. McMAHON (1893-)

THE HOLY SPIRIT IS PERSONALLY PRESENT WITHIN US

We owe it to the Holy Spirit to believe that He is in us, not merely by His graces and gifts, but *personally*, and as really as Jesus Christ is in the Tabernacle, though in a different way. Every soul in the state of grace is a living tabernacle of the Holy Ghost, and as we are obliged to adore and honour Jesus Christ on the altar, so too are we bound to honour the Holy Ghost in our souls.

The presence of Our Lord in the Blessed Sacrament on the altars of the wide world, present day and night, is proof of the boundless love of God for us. But the presence of the Holy Ghost in our souls is still more amazing because God's presence in the Blessed Sacrament will cease on the last day, whereas the presence of the Holy Ghost in our souls will never cease. It will last for all eternity. . . .

Many times each day let us resolve to light Him lamps of love by our acts of love, by short aspirations of adoration, of sorrow for our sins and faults, a word of love, a call of desire: "Dear Guest of my soul, dear Friend of all my years, I adore You within me, I am sorry for my sins and my neglect. I love You, I need You. I want You, Holy Spirit."

He will increase His graces and fill the home of our hearts with His light and warmth, a guide to our minds and a glow in our hearts.

Holy Spirit, God of Love, I adore You really and truly in my soul,

O give me Your Holy Love.

Holy Spirit, God of Peace, really and truly in my soul, give me Your blessed peace which surpasses all understanding.

Holy Spirit, God of Light, really and truly in my soul, give me Your blessed light that I may see all things clearly.

Holy Spirit, God of joy and consolation, really and truly in my soul, fill me with Your joy and consolation.

Holy Spirit, God of strength, really and truly in my soul, give me Your divine strength that I may do all I do well.

Holy Spirit, living within me, whisper to me, prompt me, inspire me to hear with my ears, to heed with my heart, and to act with my will.

Holy Spirit, truly and really in my soul, restrain my impetuousity until I consult You before I act.[2]

ROBERT EDWARD BRENNAN, O.P. (1897-1975)

The Holy Spirit as Spiritual Director

Christians find it hard, often impossible to get personal direction in the affairs of their souls. . . . Growth in Christian virtue has become largely a matter of private relationship between God and the soul. . . . One may have the benefit of counsel on occasion; in most cases, however, the followers of Christ must rely on the inspirations of the Paraclete for their advance in perfection. . . . .

Someone once asked the saintly Irish workman, Matt Talbot, the name of his spiritual director. "The Holy Ghost," said Matt. Just so. And for most of us, it must be the same Divine Comforter who shows us our end in life, and gives us the means of attaining it. This he does by creating in us certain dispositions to goodness; and more particularly, by giving us sanctifying grace and his sevenfold system of virtues and gifts.[3]

SISTER MARY OF THE HOLY TRINITY (1901-1942)

God Speaks: Our Roots Must Be Planted in God

"My little daughter, thank Me in that you have no longer anything to do with money and material arrangements; thank Me that you are able to be entirely at the service of the Spirit.

"Be thankful and rejoice; the joys of the Spirit await you, you who have followed me . . .

"See with what materials I founded My Church; a few souls of goodwill—grace flowing through the Sacraments (so soberly instituted)

"The redemptive work of the Cross—

"The Omnipotence of the Holy Spirit, My Spirit—that is all!

"Was it a well coordinated organization? Not even that.

"Nevertheless My Church was founded, surrendered to the impetuous breath of life, to the initiative of those who are Mine.

"It was founded because its roots were established."

"When you work, you are inclined to think too much that the fruit depends on the branches; it is the roots that require care. They must be planted in God."[4]

ALBERT DONDEYNE (1901-)

To believe in the Holy Ghost means that we believe that the Spirit of God is still present in the Church in this twentieth century, and that He is at work in it as He was in the first Christian community. We believe that the Spirit of God is now present wherever God's word is preached in the Lord's name and is listened to with faith, and that He insures man an effective salvation, liberation, and resurrection. It is in the last analysis this concurrence of the proclamation of God's word and the resurrectional presence of the Spirit of God that constitutes the significance of Christianity as God's message and work of salvation . . .

However, the Spirit of God is not a magic force which befalls man from the outside. What the Holy Spirit operates in us, says St. Paul, is rather something like an inner disposition, a longing for the things of the spirit. He prompts us to seek the things that are above . . . And in fact the gift of the Spirit of God is nothing less than the presence of God's love in man which enables him to love the things of God . . .[5]

FRANCES CARYLL HOUSELANDER (1901-1954)

THE HOLY SPIRIT AND THE EUCHARIST

Love must begin from within. It must be sown in the inmost darkness of the human heart, and take root and flower from the dust that man is.

This can only happen if the Holy Spirit descends from heaven and penetrates human nature, as the rays of the sun and summer rain come down into the earth, warming and irrigating the seed that is sown there and quickening it.

Christ sowed the seed of His life in us when He sowed the world with the drops of His Blood from the Cross. Now it is Christ in the

Host who draws down the Holy Spirit. For the Holy Spirit is the Eternal Love between the Father and the Son. Love which cannot resist the plea of the silence, the patience, the obedience of the Sacred Host.

In the Host Christ gives Himself to live the ordinary life as it is today, to live it fully in all its essentials, and to take into Himself, into His own living of the Host-life, the most ordinary, the most numerous, seemingly the most mediocre lives, bestowing upon them His own power to bring down the Spirit of Love.[6]

FATHER CYRIL PAPALI, O.C.D. (1902-)

PLEA FOR A NEW PENTECOST, 1957

The Holy Ghost has a way of defeating human calculations. Often it is just when your archeologists are preparing to shelve the Church as an interesting fossil, that she erupts into unprecedented activity. That is almost what is happening at present. It is only the beginning yet; but everything seems to indicate that a Pentecost is just around the corner. In his radio broadcast of December 8, 1954, to the Young Women of the Italian Catholic Action, the Pope pronounced these almost prophetic words: "And We too pray that the divine breath of grace, like with 'rush of a mighty wind' at Pentecost may fill not only your *Domus*, your house, but the whole Church. We pray Jesus to hasten the day—which must come—in which a new mysterious effusion of the Holy Ghost will envelop all the soldiers of Christ and send them—bearers of salvation—among all the suffering of the world. And these will be better days for the Church; and they will be—through the Church—better days for the whole world."[7]

LEON CARDINAL SUENENS (1904-)

THE SPIRIT, GUIDE OF THE EVOLUTION OF THE CHURCH

The Holy Spirit has been given to the Church, in particular to guarantee its fidelity to the mission which has been confided to it and which it accomplishes through all the contingencies of history. But it belongs also to the Spirit, we have said, to guide it and introduce it progressively in the plenitude of the truth. There is a delicate discernment to accomplish between that which belongs to authentic tradition and that which upholds purely human tradition. Much confusion comes from the fact that customs and usages of only a century or less are confused with true tradition which goes back to the origins, and which in the course of the ages, has sometimes been obscured. Very often, that which appears revolutionary is only a return to the sources, beyond customs without roots in the past. . . . The Lord has not wished to leave the travail of discernment to the sole play of an individual interpretation. It is his Spirit which leads each phase of the evolution. It is He who helps in extricating the response truly conformed to tradition, gradually, as new problems arise. . . .

We must open our souls to the Spirit who speaks, who works, who leads his Church.[8]

YVES MARIE JOSEPH CONGAR (1904-)

The Living Water

The Fathers had a predilection for comparing the Holy Spirit's action with that of the rain or the sun from which every created being benefits according to its nature, or to that of the mind and nervous system which affects each part of the body according to its function and needs. . . .

If the Church is alive and fruitful, if she is to have a message and a special love for everything which comes into existence through space and time, if the Spirit is that living water in her that was promised by Jesus, and which, as it streams along, endlessly renews the foliage of the living trees whose leaves, according to the Apocalypse, serve for the healing of the nations, then just as the sap rises up into the branches, producing a constant succession of leaves, flowers, and fruit, so the Spirit is constantly creating initiatives of every kind, every sort of activity and movement. . . .

The Spirit of Communion

The Holy Spirit is the conductor of the full orchestra of the Church's life, and the invisible controller of her communion.

Nothing less than the Spirit of God could have the power to bring so many different realities into unity and yet to respect their differences, and this, in fact, is the Spirit's special work. We have seen that he is given to the whole and to every part with regard to that part's function in the whole (for the building up of the body). He is intrinsically a Spirit of Communion . . . As Spirit he is the inner law of the mystical Body, as a whole and in its parts. It is not surprising that St. Thomas considered that the grace of the Spirit is the essential element in the new law, and that tradition has often perceived in the Christian Pentecost, the successor of the Jewish Pentecost, the feast of the gift of the law, the coming of the new law, the communion of the most widely differing members in the same unity. This indeed is the Holy Spirit's special work: to bring plurality and diversity into unity—without violence, and by an interior stimulation that acts as a spontaneous and joyful initiative in the individual.

By his nature he is the communication of a unity to many, who retain their manifold distinction, a unity which these many discover to be their fulfillment and joy. He is essentially Communion. That is why the most profound and comprehensive remark about him is that which concludes the First Epistle to the Corinthians: "The grace that comes through our Lord Jesus Christ, the love that is God, and the fellowship (i.e. the communion, the communication) that is ours in the Holy Spirit be with you all!"[9]

KARL RAHNER (1904-)

THE SPIRIT: THE SOURCE OF OUR PRAYER

The Spirit of God dwelling within us as a great light in all our darkness, is the source of our prayer. He is not only God before Whom we kneel in supplication; He is working in us and for us, by His inspirations, especially when we are engaged in that most important of all our activities—prayer. In itself, our prayer consists of but dry words in arid minds; our pious feelings are in themselves but sickly plants languishing in the poor soil of our souls. But, through the power of the Holy Ghost within us, the words of our prayers become winged words, light-filled words, words that rise to the throne of God; and our pious feelings take deeper root, and blossom into spiritual strength and beauty. Thus, through our prayer, the Holy Spirit within us worships the Father and pleads for us "with unspeakable groanings;" and sometimes in our prayer we shall experience something of God's eternal joy in His own infinity and splendour. Herein is the secret of the great dignity of human prayer. . . . Mighty things, far beyond our understanding, occur within us when we say: "Our Father." They may seem to us to be drily spoken and to savour of presumption; but when sincerely spoken, the inner reality to which they correspond is something glorious. We are baptized children of God, professing our belief in Him and our love for Him; therefore the Spirit of God truly lives within us and speaks in us. Through the Holy Ghost dwelling within us, the words: "Our Father" are filled with a power of worship which links them with the praise of God by the Angelic choirs in Heaven. . . .

The Holy Ghost is our help in prayer. When we are overcome with fatigue and spiritual dryness, so that the words we speak seem to fall heavy and lifeless about our feet, He prays within us with that freshness of praise we cannot command. When our lack of faith seems to wither the prayer on our very lips, He speaks words within us and for us which are not the image but the very substance of Divine Worship worshipping the Divine. Sometimes what we really think and feel seems to lag far behind the fervent words we speak in our prayer: we say—"My God, I love Thee"—and feel that the words are echoing only in our own hollowness. We then find courage and strength in the realization that the Holy Ghost dwelling within us is giving the true meaning to the words, speaking them with us in an adoring rapture of love. Always when we pray sincerely, from however dry a heart, the Spirit of God prays within us.

The Holy Ghost helps us, not only in our interior experience of prayer, but also by giving to our prayer a new and more exalted significance. Through Him, our prayer becomes one with the pure harmony of angelic prayer eternally rising like incense to the Blessed Trinity. The Spirit of God prays in us. This is the source of the confidence which enables us to pray. The Spirit of God prays in us. Herein is the sublime dignity of our prayer, and the inspiration urging us "always to pray and not to faint." The unfailing power of our prayer is the Spirit of God praying within us. Because of this, our prayers are real, however arid the words on our lips and however dry our hearts. Because the Spirit of God prays within us, our prayer will become as a fountain springing up unto life everlasting.

We must find a place in our lives for the Holy Spirit, that this Spirit may pray in us and with us. There is a craving for the divine deeply stamped in our nature, whether we acknowledge it, or choke it with sin and worldliness; there is a divine discontent in us which made St. Augustine cry out: "Thou hast made us for Thyself, O Lord, and our hearts are restless until they rest in Thee." Only when the gates of our life are flung wide to the Spirit of God can this discontent be allayed; only when our souls become living temples of the Holy Spirit can that rest be ours.[10]

The Spirit and the Charismatic

The Spirit of God breathes where He will; He does not ask our permission; He meets us on His own terms and distributes His charisms as He pleases. Therefore, we must always be awake and ready; we must be pliable so that He can use us in new enterprises. We cannot lay down the law to the Spirit of God! He is only present with His gifts where He knows that they are joined with the multiplicity of charisms in the one Church. All the gifts of this Church stem from one source—God. What Paul says in the twelfth chapter of his First Epistle to the Corinthians is still true today! This should give us the strength to overcome every form of clerical jealousy, mutual suspicion, power-grabbing, and the refusal to let others—who have their own gifts of the Spirit—go their way. That is what the Spirit wants from us! He is not as narrow-minded as we sometimes are with our recipes! He can lead to Himself in different ways, and He wants to direct the Church through a multiplicity of functions, offices, and gifts. The Church is not supposed to be a military academy in which everything is uniform, but she is supposed to be the Body of Christ in which He, the one Spirit, exerts His power in all the members. Each one of these members proves that he really is a member of this Body by letting the other members be. . . .

Surely, we should also realize that true charismatic impulses, which are never capricious and fond of innovations, are connected with sacrifice, renunciation, penance, humble love, and obedience to the Church and her official organizations. The Church needs the charismatic and the unexpected. God has not resigned in favor of the Church's administrative apparatus. Nor has He abdicated in favor of the direction promised to the Church through the Holy Spirit! He Himself is the Spirit Who breathes where He wills and descends upon children and fools, upon the poor and the simple, and perhaps even upon this or that theologian. But all charismatic and pentecostal gifts must remain IN the Church: They must remain in the constitutional, legally organized, authoritarian Church. Only when the charismatic observes the proper order, and when the official Church directs and supports the charismatic, is the life of the Church everything that it should be.[11]

HANS URS VON BALTHASAR (1905-)

The Spirit, the Author of Salvation History

In the perspective of Father and Son, of creation and redemption, the work and position of the Spirit is revealed to us as the centerpoint of reference where all perspectives meet. For it is the Spirit who makes history into the history of salvation, which is to say prophetically oriented towards the Son; and it is he who places the Son in those situations which fulfill the Promise. Because he is the Spirit of the Father and the Spirit of the Son in personal unity, he can, at the same time, be the heart of the Father's command and the heart of the Son's obedience, of the Father's promise in history pointing towards the Son and of the Son's fulfillment of history pointing towards the Father. He is the act which seals the Covenant and exposes the divine "name" and "honor" to the danger of the world, which by wounding and "grieving" the Spirit of God leads to the Passion of the God-man. True history now has three dimensions, a trinitarian structure, which confers upon history in the created world a divine spaciousness and capacity for development. . . .

The Spirit and the Bride

The workings of the Spirit are not arbitrary and subjective, for He is the Spirit of Christ, of the Logos. For all that, he blows where he lists, yet he does not speak on his own authority, but interprets what is the Lord's. And in his interpretations the Spirit is not only subjective and personal, but objective, absolute Spirit, containing in Himself a whole cosmos of super-personal truth. He is, first of all, the one who forms and gives life to the Church founded by Christ, which proceeds from his humanity sacrificed on the Cross. . . . The whole structure of the Church's being is formed of his inmost spirit. She embodies the meaning of his coming, of the fact that he is, of the way that he is. With all her organs and all the means of which she disposes, she is a faithful copy of his humanity, a being in whom he can recognize himself and to whom, leaving Father and mother, he can cleave, becoming ONE flesh.

This flesh, this Bridge, is formed for him by the Holy Spirit. The Church is not merely a formal framework within which the Spirit personally molds and inspires the individual; with her unbreakable faith, she is, as it were, the collective consciousness of all believers.

The Spirit Will Not be Limited

The Spirit mocks all human attempts to delimit him. Upon those who are truly poor, who truly thirst after it, the Spirit pours out the consolation of his truth in such breath-taking, ever increasing abundance that the very notion of "using it up," if it ever occurred to them, could only strike them as ludicrous blasphemy. Man is led into the "deep things of God" in the way described by St. Paul, by being overwhelmed by what has never been seen, heard or felt. . . . The believer in the Church must always be ready to make the leap from the old and familiar into the essentially new—the METANOEITE which lies at the very source of the Gospel—in order to be obedient to the Holy Spirit; leaving the matter of continuity entirely to him, and not turning it into a merely natural category. Not doing theology with the idea that one takes certain given and established promises and draws some kind of automatic conclusion from them, but taking every step in one's thinking as a direct hearing and obeying of the living Spirit of Jesus Christ.[12]

DIETRICH BONHOEFFER (1906-1945)

The Spirit: the Pledge of the Abiding Presence of Jesus

Although for the candidate baptism is a passive event, it is never a mechanical process. This is made abundantly clear by the connection of baptism with the Spirit. The gift of baptism is the Holy Spirit. But the Holy Spirit is Christ himself dwelling in the hearts of the faithful. The baptized are the house where the Holy Spirit has made his dwelling. The Spirit is the pledge of the abiding presence of Jesus, and of our fellowship with him. He imparts true knowledge of his being and of his will. He teaches us and reminds us of all that Christ said on earth. He guides us into all truth, so that we are not without knowledge of Christ and of the gifts which God has given us in him. The gift which the Holy Spirit creates in us is not uncertainty, but assurance and discernment. Thus we are enabled to walk in the Spirit, and to walk in assurance. The certainty which the disciples enjoyed in their intercourse with Jesus was not lost after he left them. Through the sending of the Spirit into the hearts of the believers that certainty is not only perpetuated, but strengthened and increased, so intimate is the fellowship of the Spirit.[13]

ALFRED DELP S.J. (1907-1945)

Prison Meditations on the "Veni, Sancte Spiritus"[14]

Come, Holy Ghost

The Holy Ghost is the breath of creation. As in the beginning the spirit of God moved on the face of the waters, so now—but in a much closer and more intimate way—God's Spirit reaches the heart of man bringing him the capacity to grow to its fulfillment.

Theologically, this is clear—the heart of grace is the Holy Ghost. That which makes us like Christ is the same indwelling Spirit—the principle of supernatural life in him and us. Believing and hoping and loving, the heart beats of the supernatural life, are the created being's participation in the self-affirmation of God which is expressed in the Holy Ghost.

The cry "come" can be interpreted in this way. It embodies the intensified hungry Advent-yearning. It is the will to break through barriers, to escape from fetters and confinement.

And Send from Heaven

From heaven—out of this world, of God's reality. From that place where all things are united in one, not scattered over the earth. The created being must cry out to some power beyond itself in order to acquire its share of strength; when man realizes and acknowledges that his natural powers on their own are inadequate he has taken the first step towards salvation. He needs the mission and the assignment God gives him, the permanent guidance and healing of God if he is to meet the forces of destiny on equal terms. . . .

Send Thy Radiant Light

Light is symbolic of one of the great longings of human life. Again and again we find ourselves benighted, sunk in deep gloom, without light to guide us. How could we even desire light if it were not for the eternal gift of grace which gives our spirit a vague intuition that darkness is not its natural and final state, that even in the darkest hour there is something to be hoped for, a state of fulfillment towards which the spirit must aspire. God created man as a light-endowed, radiant being, and as such sent him forth into the world; but we have blinded ourselves to this truth. Only a faint inkling remains. Man is never more soul-sick than when he becomes confused and finds himself helpless to cope with a situation. That is the primary meaning of this prayer—it is a despairing cry for divine help to dispel our self-imposed, sinful darkness, wiping the dreams and the fear from our eyes so that they may see again. But there is another imperative need for light in our lives; God's radiance dazzles us. We get presentiments and glimpses but they are transitory and usually lead nowhere. Men who are dedicated and prepared pray for divine light which will heighten their perception and raise them to realization of that fullness they have hitherto only dimly guessed at. Once a man has arrived at this stage he knows what the strength of God is even in the darkest and most hopeless situations of his life. . . .

Come Thou Father of the Poor

This cry is the arc that connects the created being with the Creator's divine fullness. In it the two realities meet in a simple and fundamental relationship. Man recognizes himself as a pitiful creature incapable of satisfying even his most pressing needs by his own effort. . . .

To the man in need, God's spirit appears fatherly, that is as all-providing strength and power directed by love. That is as it should be. When man acknowledges his need, presenting himself without vanity, self-assurance and so on in all his naked helplessness, God manifests himself in miracles of love and pity. The effects may range from the ease of heartache and spiritual illumination to the satisfying of physical hunger and thirst. When we send this cry we call upon the Spirit of creation. We are desperately poor; let us acknowledge our poverty and offer up our prayer for ourselves and our race.

Come Bounteous Giver

Three times the "poor soul" sends up its cry to the Creator and three times the healing, omnipotent Fathers hears that prayer. It is good for the soul to persist in its pleading. The Holy Ghost is the Spirit of fulfillment, inner strength, infinite abundance; it is the Spirit of fulfillment in its divine essence. God comes to the summit of expression in the Holy Ghost; all the passionate adherence of God to himself is affirmed and confirmed by the third Person of the Trinity. . . .

Nietzsche's declarations and his dreams concerning superman eventually depress and bore us—indeed in the end they seem despicable. There is one way to progress and that is by prayer, and praying in the right way. In my present situation what help can I get from a concept of the greatness to which man should attain—what use is that in this isolation and loneliness? But to feel the warm presence of the Spirit, to be aware of his strengthening breath does help me along this lonely road. When we remember that we can call on God as the bounteous giver, *dator munerum*, the dispenser of blessings and strength, then adverse circumstances lose their power. The Holy Spirit finds ways and means to give us comfort; he has resources of tenderness and attention far exceeding the arts of human love.

Come Light of Our Hearts

Once again, we find God symbolized by light—it occurs again and again. And the wonderful words "light of our hearts" indicate that we are here concerned with the Spirit of God in the very center of life, bringing healing to its roots and source. . . .

It is the nature of the Holy Spirit to penetrate and blend with the life impulses, purifying and completing them and thus imbuing them with its own intensity and assurance. *Light of heart.* We cannot pray for it too often or be too earnest in our plea that our hearts may keep their harmonious rhythm and their power of right feeling. Feeling is here the operative word—statement and explanation are of minor importance; feeling and instinct are the things that count. When the heart is in the right place, as they say, everything is in order. May the Holy Spirit have pity on this poor, foolish, hungry, frozen, lonely and forsaken heart and fill it with the warm assurance of its presence.

Best Comforter

Comforter. We ought to take this word in its simplest and most straightforward sense . . . the essence of comfort is that the mind and spirit are no longer troubled, that they are in a state of security, order and fulfillment. The genuine comforter must either establish this new state or so harmonize the old state with existing circumstances that the misery vanishes and the whole situation takes on a new character. Both depend entirely on the action of the Spirit in us. . . .

Sweet Guest of Souls

He is comfort and comforter. *Guest of souls*; actually present and present in a singularly personal way. True mystical experience is nothing less than the shatteringly conscious awareness of this continuous presence. . . .

Sweet Refreshment

This phrase can only be really appreciated by those fortunate enough to know one of those people whose very presence is so infective that it makes him a source of strength, security, joy, and trust, so inspiring that it changes the whole atmosphere, dominating it. . . .

What warmth and shelter are to the wounded who have suffered exposure, the comfort of the Holy Spirit is to the soul; only the soul, being more sensitive, feels this far more acutely than the body. . . .

Rest in Labor

We have lost the freedom for which we were created and condemned ourselves to perpetual bondage and fatigue. . . .

Factories are the new cathedrals, machines are the magic symbols of today and man is the most easily convertible currency on this utilitarian world of machinery. Everyone has been drawn into this new order and none can escape its dictatorship. Life has opened a machine-gun fire of demands on us and we cannot withstand the onslaught—unless help comes from the hills. Unless man turns to the inner strength that lets him rise above all the trials that beset him. Only from within can we draw the calm that will lift us above the hectic rat race even when we fulfill its demands and carry out our duties . . . The Holy Spirit will give us the great virtue of perseverance. With his help we shall prove stronger than the forces ranged against us, swifter than the hounds of care that pursue us in this desperate hunt our lives have become. . . .

The one indispensable condition is that we remain receptive, listening for the inner voice, otherwise we shall be drawn up in the sterile and stifling world of everyday realities. God's spirit will pour itself through our every need, drown every noise, overcome all fatigue if only we will turn to it in faith and with desire. That is why our prayer today must be to the Creator Spirit, he who works in us and fulfills our needs bringing us to our true selves in our personal lives. . . .

God within us is like a fountain and we are guests invited to rest and refresh ourselves. We must discover this fountain within ourselves and let its healing waters flow over the parched land of our lives. Then the desert will blossom. He wants to quicken you. The word of God, given long ago, is fulfilled by his free-flowing Spirit. From within you will receive the strength and the spiritual assurance to conquer. . . . Unless we find these inner fountains, these healing waters, no outward rest, no relaxation, will help us. But when the divine Spirit dawns on man's consciousness then he is able to surpass himself. He is filled with that peace, that holy and restoring stillness which we associate with God's presence—in a cathedral for instance, in a magnificent countryside, in a cherished friendship.

Coolness in Heat

This is the second fundamental need of poor, exposed defenseless man. He is at the mercy of inner driving forces that alternately harass and handicap him till he is almost exhausted. These compulsions come from within; the sleeping volcano bursts into life and stirs up explosive energies which send the tattered remnants of reality flying in all directions. Hot blood and violent anger, the sudden assertion of the inborn urge to tyrannize—these and many other smouldering human impulses may turn into consuming fires. . . .

Coolness in heat; the Holy Spirit as the source of our power to cope with the contingencies of life. God's passion for himself which finds expression through the spirit of man, burns up a man's incipient passions.

This is really a case of fire fighting fire. The Holy Spirit appeared at the beginning as tongues of fire. That is God's way of dealing with the situation. God is no destroyer of the beings he has created. His will is that all shall be forgiven and redeemed and hence his fire is not consuming but healing. And in the breath of the Spirit man grows till he can control his demoniac wildness. . . .

Solace in Woe

I vividly recall that night [of torture] in the Lehrterstrasse and how I prayed to God that he might send death to deliver me because of the helplessness and pain I felt I could no longer endure, and the violence and hatred to which I was no longer equal. How I wrestled with God that night and finally in my great need crept to him, weeping. Not until morning did a great peace come to me, a blissful awareness of light, strength and warmth, bringing with it the conviction that I *must* see this thing through and at the same time the blessed assurance that I *should* see it through. *Solace in woe*. This is the Holy Spirit, the Comforter. This is the kind of creative dialogue he conducts with mankind. These are the secret blessings he dispenses which enable a man to live and endure. . . .

O Blessed Light

There are summer days when the light seems to envelop us like a tangible blessing. It can happen in a lovely alpine meadow or a rippling field of ripening grain or floating silently in a boat on a beautiful lake. Man's consciousness is intensified and he feels at one with nature and has a marvellous cognition of the ripening, healing, and sanctifying powers the cosmos contains. Only a receptive, a reverent and observant man can experience this. It is a faint reflection of the saint's experience of blessed light—an awareness that there are times when God enfolds his children in waves of tenderness flooding their hearts and filling their whole being with the blessed current of divine life. . . .

Fill our Inmost Heart

Under the influence of this inner illumination man becomes more clear-sighted, more intuitive, wiser. He is enabled to strip the mask from falsity in circumstances and in men; he is equal to any emergency and can deal with problems more kindly than if he were in an unenlightened state—because he now knows their rightful place in the scheme of things, meets them on their own ground as it were, and sees through them to the very core of their secret hearts. . . .

Thy Faithful

Like all intimacy this relationship with the Holy Ghost rests on trusting surrender and receptivity. God's Spirit never coerces even for man's own good or to hasten his self-realization. . . .

Any man who tries to enter this dialogue with coarse thoughts and uncouth habits will lose much grace and blessings. He will miss so many whispered words of warning, silent indications of the tender solicitude and good will of God. There are times too when God's light will break like lightning over man, descend suddenly and violently, affecting his whole existence like a great boulder torn from a hillside and crashing into a lake.

Without Thy Grace

We elected to live gracelessly, we trusted solely to our own strength, were bound only by our own laws, surrendered to our own whims and followed our own instincts. . . .

And the outcome? Precisely without thy grace—a graceless life, a pitiless age, an age of inexorable fate, a time of horror and violence, of worthless life and senseless death. We ought not to be surprised that such a graceless life has translated itself into the kind of manifestation we are now enduring. And we who have been dragged down into the universal collapse—which perhaps we did not try to prevent by every means in our power—must in the midst of our destiny overcome that destiny, turning it into a cry for grace and mercy, for the healing waters of the Holy Ghost. . . .

Nothing Is in Man

Man has it in him to conceive high ideals and work for their realization but if he is honest he will recognize the fact that he can do nothing on his own. Left to himself he is incomplete, not quite a man. God is part of the definition of a man; inner unity with God is the primary condition for a fulfilled and successful life.

Nothing Is Harmless

We all know, individually, that there are times when everything we attempt seems to go wrong. All our efforts turn against us, and end in bitter disappointment. It also sometimes applies to whole generations, to spiritual movements, to social and economic projects and so on. We see things getting out of hand; intentions, and programs misfire, not only because the ideals have been betrayed by leaders and people, but because reality itself, proving too strong, has suddenly become antagonistic, difficult, intractable. . . . In the last analysis there is no such thing as neutrality—there is absolutely nothing that does not matter. Decisions, conduct, intentions, all have either a positive or negative value and if negative they are harmful and dangerous. . . . Man in a state of grace, through the Holy Ghost, is more capable of conducting his own life successfully and is also better equipped to help others. In his handling of everyday affairs he has clearer insight and better judgment, he is kinder and more generous. He bestows blessings and receives them.

Wash What Is Stained

The Holy Ghost floods our being like a healing stream and no blemish can withstand its cleaning power. *Wash what is stained.* This must be the prayer of all who long for unity with God in the core of their being. Great benevolence and grace are called for and God does not withhold these from his creation. Man cannot live without this creative contact with His Maker and these fountains are unsealed by honest and complete surrender. This is the indispensable act on man's part—surrender and prayer.

Water What Is Barren

There are months of exaltation and inspiration when the world seems almost too small and the stars are very near—but this is often a kind of creative drunkenness quickly dispelled on sober awakening to the realities of human weakness. . . .

When song dies in the heart and the inner fountains have dried up, the wasteland of our life becomes a barren wilderness swept by raging storms. . . . These wildernesses must be mastered—that of loneliness, of fear, of depression, of sacrifice. God who created wildernesses also made the streams that bring forth fruitfulness when they flow over barren land. Prayer and trust in his goodness bring his promises to pass.

Heal What Is Wounded

Man should never despair even in his darkest hours. He should remember that God shares his life, that through the Holy Ghost he can be on the most intimate terms with God and that God is always there, when outward pressure is at its worst, helping him to carry his burdens over the roughest places on his weary road. There is no fiber of his being that the healing Spirit cannot reach as long as he is willing to let it do its creative healing work. It goes on in silence within him and he should remind himself constantly that in alliance with God he possesses powers of recuperation which enable him to endure the most grievous wounds without flinching and go on meeting the demands life makes on him. He should have this inner confidence, not [because of] mere self-reliance, but because he knows beyond a shadow of a doubt that God is sharing his life with him.

Bend What Is Rigid

Man can be rigid in many ways. He can have a one-track mind like the rich young man in the gospel. God would be doing such a man a kindness in destroying his possessions before calling him to the last judgment. This paralysis in the realm of things, this fixation about property, riches, gold, jewels, art and good living was characteristic of the last century. One half of the world's population lost their souls to material possessions; the other half spent their time protesting, not at the danger to mankind through this kind of bondage, but at the fact that it was not possible for them to lose their souls in the same way because they had not yet succeeded in gaining such possessions. . . .

Even more dangerous is that inner paralysis which induces man to betray the fundamental laws of his existence. No longer "living to all truth, to all goodness," he pulls up short, sets himself apart, rests on his laurels and leads the life of a pensioner. He no longer strains with all his might to achieve ideals, reaching for the stars. The command to love God with all his heart, with all his mind and with all his strength no longer has any meaning for him; he treats it as something handed down like a legend, something that has served its turn and can be thrown aside. . . .

Destiny, and God's Spirit operating from within, can save this kind of man from the hard fate in store by rekindling the divine spark in his heart. Here is a case that emphatically calls for bending, loosening, melting, making the intractable pliable. Present day man's incapacity for love, for reverence, for appreciation has its roots in arrogance and in this petrifying of existence.

When man's heart softens and loses its numbness he actually brings about his own liberation. Like all surrender that is not prompted by creative assent this can be a painful business. But it is restorative and a step towards freedom—the torrent at last finds an outlet to its own ocean. The overcoming of icy isolation, of lack of love and self-sufficiency—that is the task of the Holy Ghost in man.

Melt What Is Frozen

Love turned cold is the deadly fate that threatens all life and must be overcome at all costs. Man should recognize clearly what this horror means, whence it comes and how devastating it can be.

It is not easy to revive a smouldering fire. When man has strayed from the current of reality he can do nothing about it at any rate on his own. At best he can revive his memory, give the assent of his will and pray for the fire from heaven that prepares, transforms and rekindles.

The Holy Ghost is God's passion for himself. Man must make contact with this passion, must play his part in completing the circuit. Then true love will reign again in the world and man will be capable of living to the full. The indwelling presence of God must take possession of our senses, draw us out of ourselves, in order that we may be capable of genuine assent and contact. God must ratify himself in us and through us; then we shall live as we should. Then the holy fire will again become the heart of the earth and remain so.

There are so many men the heat of the fire has not yet reached. A new alert type of man must be born of this trial of fire and of the penetrative radiance of the Spirit. He must be awake and alive, this new man, fully responsible, with far seeing eyes and a listening heart. His soul must respond to the marching song and his spirit must carry the standard of freedom he has found and to which he has sworn allegiance. . . .

Correct What Is Wrong

One of the saddest and most significant things about modern life is that it lacks instinct. . . . The mechanization and reorganization of our religious life has taken away our supernatural instinct as well. . Very seldom is a natural taste for religion (which is a characteristic of the man who consciously yields himself to the indwelling Spirit) met nowadays. The certainty which enables us to distinguish between good and evil by our own inner standard, to decide between useful and harmful, between wisdom and folly, has vanished. . . .

Among the gifts of the Holy Ghost are listed prudence, wisdom and piety. These are natural attributes which provide penetration, the power to see connecting links to divine underlying factors and basic causes. These are the "intuitive" faculties with which the Holy Ghost endows us and which he keeps alive in us by his own life. They give us the "single eye" and safeguard us against blind conflict with reality which must in the end do us harm.

Give to Thy Faithful

Faith is man's first step away from himself and towards God as center and absolute reality, to the exclusion of self and all pseudo-realities. And the decision has to be translated into one personal thing—unconditional loyalty. . . . Give to *thy* faithful the prayer says. It is exactly like the intercourse of two healthy human beings—the heart dares to mate with another because it finds itself at home with the chosen comrade whose worth is recognized. The Spirit does not use force, breaking in like a thief. God's holy Will never coerces but responds to the cry of willing assent. And when that cry is raised the slightest movement of the heart is sufficient to stir the ocean of God's munificent love into full flood.

Who Trust in Thee

The relationship between man and God, in spite of the distance between them and the humble reverence necessary on man's part, is a relationship built on personal trust. God bases many of his promises on the trust man should place in him. Many miracles and graces depend on the trust with which they are prayed for and expected. In this respect man has a certain advantage over God—an advantage he rarely realizes and so often fails to make use of. Our Lord called his disciples men of little faith when they did not trust him to cope with a few manifestations, laws of nature, or consequences of natural logic. We must at the very least arrive at a state of mind that will make *certain* things do not fail because we had sufficient faith to let God handle them.

Realization of our wonderful life in the Holy Ghost also rests on our trust. Despite our indwelling Spirit we often feel tired and frightened and disheartened because we do not trust the Spirit of God sufficiently for him to be able to make something of us. We believe more in our own unworthiness than in the creative impulse of God—who is living our lives jointly with us. It all hinges on trust, on whether we are willing to receive God's creative blessing and let it fulfill our lives making us efficient, living souls. Blessed are those that hunger and thirst. . . .

SIMONE WEIL (1909-1943)

THE KINGDOM OF GOD

The Kingdom of God means the complete filling of the entire soul of intelligent creatures with the Holy Spirit. The Spirit bloweth where he listeth. We can only invite him. We must not even try to invite him in a definite and special way to visit us or anyone else in particular, or even everybody in general; we must just invite him purely and simply, so that our thought of him is an invitation, a longing cry. It is when one is in extreme thirst, ill with thirst; then one no longer thinks of the act of drinking in relation to oneself, nor even of the act of drinking in a general way. One merely thinks of water, actual water itself, but the image of water is like a cry from our whole being.[15]

CARLO CARRETTO (1910-)

There is a third Presence in heaven and on earth. In addition to Jesus and the Father, there is a third Person seeking us,

It is the Holy Spirit.

Jesus Himself told us about Him, giving witness to His life. . . .

When He speaks of the Spirit, Jesus seems to want to announce a time of fullness, a time which is more extraordinary, a time which is more complete for man. . . .

We could say that without this third Person, there would be no progress, that the truth revealed by Jesus could not reach its fullness, that we could not even understand what He said, that, well, there's something missing, yes, missing.

Moreover, this third Person who is to come, whom the Father will send in the name of Jesus, never acts alone nor speaks on His own. . . .

That is strange to anyone who does not understand, but it is not strange to anyone who understands that Jesus never seeks a personal autonomy, but always refers to others, to a kind of council. . . .

First, during the years that He lived with His own, He always referred to the Father . . . Then at the end of His earthly life, in the intimacy of His last hours living among men, when He was already heading towards the beyond, He refers to the Spirit.

Speaking of Him, He testifies clearly and without reticence, that this Person, the Spirit, ' "will not be speaking on his own. . . ." ' (John 16:13).

This is an evident reference to the convergence of the Divine Persons, which theologians call the Trinity, and to what the unexpected overflowing of the Spirit reveals from within it . . .

Indeed, the Trinity is love, and only love can reveal it to us. . . .

Only God's love for me can open the doorway of His intimate life. And the Holy Spirit is the love which opens that door and allows me to contemplate the intimate life of God.

Only the love He diffuses in me, through the grace given by Christ, can enable me to see the 'things of above.'

The Holy Spirit is communication: communication between the Father and the Son, and communication between us and God.

If He is there, everything is clear; if He is not, everything is dark.

Do not ask me to understand on a human level. I can't.

It is enough for me to contemplate, and it is the Spirit who gives me the power to contemplate: He is the love of God in me.

The catechism is not enough, theology is not enough, formulas are not enough to explain the Unity and Trinity of God.

We need loving communication, we need the presence of the Spirit.

That is why I do not believe in theologians who do not pray, who are not in humble communication of love with God.

Neither do I believe in the existence of any human power to pass on authentic knowledge of God.

Only God can speak about Himself, and only the Holy Spirit, who is love, can communicate this knowledge to us. . . .

It is so difficult to speak of these things. We have to babble like children, but at least, like children, we can say over and over again, tirelessly, 'Spirit of God, reveal yourself to me, your child.'

And we can avoid pretending that knowledge of God could be the fruit of our grey matter.

Then, and only then, shall we be capable of prayer; borne to the frontier of our radical incapacity, which love has made the beatitude of poverty, we shall be able to invoke God's coming to us, 'Come, creator Spirit!'[16]

THOMAS MERTON (1915-1968)

SELF CONQUEST: CONQUEST BY THE HOLY SPIRIT

Real self-conquest is the conquest of ourselves not by ourselves but by the Holy Spirit. Self-conquest is really self-surrender.[17]

There is no true spiritual life outside the love of Christ. We have a spiritual life only because we are loved by Him. The spiritual life consists in receiving the gift of the Holy Spirit and His charity, because the Sacred Heart of Jesus has willed in His love, that we should live by His Spirit—the same Spirit which proceeds from the Word and from the Father, and Who is Jesus' love for the Father.[18]

. . . The only way in which we can become "spiritual" in the true sense of the word is to possess within us a *pneuma* or spirit which is formed by the coalescence of our spirit with the Spirit of God in one principle of supernatural action.[19]

The Spirit: Source of Deliverance and Freedom

The Holy Spirit comes to set the whole house of our soul in order, to deliver our minds from immaturity, alienation, fear, and tenacious prejudice. If Christ is the Lamb of God Who takes away the sins of the world, then surely He sends His Spirit to deliver our souls from obsession with our feelings of guilt. This is the thing so many Christians refuse to see. They think Christ's power to deliver us from sin is not a real liberation but an assertion of His own rights over us. The truth is that it is both, for when God asserts "His rights" over us we become free. God is Truth and "The truth shall make you free."[20]

The Divine Spirit purifies the image of God in my soul by faith. He cures my spiritual blindness, opens my eyes to things of God. He takes possession of my will so that I no longer remain captive of my own passions and compulsions, but am able to act in the fruitful tranquility of spiritual freedom. In gradually teaching me charity He perfects the likeness of God in my soul by conforming me to Christ. For my union with Christ is much more than imitation of His virtues as they are described in the Gospel: it must be a union created in me by the transforming action of His own Spirit. And the Life which the Spirit breathes into my spirit, is Christ Himself, mystically present in my own being and my own person.[21]

The Spirit and Our Life in Christ

The Holy Spirit is sent from moment to moment into my soul by Christ and the Father dwelling in the midst of my soul, the way the blood of life is sent out into all the parts of my body from my heart. And this Spirit draws me back into Christ and binds me to the Father in Him, so that my life is hidden with Christ in God. And yet I travel out from Him, in His Spirit, to do his work and fulfill His will among men. And then the time comes, according to his will, He draws me back into Himself again.

If I have this life in me, what do the accidents of pain and pleasure, hope and fear, joy and sorrow matter to me? They are not my life and they have little to do with it. Why should I fear anything that cannot rob me of God, and why should I desire anything that cannot give me possession of Him?[22]

As a magnifying glass concentrates the rays of the sun into a little burning knot of heat that can set fire to a dry leaf or a piece of paper, so the mysteries of Christ in the Gospel concentrate the rays of God's light and fire to a point that sets fire to the spirit of man. And this is why Christ was born and lived in the world and died and returned from death and ascended to His Father in heaven. . . . Through the glass of His Humanity He concentrates the rays of His Holy Spirit upon us so that we feel the burn, and all mystical experience is infused into the soul through the Man Christ. . . .

The glass of that Humanity seeks out spirits that are well prepared, dried by the light and warmth of God, and ready to take flame in the little knot of fire that is the grace of the Holy Ghost.[23]

The Spirit Prays Within Us

Contemplative prayer is the recognition that we are the Sons of God, an experience of Who He is, and of His love for us, flowing from the operation of that love in us. Contemplative prayer is the voice of the Spirit crying out in us, "Abba, Pater." In all valid prayer it is the Holy Ghost who prays in us: but in the graces of contemplation He makes *us realize* at least obscurely that it is He who is praying in us with a love too deep and too secret for us to comprehend. And we exult in the union of our voice with His voice, and our soul springs up to the Father, through the Son, having become one flame with the Flame of their Spirit. The Holy Ghost is the soul of the Church and it is to His presence in us that is attributed the sanctity of each one of the elect. He prays in us now as the Soul of the Church and now as the life of our own soul—but the distinction is only real in the external order of things. Interiorly, whether our prayer be private or public it is the same Spirit praying in us: He is really touching different strings of the same instrument.[24]

. . . . In primitive Christian literature, and especially in the New Testament, we read not so much of receiving grace as of receiving the Holy Spirit—God himself.

We would do well to emphasize *uncreated* grace. The Holy Spirit present within us, the *dulcis hospes animae*, the "sweet guest dwelling in our soul." His very presence within us changes us from carnal to spiritual beings, and it is a great pity that we are so little aware of this fact. If we realized the meaning and import of his intimate closeness to us, we would find in him constant joy, strength, and peace. We would be more attuned to that secret, inward "inclination of the Spirit which is life and peace." We would be better able to taste and enjoy the fruits of the Spirit. We would have confidence in the hidden One who prays within us even when we ourselves are not able to pray well, who asks for us the things we do not know we need, and who seeks to give us joys we would not dare to seek for ourselves.

To "be perfect" then is not so much a matter of seeking God with ardor and generosity, as of being found, loved, and possessed by God, in such a way that his action in us makes us completely generous and helps us to transcend our limitations and react against our own weakness. We become saints not by violently overcoming our own weakness, but by letting the Lord give us the strength and purity of his Spirit in exchange for our weakness and misery. Let us not then complicate our lives and frustrate ourselves by fixing too much attention on ourselves, thereby forgetting the power of God and grieving the Holy Ghost.[25]

The Law of the Spirit: A New Law of Love

. . . Now that Christ has laid down his life and risen from the dead, to take possession of us by his Spirit, the Spirit himself, dwelling in us, should be to us a law. This interior law, the "New Law" which is purely a law of love, is summed up in the word "sonship.". . . .

The Holy Spirit does not abolish the Old Law, the *exterior* command: he makes that same law *interior* to ourselves, so that doing God's will becomes now no longer a work of fear but a work of spontaneous love.

Hence the Holy Spirit does not teach us to act contrary to the familiar dictates of law. On the contrary he leads us to the most perfect observance of Law, to the loving fulfillment of all our duties, in the family, in our work, in our chosen way of life, in our social relationships, in civic life, in our prayer, and in the intimate conversation with God in the depths of our souls.

The Holy Spirit teaches us not only actively to carry out the will of God as signified to us by precept, but also lovingly to accept the will of God in providential events beyond our own control.[26]

The laws of the spirit are laws of humility and love. The spirit speaks to us from a deep inner sanctuary of the soul which is inaccessible to the flesh. For the "flesh" is our external self, our false self. The "spirit" is our real self, our inmost being united to God in Christ. In this hidden sanctuary of our being the voice of our conscience is at the same time our own inner voice and the voice of the Holy Spirit. For when one becomes "spirit" in Christ, he is no longer himself alone. It is not only he who lives, but Christ lives in him, and the Holy Spirit guides and rules his life. Christian virtue is rooted in this inner unity in which our own self is one with Christ in the Spirit, our thoughts are able to be those of Christ and our desires to be his desires.

Our whole Christian life is then a life of union with the Holy Spirit and fidelity to the divine will in the depths of our being. Therefore it is a life of truth, of utter spiritual sincerity, and by that token it implies heroic humility, For truth, like charity, must begin at home. We must not only see ourselves as we are, in all our nothingness and insignificance; we must not only learn to love and appreciate our own emptiness, but we must accept completely the reality of our life as it is, because it is the very reality which Christ wills to take to himself, which he transforms and sanctifies in his own image and likeness.

If we are able to understand the presence of evil within us, we will be calm and objective enough to deal with it patiently, trusting in the grace of Christ. This is what is meant by following the Holy Spirit, resisting the flesh, persevering in our good desires, denying the claims of our false exterior self, and thus giving the depths of our heart to the transforming action of Christ. . . .

Hence, when we are united to Christ by baptism, faith, and love, there may be many evil tendencies still at work in our body and psyche —seeds and roots of "death" remaining from our past life: but the Holy Spirit gives us grace to resist their growth, and our will to love and serve God in spite of these tendencies ratifies his lifegiving action. Thus what he "sees" in us is not so much the evil that was ours but the good that is his.[27]

The Spirit within Us

The activity of the Spirit within us becomes more and more important as we progress in the life of interior prayer. It is true that our own efforts remain necessary, at least as long as they are not entirely superseded by the action of God "in us and without us," (according to the traditional expression). But more and more our efforts attain a new orientation: instead of being directed towards ends we have chosen ourselves, instead of being measured by the profit and pleasure we judge they will produce, they are more and more directed to an obedient and cooperative submission to grace, which implies first of all an increasingly attentive and receptive attitude toward the hidden action of the Holy Spirit. It is precisely the function of meditation in the sense in which we speak of it here, to bring us to this attitude of awareness and receptivity. It also gives us strength and hope, along with a deep awareness of the value of interior silence in which the mystery of God's love is made clear to us.[28]

DANIEL BERRIGAN (1921-)

Pentecost

All their lives rounded in a backcountry brogue
now to see, at crowd's edge.
the fine Athenian profiles
agape as bumpkins,
scenting their delicate language
like odor of muscatel
or honey.

Peter and John
it is babel crashing about your ears.
The Spirit
impatient of gross and exquisite tongues
of known and unknown gods
has riven the abominable tower
with His descent.

Now the undivided tongues
are abroad
are a wildfire
front the twelve winds
front the twelve winds from these transfigured faces.

Never again to be constrained
by scarecrow gestures
by hem or haw.
Forever to see agonized at the crowd's edge
the profiles emptied of guile
their human wisdom consumed in a stench of straw.[29]

HANS KÜNG (1928-)

The Spirit Effects a New Creation

The Spirit is . . . the earthly presence of the glorified Lord. In the Spirit Christ becomes Lord of his Church, and in the Spirit the resurrected Lord acts both in community and in the individual. The power of his resurrection is more than a power of ecstasy and miracle; it produces a new creation. The Spirit opens up for the believer the way to the saving action of God in Christ. He does this not as a magic power which men cannot resist; he creates the possibility of man's replying with a responsible and conscious affirmative. He gives him through the knowledge of the crucified Christ, the realization that in Jesus Christ God acted for him.[30]

The Church Cannot Regiment the Spirit

The Spirit works *where* he wills. The Spirit of God cannot be restricted in his operation by the Church; he is at work not only in the offices of the Church, but where he wills: in the whole people of God. . . .

The power of the Spirit of God can pass through *all* walls, even church walls. It is true that the Holy Spirit has his dwelling and his temple in the Church, which he fills and which he governs. Here his power is especially revealed, since in the Church and through the Church the word of God is preached and his sacraments are administered. But the Spirit of God, if domiciled in the Church, is not domesticated in it. He is and remains the free Spirit of the free Lord not only of the "holy city," not only of Church offices, not only of the Catholic Church, not only of Christians, but of the whole world. . . .

The Spirit is at work *when* he wills. The Spirit of God is not, of course, a Spirit of arbitrariness or apparent freedom, but of real freedom; he is a Spirit of order, not chaos; peace, not contradictions, in the Church as well as in the world. This is what Paul had to remind the Corinthians, who, proud of their spiritual gifts, had neglected order in the Church: "God is not a God of confusion but of peace." Arbitrariness, disorder and chaos in the Church cannot be the work of the Holy Spirit.

At the same time, God's Spirit does not blow when he *must*, but only when he *wills*. . . .

The Church cannot dictate to the Spirit or regiment it. It can only pray and beg: Veni! God's Spirit may dwell in the spiritual house of the Church, and remain with the Church and work through it. But he dwells and remains and works there not on the basis of a law, because he must, but on the basis of his faithfulness, because he wills.[31]

Factions Drive Out the Spirit

In the Spirit, God himself and the Kyrios are effectively present in the community of believers, despite all their human weakness. The Church is the place of God's special presence on earth. Just as God was once thought of as dwelling in a stone temple, both in the Jewish and Gentile religions, he now lives in the community of Christ. It no longer needs a stone temple, it is itself the new spiritual temple. For this very reason the community has the responsibility of maintaining the temple in brotherly unity. "If anyone destroys God's temple, God will destroy him. For God's temple is holy, and that temple you are." Any Church which like the Corinthians destroys the unity of the community by making factions drives out the Spirit. Anyone who drives out the Spirit destroys the temple, destroys the community and ultimately destroys himself. The fact that the Church, the community, is a building of the Spirit, implies a charge upon the members of the community: since they are spiritual, they must lead spiritual lives. . . . The Church is a building which exists in the Spirit and through the Spirit and by virtue of the Spirit of the Lord. The glorified Lord sends his Spirit and turns his fellowship of disciples into a Church. It is through the Spirit that the reconciliation effected by Christ between Jews and Gentiles becomes effective and fruitful. In *one* Spirit and in *one* body they all have access to the one God.[32]

DOROTHY DOHEN (1923-)

WOMAN AND THE HOLY SPIRIT

The young woman was pregnant with her first child. "Just think," she said, "the baby grows without my doing anything about it. There is nothing for me to do but just wait." This attitude of passivity, of patient waiting, is the attitude preeminently of the expectant mother. . . . Various reasons have been advanced to account for the fact that the greater number of mystics in the Church have been women. One telling reason certainly is that a woman is conditioned psychologically for that complete surrender to the Holy Spirit which is the indispensable prerequisite for the mystical life. In marriage and childbirth she knows what it is to let herself be acted upon, to develop a spirit of patient waiting, of silent expectation . . . She is disposed to let the Holy Spirit form Christ within her.

The woman who surrenders herself completely to the Holy Spirit lives in a constant state of receptivity. But, lest her passivity degenerate into quietism, and receptivity into mere inertia, she must keep herself vivified by *hope*. In lively confidence that what He has promised will come to pass, in fervent expectation that the Holy Spirit will form Christ within her, in silent, joyful waiting she looks forward to His coming.[33]

SISTER M. PAULINUS

Veni, Sancte Spiritus

True ghostly joy is armor buckled on:
Armor of gold as that which shone upon
The Grecian front when winning Glaucus forth.
More splendorous, this, lighter, more surely wrought.

Then come, Spirit of Bliss, clothe us in mail
(So let our foemen's swords splinter and fail)
O be Yourself Coat, Helmet, Golden Shield,
And let us wear and bear You in the field.[34]

BORIS BOBRINSKOY

The Holy Spirit of the Pentecost

The great event of the New Covenant, sealed by the bloody and glorious Pasch of the Incarnate Logos, is the lightning bolt which totally transformed a fraternity of disciples and friends of Jesus, faithful to His memory, into a Church, the People of God, the Chosen People, a royal priesthood, sanctified by the Blood of Jesus Christ; it is the violent eruption of the Holy Spirit, at the Cenacle, the morning of the Pentecost.

All the richness of the teaching of the prophets, of the sacred writers about the Spirit of God, the words of Jesus Himself announcing the imminent and necessary coming of the Holy Spirit, the Consoler, the Spirit of Truth, this teaching was only able to become a lived reality when He who had been proclaimed and awaited had finally come and descended individually on each member of the apostolic community, in the form of tongues of fire. It was at this moment that the Church, baptized and regenerated in the Blood of Christ, was confirmed and fortified once and forever in the new life which is the life of the Spirit, life in the Spirit of God.

The Holy Spirit in Man

Before being the term and the end of our prayer, the Holy Spirit is its source, its force, its elan, its inspiration; the Spirit, we would say, is He who prays in us, who intercedes in us and for us next to the Father . . . The Holy Spirit is the great pedagogue and communion with Christ and through Him, with the Father.

The Holy Spirit is also the object of prayer, of our spiritual quest.

To acquire the Spirit of God: this is the goal of the Christian life (St. Seraphim of Sarov).

According to a variant of the Gospel of Luke, reported by St. Gregory of Nyssa, in place of Kingdom of God, the second demand contains the following words: "That thy Holy Spirit come upon us and purify us." (Luke XI: 2). To ask for the Kingdom of God then is to ask for the Spirit of Christ. Everything else flows from this. It is the global prayer of confidence, above and beyond all uttered speech, in the silence of love.

The Holy Spirit is also He to whom the Christian addresses himself in his prayer. Prayer to the Holy Spirit is, we would say, prayer desiring prayer, the placing in a state, in a condition for prayer, the orientation of our total being toward dialogue.

And finally, the Holy Spirit is also the interior force which gives birth to vocations, which permits the child to perceive the attraction of God and His call, gentle but persistent, which gives him the desire for the priesthood, a savor for the Church, a certain interior experience, the joy of the presence of God. Little by little, this call becomes sharper, more pressing, but it can also be rejected, suffocated . . .

This gentle breeze is capable of changing itself into a storm. This watchful flame can ignite into a raging incendiary; it is in every man, Christian or pagan, always at work, forming man for the good, toward the best in himself, for the truth, for love, opening his eyes to recognize and love Christ, awakening his dormant faith and fortifying and guiding him.

The Holy Spirit: Our Hope for Unity with Orthodox Brethren

Our generation is perhaps particularly marked in all Christian sects by a profound return to an awareness of the Holy Spirit. We are actually reaping the fruits of an entire period of return to biblical sources, to the Fathers, to the ancient liturgies, or let us rather say, to the spirit of the Scriptures, to the spirit of the Fathers, to the spirit of the liturgy, to its communal sense, to its internal cohesion, to its authentic and realistic symbolism. In the measure of this return, of this attentive study of sources it is the Holy Spirit who emerges, bursts forth, illuminates, pacifies and unifies the entire body of Christ, divided Christianity.

Religious literature, as much Catholic and Protestant as Orthodox, abounds with works of every sort and at all different levels, on the Holy Spirit—articles, biblical studies, generalizations or erudite works.

Numerous are the days of study, the ecumenical sessions or the permanent, specialized commissions, the retreats of priests, pastors, students and laity, who choose as their theme of communal reflection the Holy Spirit. This is all the more remarkable since just so recently the Holy Spirit was "the great unknown," as a Catholic expert at Vatican II has named Him, "He of whom we don't know how to talk and about whom the words resound hollowly." . . .

Certainly what happens at Rome or Geneva is of the utmost concern to us and we must not imagine that "Oriental" historical Orthodoxy can remain impassive before the common striving of the Christian world toward a rejuvenation of its ecclesiastical life by the renewed vigor of the Spirit which pushes and solicits it.

Whether it be a question of collegiality or of the role of the laity or of the marriage of priests or of the interpretation of Scripture or of the place of authority and its limits in the Church, a great course remains to be pursued which has just begun to be hewed out. Orthodoxy is confident that one day the traditionally Occidental Christianities, having rediscovered the essential in the theology of the Holy Spirit, will know how to reply to these questions as to so many others which the modern world poses to them, in a strong, well-formulated proclamation and an ever greater interior witness.[35]

FREDERICK DALE BRUNER (1932-)

The Pentecostal Movement and the Gift of Tongues

Theologically, the adherents of the Pentecostal movement unite around an emphasis upon the experience of the Holy Spirit in the life of the individual believer and in the fellowship of the church. The Pentecostal does not normally care to distinguish himself from evangelical believers in the fundamentals of the Christian faith. . . . But the Pentecostal finds his distinct *raison d'etre* in what for him is crucial: his faith in the supernatural, extraordinary, and visible work of the Holy Spirit in the post-conversion experience of the believer today as, he would insist, in the days of the apostles.

What is this work? The distinctive teaching of the Pentecostal movement concerns the experience, evidence, and power of what Pentecostals call the baptism in the Holy Spirit. . . . .

In terms of the church's theology and mission Pentecostalism's significance may be that it incarnates a neglected reality of the New Testament church: the Holy Spirit in the experience of believers. What to some may seem an overemphasis of the Spirit and especially of the

Spirit's more noticeable operations may, perhaps, be intended to startle the church into an awareness of its little emphasis of the same Spirit. Perhaps in the divine perspective a church that gives too much attention to the Spirit is no more culpable—perhaps less—than a church that gives him too little. Perhaps the Pentecostal movement is a voice —albeit an ecstatic and at times a harsh voice—calling the people to hear what the Spirit is capable of saying to and doing with a church that listens.[36]

DOROTHY HOLLAND

PENTECOST

With punishment; with favor; by prophets
I wooed you.
But the day was long and you were weak.
I sent you then the knowledge of Myself
You nailed It to a Tree.
And now—I send you Love,
The very Breath I breathe.[37]

DAVID WILKERSON (1931-)

WILKERSON'S DISCIPLE NICK PREACHES TO DRUG ADDICTS

"If you want power in your life . . . if you are on the needle and really want to change, then listen to this. The Holy Spirit is what you need. And when you receive Him, you will also receive ten special gifts which you can depend on. I'm going to tell you about them. If you have a pencil and paper you can copy down the Bible references that show where I got them.

"First of all you have power. You can read that in Acts I:8. You shall have power when the Holy Spirit comes upon you.

"Then, you're going to have a Comforter. John XIV:26. A Comforter doesn't mean someone who will make you comfortable, it means someone who will stand by you and give you strength.

"Next you will have protection. Read in Acts XVI:6 how the Holy Spirit forbids the apostles to take a step which would have been tragic. He will guide you like this, too.

"And here's an important one: you will no longer be hounded by the mind of the flesh, but you will have spiritual values. Read it in Ephesians II:3-6.

"You will have life. Now you are headed for death, but with the

Holy Spirit, it says in Second Corinthians III:5-6 that you will have new life.

"And you will be living with the Spirit of Truth. The needle holds out a promise to you that is never fulfilled. You don't get release in a drilling session, it just gets worse. John XVI:13 tells you that you will have Truth.

"Access to the Father will be yours. Read Ephesians II:18.

"And the last three: You will have Hope. How many of you have that now? Not many. You will have Hope, says Romans XV:13.

"And the point of all this is found in Second Corinthians III:17. You, you boys out there now, will have liberty!

"And how does this come about? Through a dramatic, sudden overpowering experience. Read about it for yourselves in Acts X:44."

Then Nicky stopped. His voice dropped and he spoke in almost a whisper. "That's what's ahead for you in this new life," he said. "But here tonight I don't think we want to *read* about it. And we don't want to *talk* about it. We want to *do* it!

"If you want this change and power and hope and freedom in your life, get on your feet and come up front. I'm going to lay my hands on your head just like St. Paul did and the same thing is going to happen to you that happened to the new Christians in his time. You're going to receive the Holy Spirit!"[38]

PAUL EVDOKIMOV 1901-1970)

THE PRAYER THAT HAS NEVER BEEN REFUSED

According to the Father, the Holy Spirit is the very essence of the gift of God. That is why there is one prayer that has never been refused, one which the Father always answers immediately, and that is the request for the Holy Spirit, the *epiklesis*. The man who seeks honestly and sincerely, who knows how to listen to the silence of his mind, can formulate the prayer of his heart in a conditional form: "If Thou art, answer me, and send the Holy Spirit."

The spiritual life comes from above. God inaugurates it by the gift of his presence. Man receives this revelation-event and answers by his act of faith. He formulates and confesses the Creed, the saying of the Father's *Thou* with his Son and his Spirit. A liturgical dialogue, productive of unity, is begun. . . .

When we confess in the Apostles' Creed that "I believe in the Holy Spirit, in the Holy Catholic Church," we mean "in the Holy Spirit that descended on the Church on pentecost," and this is pentecost perpetuated and the *parousia* begun in action in history. This time does not withdraw man from the world, but it lightens the weight of the world, making man more joyous by the breath of the Spirit. It is our world of television, guided space craft, supersonics, interplanetary journeys, in this world that is at the same time atheistic and believing, paradisiacal and infernal, but always loved by God, that man is called upon to live the miracle of his faith. Like Abraham in former times, he starts out, without knowing where he is going or why; but he knows that he bears in his heart a flame of fire, and he can only repeat the winged words of St. John Climacus, "I go forward singing to you . . ."[39]

MICHAEL WALKER (1932-)

Pentecost

Lord, we want another Pentecost, a revival of the Spirit's power among us,
so we look back with nostalgia to the first
Pentecost, envying the apostles that experience
that seems to elude us;
for we want to hear the wind in the streets,
rattling the windows and banging the doors, blowing
gusty and invigorating from the mountain of the Lord,
we want to see the tongues of fire over each
other's heads,
we want to preach the word that converts, renews, convicts,
redeems,
Lord, we want another Pentecost . . .
At least, Lord, that's what we ask for,
I'm not sure whether we really want it;
I ask myself, Lord, do I know what I am praying for?
—the wind, Lord, the wind,
blowing open doors I thought were safely shut;
hurling neat plans, agendas, committee reports
into the air;
rushing down by-ways where men have been snoring
peacefully in the siesta of middle-age;
—and the fire, Lord,
that flame that is not a cosy glow,
keeping me pink and warm, but a flame that
sears, scalds, consumes (remember Malachi, Lord:
refining fire and fuller's soap, the men nearest
to God purged and scrubbed);

that flame that makes me shield my eye, and
sweat.
Lord, this is what I am asking for,
may I also want it;
and if You come, Lord, still as wind and fire, yet
unannounced and unseen by others, may I recognize You;
as I look for the renewal of Your Church, Lord may I
be prepared for the renewal within myself: the wind
that drives out the dust and debris of my half-hearted
efforts and my shabby compromises, that makes me
catch my breath and clutch again for the security of the Rock;
and the fire, Lord, the passion for You and the people which
might by Your grace, forge something of lasting gold in my life.
Lord, we want another Pentecost
that, renewed by wind and fire, we may
preach the Good News,
and men may hear,
and hearing, may see visions and dream dreams.
A Prayer for Others:
that the Church that prays for the coming of the Holy
Holy Spirit
may be given grace to endure His coming
and may He be poured out on
all men.[40]

NOTES

1. "Invitation to the Paraclete," in *A Child Asks for a Star* (Denville, New Jersey: Dimension Books, 1964), p. 21.

2. *The Gift of God* (Westminster, Md.: The Newman Press, 1958), pp. 30-33.

3. *The Seven Horns of the Lamb. A Study of the Gifts Based on Saint Thomas Aquinas* (Milwaukee: Bruce Pub. Co., 1966), p. 3.

4. *The Spiritual Legacy of Sister Mary of the Holy Trinity. Poor Clare of Jerusalem (1901-1942).* Edited by Silvere van den Broek (Westminster: The Newman Press, 1950), pp. 234, 262.

5. *Faith and the World* (Pittsburgh: Duquesne University Press, 1963), pp. 52-54.

6. *The Passion of the Infant Christ* (New York: Sheed and Ward, 1949), p. 134.

7. "The Church Militant Mobilizing," *Spiritual Life* (June, 1951), p. 172. First appeared in *Wuntes Docete*, Anno X, (1957), facs. III.

8. "Esprit-Saint et renouveau conciliare," *Documentation Catholique* LXII (September 5, 1965), pp. 1511-1512, 1515.

9. *The Revelation of God.* Translated by A. Manson and L.C. Sheppard (New York: Herder and Herder, 1968), pp. 159, 166-167.

10. *On Prayer* (New York: Paulist Press, 1968), pp. 28-29, 21.

11. *Spiritual Exercises*. Translated by Kenneth Baker (New York: Herder and Herder, 1966), pp. 255, 168.

12. *A Theology of History* (New York: Sheed and Ward, 1963), pp. 60, 99-100, 104.

13. *The Cost of Discipleship* (New York: Macmillan, 1969), p. 259.

14. Extracts from *Prison Meditations/Letters from Prison* of Alfred Delp, S.J.© Search Press, London, 1962/1976.

15. *Waiting for God.* Translated by Emma Craufurd (New York: Capricorn, 1951), pp. 217-218.

16. *The God Who Comes* (Maryknoll, N.Y.: Orbis Books, 1974), pp. 75-79.

17. *Thoughts in Solitude* (New York: Farrar, Strauss and Cudahy, 1958), p. 29.

18. *Ibid.*, p. 36.

19. *The New Man* (New York: Farrar, Strauss and Cudahy, 1962), pp. 199-200.

20. *Ibid.*, pp. 43-44.

21. *Ibid.*, pp. 169-170.

22. *Seeds of Contemplation* (Norfolk, Conn.: A New Directions Book, 1949), p. 96.

23. *Ibid.*, p. 91.

24. *The Sign of Jonas* (New York: Harcourt, Brace, 1953), pp. 291-292.

25. *Life and Holiness* (New York: Herder and Herder, 1963), pp. 30-32.

26. *Ibid.*, pp. 37-38.

27. *Ibid.*, pp. 86-88.

28. *The Climate of Monastic Prayer*, Cistercian Studies Series, No. 1 (1969), pp. 58-59.

29. "Pentecost," in *Time Without Number* (New York: Macmillan, 1957), p. 5. Copyright: The Catholic Poetry Society of America. *Spirit*, 1956.

30. *The Church* (New York: Sheed and Ward, 1967), pp. 166-167.

31. *Ibid.*, pp. 176-178.

32. *Ibid.*, pp. 170-171.

33. *Women in Wonderland* (New York: Sheed and Ward, 1960), p. 250.

34. "Veni, Sancte Spiritus," in *America*, CIII (July 30, 1960), p. 474.

35. "The Holy Spirit, Life of the Church," *Diakonia*, VI (No. 2), pp. 304-305, 316-318.

36. *A Theology of the Holy Spirit. The Pentecostal Experience and the New Testament Witness* (London: Hodder and Stoughton, 1970), pp. 20-21, 33.

37. "Pentecost," *Torch*, XL (No. 6), p. 21.

38. *The Cross and the Switchblade* (Old Tappan, New Jersey: Fleming H. Revell, 1972), p. 181. John and Elizabeth Sherril co-authors.

39. Paul Evdokimov, *The Struggle with God*. Translated by Sister Gertrude, S.P. (Glen Rock, New Jersey: Paulist Press, 1966), pp. 39, 92.

40. *Hear Me Lord. Prayers from Life* (Old Tappan, N.J.: Fleming H. Revell, 1969), p. 108.

INDEX

Spirituality